Barney Warf
Post-Truth Geographies

Digital Geographies

———

Edited by
Barney Warf

Volume 1

Barney Warf

Post-Truth Geographies

—

DE GRUYTER

ISBN 978-3-11-163124-0
e-ISBN (PDF) 978-3-11-074984-7
e-ISBN (EPUB) 978-3-11-074990-8
ISSN 2749-3253

Library of Congress Control Number: 2023938848

Bibliographic information published by the Deutsche Nationalbibliothek
The Deutsche Nationalbibliothek lists this publication in the Deutsche Nationalbibliografie;
detailed bibliographic data are available on the internet at http://dnb.dnb.de.

www.degruyter.com

For Karen, Suzanne, and Phil, comrades in octopus arms.

Contents

List of Figures —— XI

Chapter 1
Introduction —— 1
    Truth and its Uses —— 3
    Post-Truth: A Brief Introduction —— 4
    Post-Truth Geographies —— 6
    This Volume's Argument —— 7
    Outline of Chapters —— 8

Chapter 2
The Meanings and Philosophies of Truth(s) and Post-Truth —— 14
    What does "Truth" Mean? Varying Views of Truth —— 15
    Correspondence Theory of Truth —— 17
    Coherence Theory of Truth —— 18
    Pragmatist Theory of Truth —— 18
    Consensus Theory of Truth —— 20
    The Enlightenment, Empiricism, and Positivism —— 20
    The Problem of Pseudo-Science —— 26
    Marxism and Truth —— 29
    The Relativization of Truth —— 31
    Foucault and the Social Construction of Truth —— 35
    Feminism and Truth —— 38
    Post-modernism and Truth —— 40
    Post-structuralist Truths —— 46
    Post-truth as Epistemology and Ontology —— 48
    Chapter Conclusion —— 53

Chapter 3
The Historical Geography of Fake News and Post-Truth —— 56
    What is Fake News? —— 56
    The Early History of Fake News —— 58
    Yellow Journalism —— 62
    Fake News and Politics —— 65
    Fake News and Immigration —— 70
    Military Propaganda and Fake News —— 71
    Corporations and Fake News —— 79

Modern Day Tabloids —— **84**
Fake News and the Internet —— **86**
Chapter Conclusion —— **89**

Chapter 4
Right-wing Post-truth Geographies —— **90**
Anti-Intellectualism and its Aftermath —— **90**
Science Denialism —— **93**
Denial of Climate Change —— **97**
The Right-Wing American Mediasphere —— **102**
Howling at the Moon: Right-Wing Conspiracy Theories —— **108**
Fake News and the 2016 and 2020 U.S. Presidential Elections —— **110**
Donald Trump's Lies and their Fake Geographies —— **114**
Right-Wing Covid Denialism —— **124**
Fake News and Brexit —— **127**
Chapter Conclusion —— **131**

Chapter 5
The Urban and Rural Landscapes of Post-truth —— **133**
Cities and Cognitive-Cultural Capitalism —— **134**
Cities, Rural Areas, Diversity, and Tolerance —— **135**
News Deserts —— **138**
The Spatiality of Gullibility: Explaining Susceptibility to Fake News —— **140**
European Urban-Rural Dichotomies —— **144**
Chapter Conclusion —— **146**

Chapter 6
World Regional Geographies of Post-Truth —— **147**
Neoliberalism and Post-Truth —— **148**
European Landscapes of Post-Truth —— **151**
Russian Fake News —— **153**
The Spatiality of Post-Truth in Asia —— **157**
Posverdad: Latin America Grapples with Post-Truth —— **160**
آخر الحقيقة: Post-truth in the Middle East —— **165**
Post-Truth with African Characteristics —— **169**
Chapter Conclusion —— **171**

Chapter 7
Conclusions: Contours of Geography in the Age of Fake News —— 173

References —— 180

Index —— 216

List of Figures

Figure 3.1: *New York Sun* Lithograph of the Great Moon Hoax of 1835. Source: https://commons.wikimedia.org/wiki/File:Great-Moon-Hoax-1835-New-York-Sun-lithograph-298px.jpg —— **61**

Figure 3.2: The Yellow Kid. Source: https://commons.wikimedia.org/wiki/File:Yellow_Kid_1898-01-09.jpg —— **63**

Figure 3.3: 1910 Cartoon of William Randolph Hearst. Source: https://commons.wikimedia.org/w/index.php?search=%22yellow+journalism%22&title=Special%3ASearch&go=Go&ns0=1&ns6=1&ns12=1&ns14=1&ns100=1&ns106=1#/media/File:The_Yellow_Press.jpg —— **64**

Figure 3.4: President Truman holding newspaper falsely announcing his defeat, 1948. Source: https://commons.wikimedia.org/wiki/File:Dewey_Defeats_Truman_(AN-95-187)_resized.jpg —— **68**

Figure 3.5: U.S. Anti-German Poster, 1917. Source: https://commons.wikimedia.org/wiki/File:Harry_R._Hopps,_Destroy_this_mad_brute_Enlist_-_U.S._Army,_03216u_edit.jpg —— **74**

Figure 3.6: An 1889 Advertisement for "Arsenic Complexion Wafers". Source: https://commons.wikimedia.org/wiki/File:18891109_Arsenic_complexion_wafers_-_Helena_Independent.png —— **80**

Figure 4.1: Orlando Ferguson's Depiction of a Flat Earth, 1893. Source: https://commons.wikimedia.org/wiki/File:Orlando-Ferguson-flat-earth-map_edit.jpg —— **96**

Figure 4.2: Trump Supporters Storm the Capitol Building, January 6, 2021. Source: https://commons.wikimedia.org/wiki/File:DC_Capitol_Storming_IMG_7960.jpg —— **114**

Figure 4.3: Sign Opposing Brexit Lies. Source: https://commons.wikimedia.org/wiki/File:Self-serving_liars_(51123376015).jpg —— **129**

Figure 5.1: Number of Newspapers by County in the U.S., 2022. Source: https://www.washingtonpost.com/opinions/2022/12/27/newspapers-disappearing-democracy-media/ —— **138**

Figure 6.1: Internet Research Agency, St. Petersburg. Source: https://commons.wikimedia.org/wiki/File:55_Savushkina_Street.jpg —— **155**

https://doi.org/10.1515/9783110749847-001

Chapter 1
Introduction

The truth is rarely pure and never simple.
Oscar Wilde

At first glance, the notion of "post-truth" seems like an oxymoron. A fact, a claim to truth, is either true or it is not. But upon closer inspection, "truth" turns out to be problematic: there are many definitions of truth, and, since knowledge is always a social construction, what counts as true and what does not have often been a matter of historical and geographical circumstances.

Truth and its opposite, lies and deceit, have often been used to advance particular social and political agendas. More recently, the world has witnessed an eruption of post-truth, which undermines the very notion of truth, evidence, and objectivity altogether. A variety of circumstances have combined to elevate falsehoods over factual claims, conspiracy theories, and malicious denial of science. Whether we like it or not, we live in a post-truth world today, as impossible as that might seem.

This volume aims to explore a complex topic: the spatiality of post-truth, that is, the geographies of lies and falsehoods, bullshit and unfounded assertions, propaganda and conspiracy theories. Geography has always been poised between matter and meaning, the tangible and the intangible. But it has always taken those meanings to be true, whatever that might mean. What happens if we replace truth with falsehood, if such a simple dichotomy exists? What kinds of geographies would result? The boundaries between truth and non-truth – whatever they may be – have varied over time and space, and space and place are intimately wrapped up in what we think is true, and not true. There is no easy approach to this issue. Matters of truth are complex philosophically and often deeply entrenched in political debates. One party's claim to truth may be viewed by another as a set of bold-faced lies. "Truth" is historically contingent: at one point in time, it was transparently true that God exists and that the world is flat; at another, these notions are dismissed as ignorant fictions. From a social constructivist standpoint, because knowledge is not simply socially produced but also grounded in space and place (Thrift 1985, 1995; Powell 2007), the ways in which truth is produced, and distorted, vary widely over the earth's surface.

This volume is concerned with the spatiality of post-truth. While post-truth has received attention from historians (Gudonis and Jones 2020), scientists (Iyengar and Massey 2019), journalists and media scholars (Alexander et al. 2016), educators (Peters 2017; Chinn et al. 2021), media studies scholars (Gunkel 2019), and philoso-

https://doi.org/10.1515/9783110749847-002

phers (Fuller 2018), the spatial dimensions of post-truth have, remarkably, been largely unexamined. The geography of post-truth is important because it varies over time and space: like truth, post-truth means different things in different places, and its origins, causes, and impacts vary widely among countries, cultures, and social groups.

Post-truth geographies involve a wide array of topics that have long concerned geographers, including borders, landscapes, cities, nation-states, immigration, globalization, geopolitics, the environment, and networks. Each of these topics, and many others, has been subject to countless waves of false information, lies, slander, and untruths. "Climate change is a hoax!" is an example of a post-truth geography. So are "immigrants bring leprosy!", "the border wall is under construction," and "Brexit will save Britain from hordes of immigrants seeking to enter the country." Each of these, and many others, involves lies, distortions, and falsehoods that play out over space. Because knowledge, power, and space are always intertwined, deliberately false statements such as fake news invariably acquire a geographic dimension.

This topic integrates several strands of geography, including geopolitics, cybergeographies, and geographies of media and communications. Diving into the post-truth world involves a vast array of subjects, some of them outright bizarre: fake news, lies, spin, conspiracy theories, science denial, propaganda, disinformation, misinformation, rumor bombs, deepfake videos, and others. Winding through the discussion of all of these topics is a concern for how truth is (re)produced, communicated, received, (mis)interpreted, and used or abused.

Much of the book focuses on the United States. In part, this reflects the fact that post-truth is largely an American creation and is most deeply embedded in that country. To be sure, post-truth phenomena are found worldwide: like everything else, post-truth has gone global. But the U.S., due to a unique combination of factors, exhibits post-truth to a degree almost unprecedented anywhere else: a wealthy, conservative country with a strong sense of entitlement; the only rich nation that is also quite religious; a poor educational system that does a remarkably bad job teaching science; large, influential technology companies like Google and Facebook; a large conservative media ecosystem led by Fox News; a politically polarized country in which conservatives view liberals as enemies, not rivals; and, of course, the world's first post-truth president, Donald Trump. Thus, while almost all scientists agree about anthropogenic climate change, half of Americans do not. Post-truth is not an example of American exceptionalism, but its birth and growth in the country are not accidental. After all, the U.S. gave the world neoliberalism and the internet, two major pillars of the post-truth world.

Nonetheless, post-truth has escaped the U.S. to take over much of the world. It is seen and felt in Europe. Russia exports it worldwide. Autocrats around the world deploy it at will. Variations of post-truth are found through the developing world. Everywhere, post-truth has been weaponized in attacks on democracy, to delegitimize political opponents, and to further right-wing agendas.

Truth and its Uses

> It is difficult to speak the truth, for although there is only one truth,
> it is alive and therefore has a live and changing face.
> Franz Kafka

To understand post-truth, it is helpful to come to terms with the notion of truth itself, notably how and why we value it.

"Truth," from the Old English *"trouthe,"* has long signified fidelity and reliability. It is often defined as the pursuit of knowledge, a map of reality. It is a claim about the world backed by evidence. "In time the concept of truthfulness came to signify that not just your word but your *words* could be counted on" (Keyes 2004, p. 23). Truth signals honesty. It is essential in daily life, for how we negotiate the world; it is the mapping of knowledge claims to reality. In philosophical terms, truth is the bridge from epistemology to ontology, that is, from what we know (or think we know) to what we take to be real. Truth is a representation of what we think exists in the world, a knowledge claim. Truth lies at the core of scientific inquiry, education, journalism, and law.

For some, truth has instrumental value: it is useful in daily life. Truth is how we explain reality to ourselves and to others. It is fundamental to our understandings and predictions about the world. For others, truth has intrinsic value: we equate it with "the good." Truth has a moral value: we equate truthfulness with honesty, and teach children that lying is wrong. It indicates that one will keep their promises. Shakespeare advised "to thine own self be true." Telling the truth means to express oneself honestly, even courageously, if need be, as in speaking truth to power. It lies at the core of science: truth explains reality. Truth is what keeps us anchored in reality, a way of preventing us from floating away on the tides of lies and fictions. We hope advertisers, historians, business executives, and politicians are truthful, even if they often are not. Truth is fundamental to making wise decisions and choices for individuals and societies alike. As MacKenzie and Bhatt (2020, p. 217) argue, "Truth is invaluable to the integrity of the person, institution and nation, and a climate of trust to the proper functioning of democracy." It is central to the rule of law. Thus, witnesses in American courts must answer the question "do you swear to tell the truth, the whole truth, and nothing but the truth?" Telling falsehoods in court can lead to charges of perjury. We hope children learn "the truth" in classrooms. The media are expected to tell "the truth" when reporting the news. We hope that friends, family, and therapists tell us the truth when giving us advice. Truth is foundational to trust, to any relationship based on honesty; after all, no one trusts a liar. It takes much truth to forge an honest relationship, and one lie can destroy it. Truth is essential to treating people with respect, to the cultivation of social capital, and to reciprocal obligations. Truth, then, is foundational to social organization and cooperation. Truth and trust are indispensable to complex, successful societies: the contemporary crisis of truth is also a crisis of trust.

What is "true," and what is not, has been a matter of philosophical debate for millennia. For some, truth is a product of our senses, language, logic, data, facts, and evidence. Some statements are true by definition (e. g., 2+2=4); this is *a priori* truth. Others are true, or so we think, by appeal to the "facts;" this is *a posteriori* truth. Unfortunately, as we shall see, this line of thought is a bit simplistic, and takes "the facts" to be unproblematic. Yet other statements are true by consensus among a community: for the religious, it is self-evident that there is a god(s). For others, truth is a social construction, always linked to an interest, a reflection of power. Truth is many things, but one aspect is vital: truth is useful. It helps to get things done, achieve goals, build relationships, and work constructively. This is an unvarnished pragmatist theory of truth, where its value is found in its utility.

Unfortunately, truth is often treated badly: we massage the truth, embroider the truth, bend the truth, shade the truth, stretch the truth, enhance the truth, and withhold the truth. We do these things to hide mistakes, increase prestige, and prevent hurt feelings. Lying is universally regarded as morally toxic, so variations of truthfulness often serve in its stead.

Learning the truth, it turns out, is remarkably difficult. The reason is that we interpret the world through subjective lenses, and never see "objective" reality without biases. Information that we agree to be true must be trusted; to do so, it must mesh, to one extent or another, with our pre-existing beliefs. As Andy Rooney once said, "People will generally accept facts as truth only if the facts agree with what they already believe."

Post-Truth: A Brief Introduction

> Truth has been replaced by believability.
> Daniel Boorstein

If truth is so important, why would anyone be against it? The question is difficult and the answer is complex. Claims to knowledge are invariably claims to authority, that is, power and knowledge are inseparable, as Michel Foucault (1980, 1997) powerfully demonstrated. Whose truth, then, achieves respectability and popularity? Whose voices are heard, and whose are marginalized? The problem is magnified because truth is so wrapped up in power relations. In Foucault's reading, truthful claims are not necessarily popular because they are accurate, but because they serve power relations. Because truth claims involve power, it is not in everyone's interest to accept them. Truth, then, is rejected because it does not serve some interests. Battles over truth are battles over power.

"Post-truth" has a variety of meanings. Broadly, it is taken to mean an intellectual and social condition in which there is no such thing as "objective truth," in which facts, data and evidence are irrelevant, in which appeals to emotion and affect are more significant than appeals to the intellect, rationality, and science. Post-truth encompasses lies, deception, fake news, alternative facts, propaganda, conspiracy theories. None of these needs be true in order to have effects, both social and spatial. Post-truth is frequently accompanied by a deep distrust of expertise as elites and a dismissal of facts and science. If the analysis of post-truth entails the analysis of power, then "Post-truth is the latest manifestation of a long, troubled history in the relations of truth, politics, and power" (Neimark et al. 2019, p. 614). Post-truth is the antithesis of Enlightenment values that emphasize knowledge: it is rooted in ignorance, anti-intellectualism, resentment, gullibility, and fear of difference.

When the term "post-truth" first appeared around 2015, it gave rise to an enormous outpouring of works on the subject (e. g., Ball 2018; Prado 2018; Rabin-Havt and Media Matters 2016; D'Ancona 2017; McIntyre 2018). There is a remarkable consensus that emerges from these works: post-truth serves reactionary political purposes; it is more tied to emotion than facts; and it exploded with the growth of social media and the disintegration of traditional media structures that acted as gatekeepers of information consumed by the public.

The internet was once naively heralded for ushering in a new age of enlightenment; truth, it was thought, would emerge from the free marketplace of ideas. Instead, it allowed lies and falsehoods to proliferate with abandon. In many ways, cyberspace brings out the worst in people; the anonymity it affords allows sudden breaks with social norms. Many find themselves sequestered in information silos, or echo-chambers in which they rarely, if ever, encounter opposing views. The internet is the primary vehicle through which fake news circulates and lies spread at the speed of light. In short, a post-truth world is unimaginable without cyberspace.

On October 17, 2005, comedian Stephen Colbert coined the word "truthiness" to refer to "the quality of seeming or being felt to be true, even if not necessarily true" (Oxford Dictionaries 2018), that is, something that *feels* true even if it is not backed up with facts. Truthiness was the quality of a claim *feeling* true even if it lacked evidence that it was verified empirically. Truthiness in many respects is the perfect metaphor for the post-truth world.

The boundaries between truth and post-truth are fuzzy and permeable. Truth fades into post-truth gradually, like the earth's atmosphere in outer space. There is a continuum between hard, cold truth rooted in evidence and data and pure falsehoods. Very few ideas, claims, or statements fall into either extreme. This makes understanding post-truth difficult, and fascinating.

It is perhaps best to think of post-truth not as a state but a thing. Post-truth is a collection of lies, deceits, propaganda, and conspiracy theories design to maximize the political power of right-wing and conservative movements the world over. Post-truth was made to happen, created by particular actors with specific interests in mind. As such, post-truth is situated in time and space, that is, it has a history and a geography. Post-truth is flexible, malleable, and adapts to its circumstances, taking different forms in different time-space contexts. It changes over time, adopting new ideas and technologies.

What does a post-truth society look like? Essentially, it is one in which reason, facts, data, and evidence are irrelevant. "In a post-truth world, objective truth does not matter, and what is truthful or factual is opinion-based and therefore purely in the eye of the beholder" (Guadagno and Guttieri 2021, p. 168). In this world, there is no such thing as hypocrisy. Truth itself is questionable, even unnecessary. Scruton (2017) holds that "If there is no truth, then opinions are no longer true or false, but simply yours or mine, ours or theirs."

Post-Truth Geographies

What kinds of geographies come out of a post-truth society? What kinds of geographies give rise to it? This volume examines how post-truth geographies are created, by whom, and toward what ends. Delving into this issue takes one into the realms of power and knowledge, the social construction of truth, the role of the media, and the uneven spatialities that inevitably accompany these processes.

The discipline of geography's intersections with post-truth are relatively recent. Geographers have examined post-truth in light of geopolitics (Chesney and Citron 2019; Laketa 2019), political ecology (Neimark et al. 2019), environmental governance (Simon 2022), cartography (Kent 2017), and geospatial big data (Zhang et al. 2021). But there have been few attempts to examine the spatiality of post-truth systematically, to link its appearances across diverse contexts, to explore the similarities and differences that emerge in varying national and local conditions.

Post-truth geographies are not the same as fictional geographies, just as literature about the real world differs from fiction. Fictional geographies portray realities that do not pretend to be real, such as maps of the world that comprises *The Lord of the Rings*. In contrast, post-truth geographies aspire to realism in the hopes of deluding or manipulating people. However, as Laketa (2019) points out, in a post-truth world the boundaries between fantasy and reality become hopelessly blurred. Indeed, the very definition and meaning of reality itself is called into question. Because knowledge is always a social product, truths – and there are many – are created within a changing constellation of times and places. Truths serve interests; they are tied to social purposes, often political in nature.

Post-truth plays out unevenly over space, unfolding differentially among various social groups situated in diverse contexts. It takes different forms in different places at different times. It diffuses from one arena to another as actors form networks of knowledge and power. Because post-truth takes many different forms in varying spatial locations, it perhaps should not be conceived as a unitary phenomenon, but a collection of falsehoods that differ from one place to another. Nonetheless, there are broad generalities that underpin the spatiality of post-truth. Its empirical manifestations reflect the intersection of these trends with unique local circumstances.

This Volume's Argument

The central thesis of this volume – the arc that connects its chapters together – is relatively straightforward and perhaps deceptively simple. It holds that the contemporary rise of post-truth is a reflection of a perfect storm of events that has been building for years. Neoliberalism plays a central role, as it has undermined democracies around the world, enhanced social and spatial inequality, and created mass resentment among the disenfranchised. This is found in both the middle classes of the developed world, besieged as they are by deindustrialization, layoffs, and stagnant standards of living, and the large numbers of people in the developing world whom neoliberalism has oppressed. The result has been a global wave of populist movements eager to voice their fury at "elites," although in practice right-wing populism also blames immigrants, minorities, and other marginalized groups. Fake news has contributed mightily to this process, undermining democracies everywhere. Post-truth serves as a smokescreen to divert popular attention away from issues of class and toward the culture wars. It obscures unpopular political agendas such as privatization, tax cuts for the wealthy, and deregulation. In short, post-truth is a weapon of class war waged on a global scale. Just as truth was essential to the creation of modern democracies, post-truth is vital to neoliberal capitalism. The destruction it has generated across the globe is incalculable.

Given capitalism's shift under neoliberalism to a white collar, service-based, information-intensive economy, workers with abundant and sophisticated skills are more likely to succeed in what Scott (2008, 2014) calls cognitive-cultural capitalism. The producer and financial services that employ such staff are typically bound together in large metropolitan areas by the agglomeration economies found there. In contrast, rural areas and small towns have typically lagged behind, suffering higher rates of poverty, unemployment, and out-migration. These trends set the stage for the geography of post-truth within countries. Often undereducated, such populations are particularly sensitive to the fake news that circulates on conservative media channels.

In concert with this transformation, the microelectronics revolution and digital media have ushered in a new era of journalism. Mainstream pillars of the media such as newspapers have been largely eroded; some places are news deserts. In their place has arisen a vast digital ecosystem presenting a cacophony of competing voices. Lies, deception, propaganda, and fake news obviously long pre-dated the internet, but cyberspace, particularly social media, has made it much easier for like-minded peoples to find each other and form "communities of truth," even if their truth is not real. In cyberspace, fake news travels at the speed of light, turbocharging post-truth as it moves through time and space. As a result, many social media users find themselves in echo chambers in which differing views are excluded, a process enhanced by sophisticated search algorithms. The result is that news, whether fake or not, is filtered through cognitive biases that inhibit the reception and understanding of contrary opinions. Post-truth thrives in this context.

The argument made here is often passionate, because truth matters and because post-truth is so destructive. Post-truth has undermined elections, eroded trust, fomented xenophobia, led people to reject science, forgo vaccines, and deny climate change. Given its destructiveness, it is too important to ignore.

Outline of Chapters

> The truth will set you free, but first it will piss you off.
> Gloria Steinem

In keeping with the narrative arc of this project, the chapters unfold as pillars of an emerging argument. They begin on a philosophical and historical note, then delve into contemporary geopolitics, where post-truth wracks the most havoc.

Chapter 2 explores the philosophical dimensions of truth and post-truth. There are several competing philosophical traditions concerning truth, which overlap and have varying criteria for what counts as "true." The chapter summarizes the correspondence theory, by far the most common, as well as coherence, pragmatist, and consensus approaches. It then turns to the Enlightenment, when modern science and non-metaphysical views of truth gained ground. Philosophies such as empiricism and positivism, firmly reliant on the correspondence theory, underpinned the remarkable discoveries and innovations of modernity. The view of knowledge that emerged from this context, centered on a knowable, objective reality and truth as its mirror, became hegemonic worldwide. It then grapples with pseudo-science, science's evil twin sister.

The relativization of truth – the move that knocked it off its perch on objective reality – began with Friedrich Nietzsche, who introduced a perspectival notion of truth. This line of thought was carried forward by Ludwig Wittgenstein and Thomas Kuhn. Phenomenology also relativized truth by emphasizing the role of subjective, lived experience.

If these approaches did not suture truth to social relations, then social constructivism did. Marxism offers a very different view of truth, one that socialized the notion and linked it to class warfare. In particular, Michel Foucault offered a vision of truth indelibly linked to power: truth always serves an interest. The combination of power and knowledge – discourse – serves to construct the lived reality of people in some ways and not others, normalizing particular sets of practices and naturalizing (and at times, challenging) social hierarchies. In the wake of Foucault, feminists weighed in, arguing that knowledge is gendered and challenging prevailing masculinist tropes that the world must be penetrated and conquered. In its place, feminism put forth a view of knowledge as partial, embodied, and contextualized, rooted time and space.

Post-modernism took the process of relativization to new heights (or lows, depending on one's view), creating great distrust about broad metanarratives that purported to interpret the world. Postmodernism played with the very notion of reality itself, sketching a world in which the real and the hyperreal became indistinguishable and truth evaporated altogether. In the wake of post-modernism, post-structuralism restored the Foucauldian notion of truth and power and avoided post-modernism's collapse into nihilism. Finally, the chapter examines post-truth, its origins and multiple implications, its explosive growth through cyberspace, the roles of search algorithms and confirmation biases, and how feelings became a substitute for facts and evidence in holding to political beliefs.

Chapter 3 offers an historical geography of post-truth and fake news. Lies, deception, and propaganda have a long and colorful history, and misinformation has been deployed in a wide array of contexts over time. The chapter begins by interrogating the notion of fake news and its various meanings. The early history of fake news includes tales, rumors, and lies told by state actors to advance political agendas, including the Romans, medieval Europe, and the Renaissance. With the Enlightenment, it began to circulate in print in large quantities as newspapers carried lurid stories. This process culminated with the rise of yellow journalism in the late 19th century, as epitomized by William Randolph Hearst during the Spanish-American war. In the 20th century, fake news and politics became symbiotic, and every election was accompanied by a swarm of false stories, conspiracy theories, and outride lies. Fake news is also used to demonize immigrants, a favorite target of right-wing parties the world over.

Military propaganda is another form of fake news, a form of information warfare used to create fear and sow mistrust and doubt. The Nazis and the Soviets were masters of it. Other examples include Holocaust denial, anti-Communist propaganda, and American duplicity ranging from the Gulf of Tonkin incident to the myth of weapons of mass destruction in Iraq in 2003. Corporations also wage information war, whether in forms of false advertising or the denial of inconvenient problems like the dangers of tobacco and climate change.

Today, in the era of pervasive info-tainment, tabloids are a common source of fake news, which to many gullible readers appears to be true. Finally, the internet created entire new worlds of fake news, allowing it to circulate at blinding speeds and reach unprecedented audiences. The result is a mosaic of information bubbles that protect inhabitants from differing opinions, views, and facts that do not fit their preconceptions.

Chapter 4 addresses the vast right-wing apparatus for producing and conveying post-truth. Conservatives and reactionaries, of course, are not the only ones to engage in this activity: liberal and left-wing post-truth includes some vaccine deniers. But as several observers have pointed out, the vast majority of post-truth – fake news, outright lies, and such – is largely the preserve of highly conservative commentators (Manjoo 2008; Mooney 2012; Hansson 2017). This is no accident: post-truth, after all, serves neoliberalism, and conservative media are neoliberalism's prime promoters. The chapter opens by examining anti-intellectualism, the underside of the Enlightenment, and how it has led to widespread distrust of "experts" as part of some vague, mythologized "elite." Anti-intellectualism is, in turn, closely tied to populism, the evil stepchild of neoliberalism. A variant of this world view is science denialism (not healthy skepticism), which often has religious roots. Science denialism is a form of post-truth that rejects evolution, vaccines, and climate change, for example. The latter deserves special attention, given that climate change is the leading existential crisis of our era, and its denial has become an article of faith among many conservatives. This is post-truth in the service of the fossil fuel industry.

The chapter then examines the enormous conservative mediasphere that emerged in the United States. This conglomeration of television networks, webpages, and radio shows is the largest machine for producing post-truth in the world. At its core is Fox News, less a news network than a propaganda outlet for the Republican Party, although there exists a plethora of other forums such as Alex Jones's Infowars, Breitbart News, Newsmax, *The Washington Times*, and former radio commentator Rush Limbaugh.

A particularly dramatic form of reactionary post-truth is conspiracy theories. While these have circulated in politics for centuries, more recent examples have flourished on the internet. The QAnon conspiracy, for example, holds that a secretive government official, "Q", is exposing the alleged cabal of Democrats and liberals as baby-eating globalists. Another conspiracy involves 5G telecommunications. Among sections of the public that do not understand or appreciate science, or data and evidence for that matter, such conspiracies wreak enormous damage.

Conservative fake news played a central role in recent U.S. presidential elections. The Pope endorsed Trump! Democrats caught with suitcases of fake ballots! Voting machines switched votes from Trump to Biden! Dead Venezuelan president Hugo Chavez was involved (somehow)! Viewers of Fox News were particularly likely to swallow such bullshit (Calvillo et al. 2021); indeed, they are more likely to be uninformed than people who watch no news at all. Fake news also led an army of Trump supporters to storm the U.S. Capitol building on January 6, 2021, an example of vicious post-truth leading to violence.

Donald Trump is the poster boy of post-truth. No American politician has ever lied so publicly, frequently, and shamelessly. As president, he lied more than 30,000 times. The chapter examines his innumerable falsehoods and the post-truth geographies that emerged in their wake, including the border wall with Mexico, that windmills cause cancer, that Muslims celebrated the collapse of the World Trade Center, that Democrats want babies aborted after birth, that immigrants bring in most illegal drugs, and the dismissal of covid as a Chinese hoax. A lie about his inaugural crowd led Kelly Ann Conway to famously proclaim the existence of "alternative facts." Trump's endless falsehoods formed the model for autocrats the world over, such as Brazil's Jair Bolsonaro.

Perhaps the saddest outcome of right-wing science denialism and conspiracy theories concerns the covid pandemic. Trump initially minimized the threat, downplayed the need for mask mandates, promoted fake cures like hydroxychloroquine, and only embraced vaccines out of political necessity. His followers like Sean Hannity called the pandemic a liberal plot to weaken Trump. The damage continued with assaults on public health authorities and conspiracy theories about vaccines, which Fox News's Tucker Carlson called "greatest scandal of my lifetime, by far" (Hsu 2021). As a result, post-truth murdered more than one million Americans.

In Britain, post-truth assumes a different form, notably during the 2016 debate about Brexit. The Leave campaign skillfully deployed a variety of falsehoods to win voters, such as the notion that clinging to the EU would allow countless refugees from Syria and Iraq, as well as immigrants from Turkey, to pore into the country. Leave also promulgated the idea that the UK sent £350 million ($480 million) per week to the EU that could be used instead to fund its National Health Service. Tabloids promised a "global Britain" that would flourish without the restrictions of the EU. A purer form of post-truth geopolitics is difficult to find.

Chapter 5 explores the urban-rural dichotomy that defines much of the spatiality of post-truth. Borrowing Scott's (2014, 2019) notion of cognitive-cultural capitalism (and its variant, the creative class), the chapter argues that in large cities, where producer services tend to agglomerate, large pools of well educated workers are formed. Such people tend to be relatively resistant to fake news and conspiracy theories. In contrast, many small towns and rural areas have stagnated economically and suffered from prolonged outmigration. Large cities tend to be globalized centers of cosmopolitanism that draw together people from diverse cultures and are thus relatively tolerant; rural areas are often characterized by homogeneity in which cultural difference is infrequently experienced and is often met with hostility. College-educated and well-informed residents tend to leave such places. Many rural denizens view cities with suspicion, resenting the "elites" who supposedly live there, and are politically highly conservative.

These differences are compounded by the changing geographic structure of the media, in which corporatization has created new deserts in many lightly populated areas. Unsurprisingly, news deserts are typically places of low-information residents prone to distrust the "mainstream media" and to accept fake news and conspiracy theories. It is difficult, if not impossible, to challenge confirmation biases in such circumstances.

The upshot of these trends is to create differential landscapes of gullibility. Differences in educational opportunities, the ability to mingle with others from different backgrounds, and the variety and quality of news sources play a major role. The geography of post-truth is thus most heavily evident in poorer, rural areas and small towns where neoliberalism has taken its greatest toll.

Chapter 6 repurposes an old geographic tool, regions, to explore the global geographies of post-truth. It begins by detailing the connections between post-truth and neoliberalism, the central argument of this volume. Neoliberalism has also accelerated the complexity of the global division of labor, leading to a surge in producer services and associated demand for skilled labor. It is no accident that post-truth has found its most fertile ground in societies most heavily plagued by neoliberalism. Besides undermining democracy, neoliberalism has spawned a series of autocrats around the world backed by populist movements that thrive on fake news: Trump, Bolsonaro, Orban, Erdogan, Duterte, Modi, and others. These share in common an intense nationalism, contempt for minorities, distrust of experts and "elites," and xenophobia. The chapter then moves onto the global stage with a critical regional geography of post-truth. In Europe, post-truth emerged under different conditions than the U.S., including stronger social democracies, low-cost universities, and greater linguistic diversity. The growth of post-truth there has occurred in the wake of the Foxification of the media. Europe evidences a similar divide as in the U.S. between vibrant urban and stagnant rural areas, pointing to the broader acceptance of fake news in economically depressed regions. Russia has a long history of disinformation going back to the Soviet Union. Unlike the ideological propaganda of the cold war, contemporary Russian fake news is designed to meddle in the elections of other countries, spreading lies and sowing distrust. Russian interference helped Trump in 2016. Today Russia is one of the world's great generators of fake news, particularly through its Internet Research Agency, which it uses to meddle in other countries' affairs. In Asia, post-truth has erupted in a variety of national contexts, including its service to Hindutva in India, the Communist Party in China, anti-Rohingya activists in Myanmar, and the ludicrous mythology surrounding Kim Jong Un in North Korea. In Latin America, *posverdad*, the Spanish term for post-truth, is to be found among the various populist movements that erupted in the wake of neoliberalism's tortuous policies in the region. Post-truth in the Middle East and North Africa has often originated with autocratic governments that use bots and cybermilitias to spread propaganda. Syria uses an electronic army for this purpose. The Saudis spread lies after they murdered journalist Jamal Khashoggi. Turkey's President Erdoğan deploys a Twitter army to attack opponents. African post-truth has been embroiled in efforts to combat AIDS. This set of examples serves to demonstrate the malleability of post-truth, how it emerges under different circumstances.

All across the globe, post-truth has caused incalculable harm. It has undermined the public's confidence in governments and institutions, generated election denial, created skepticism about vaccines, hampered efforts to combat climate change, and spread conspiracy theories. Post-truth enters into geopolitics (e.g., Brexit, the spat between Qatar and Saudi Arabia), with nasty and unpredictable results. For these reasons, it deserves to be understood. We cannot combat post-truth unless we comprehend its origins, characteristics, and nefarious consequences.

Chapter 2
The Meanings and Philosophies of Truth(s) and Post-Truth

> Lies are the greatest murder. They kill the truth.
> Socrates

To understand the nature of a post-truth world, and post-truth geographies, we must begin with the notion of truth itself. Theorizing about truth is not some abstruse academic debate, but an issue with real-world consequences: the instrumental value of truth is that it leads to successful actions. The claim to truth forms an essential part of most assertions, statements, and beliefs. We typically associate truth with logic, evidence, and consistency. Truth is often held to be synonymous with knowledge, although these are not quite identical. Philosophers often hold that knowledge consists of justified, true belief (Lehrer and Paxson 1969): beliefs that are not justified (but accidentally "true") are not knowledge, and justified beliefs that are not true are not knowledge. Finally, truth is often contrasted with falsehoods and lies, or in the contemporary context, fake news.

These comments imply that truth is a simple and straightforward matter. Unfortunately, that is not the case. The definition and meanings of truth have changed over time, and the concept has been remarkably resistant to a clear and universal definition. Truth has long been the subject of an enormous body of work by philosophers, and there are several definitions and interpretations. "Truth," it would seem, is a simple matter, a representation of reality grounded in facts and evidence. Unfortunately, things are not so simple. There are many theories of truth, many ways of defining it, and criteria that it meets (or does not). Truth is not a timeless absolute, but always subject to interpretation. Who interprets it, under what conditions, using particular ideological and cognitive filters, is always essential. There is a spectrum from unquestionably true (*a priori* truths of mathematics) to bold lies.

Perhaps, as Scharp (2013) argues, truth itself is an incoherent concept full of semantic paradoxes. Scharp maintains that arguments that assert a truth are invariably governed by inconsistent rules. Yet this is a view grounded in analytic philosophy that posits truth as residing in an asocial Platonic realm; it makes no attempt to view truth in social terms. For this reason, it lacks relevance. Replacing truth is not so simple; truth(s) serves a purpose, or a variety of purposes, that makes it useful. We create and invent truths all the time because they serve an end, help us to accomplish things and reach goals.

https://doi.org/10.1515/9783110749847-003

This chapter outlines the complex philosophical definitions, meanings, and implications of truth in various forms. It opens with an overview of varying views of truth, including classical distinctions and contemporary views. Second, it addresses the Enlightenment and the rise of modern, rational science, which gave rise to empiricist and positivist notions of truth as statements that match "the facts." As Pinker (2018) has emphasized, this vision of the world has brought us enormous benefits. Third, it takes a brief detour into the matter of pseudo-science, the evil twin stepsister of Enlightenment science. Fourth, it turns to Marxism, and the beginnings of a social constructivist view of truth as an instrument of class warfare. Fifth, it examines the slippery slope of relativism, including Nietzsche's perspectivalism, Thomas Kuhn and paradigms, and phenomenology. Sixth, it focuses on Michel Foucault, arguably the most influential philosopher of the 20th century, whose notion of discourse forever sutured truth and power. Seventh, it summarizes feminist interpretations of truth, and alternatives to the search for objectivity in the form of standpoint theory. Eighth, it dwells on post-modernism, which slid down the slippery slope into intellectual nihilism. Ninth, it argues that post-structuralism, post-modernism's stepchild, rescued truth from the abyss of endless relativism and offered an affirmative version of truths as discourses that contend with one another. Finally, it turns to the question of post-truth, including the rise of a post-truth world and its implications.

Throughout, it explores the implications of these views for geography. There is, as Thrift (1995) notes, a geography of truth; as this volume aims to demonstrate, there is also a geography of post-truth. Geography has always been poised between matter and meaning, between the material and immaterial worlds. With the rise of social theory, geographers became epistemologically self-conscious, and concerned with the nature of knowledge, and thus truth. Different definitions and meanings of truth have given rise to varying conceptions of space and spatiality, ranging from the isotropic plains of positivist models to the rhyzomic networks of post-structuralism.

What does "Truth" Mean? Varying Views of Truth

> You will know the truth and the truth shall set you free.
> Jesus, according to John the Apostle, in John:32

Truth, unfortunately, is a fantastically difficult subject to pin down. Epistemologists have been arguing about it for centuries. Part of what makes a post-truth world challenging to comprehend is that there is no simple definition of truth, no universal understanding; rather, there are a variety of theories that seek to pin it down and define its essential qualities.

The quest to understand truth has a long history (Baggini 2017). In *The Republic* (375 BC), Plato famously laid out the Allegory of the Cave, in which prisoners, chained to a wall, only see the shadows cast by a fire behind them. Those who escape the cave see the world as it really is; Plato reserved this role for intellectuals. Unfortunately, Plato's idealist view of truth, which has been enormously influential in Western history, posited that it existed in some asocial, ahistorical, aspatial world devoid of real-world roots. Aristotle, Plato's student, wrote "To say of what is that it is not, or of what is not that it is, is false, while to say of what is that it is, and of what is not that it is not, is true" (David 2002), apparently adopting the correspondence theory of truth (see below). The Epicureans and Stoics similarly believed that truth lay in sense perceptions.

One of the most important distinctions between different types of truth is the differentiation between *a priori* and *a posteriori* truths (Müller-Merbach 2007). (These are sometimes called analytic and synthetic statements). With roots going back to Aristotle, Euclid, and Immanuel Kant's *Critique of Pure Reason*, each of these has received enormous attention from analytic philosophers. *A priori* truths are those that are true by definition and are independent of sensory experience (Thompson 1981): a square has four sides; $2 + 2 = 4$; a bachelor is an unmarried male. As Kant put it, "we shall understand by *a priori* knowledge, not knowledge which is independent of this or that experience, but knowledge absolutely independent of all experience" (quoted in Kitcher 1980, p. 4). *A priori* statements are necessarily and inescapably true, and cannot ever be held to be false, and are universally applicable. They form the bases of logic and mathematics. On the other hand, *a posteriori* truths are those that are "true" by appeal to experience and evidence. This notion, in turn, depends heavily on what we mean by "experience" and "evidence." Unlike *a priori* truths, *a posteriori* ones are open to debate. Because they rely on sense perceptions, these are contingent and can change and vary over time and space; as we shall see, connecting truth statements to facts is much more difficult than it first appears. *A posteriori* truths gained popularity with the emergence of empiricism during the Renaissance and are the foundation of contemporary science. Kant himself seemed to hold to the correspondence theory, writing in *Critique of Pure Reason* "The nominal definition of truth, namely that it is the agreement of cognition with its object, is here granted and presupposed."

There is far more to this issue than the brief synopsis presented here, but this distinction serves to remind us that there is more than one type of truth, and sets the stage for more contemporary distinctions.

More recently, five prevailing schools of thought concerning truth have emerged: correspondence, coherence, pragmatist, constructivist, and consensus.

(There are also other versions not considered here, such as the semantic theory of Tarski and the deflationary theory of Frege). Each arose under different historical and social circumstances, has different strengths and weaknesses, and variations in emphasis. Each, to varying degrees, has influenced the discipline of geography in different ways.

Correspondence Theory of Truth

By far the most commonly accepted version of truth is the correspondence theory, in which the truth value of theoretical statements is judged by their isomorphism with observed facts, that is, the correspondence between hypotheses and data (typically at the fetishized 95 % statistical confidence level). This view is highly popular in part because it is simple and seemingly self-evident, and it underlies the epistemologies of empiricism and positivism.

The correspondence theory has a long history. Its origins are often traced back to Aristotle, who famously said "To say of what is that it is, or of what is not that it is not, is true." René Descartes said in 1569 that "I have never had any doubts about truth, because it seems a notion so transcendentally clear that nobody can be ignorant of it ... the word 'truth', in the strict sense, denotes the conformity of thought with its object" (quoted in David 2002). The notion was also anticipated by David Hume in the 18th century. The correspondence theory came into its own in the 20th century, when it was formalized and popularized, notably by the Vienna Circle of scientists and philosophers. One of its most famous advocates was mathematician and philosopher Bertrand Russell (1912), who, for example, said "Thus a belief is true when there is a corresponding fact, and is false when there is no corresponding fact." The correspondence theory has the advantage of subjecting truth claims to verification (or in the Popperian version, to falsification).

Truth, in this view, unproblematically exists "out there," separate from values and opinions. Truth has a status independent of whether anyone believes in it or not, which is to say that it is held to be not a social construction but an objective, given entity. The truth is always true under all circumstances. In this view, facts are taken for granted, and truth is lodged outside the world of perceptions. Because there is only one objective reality, there can be only one truth. Truth is fixed, frozen, and eternal; in the lingo of philosophers, it is mind-independent. Such a perspective subscribes to a blunt dichotomy between theoretical and empirical languages (i.e., the data are assumed not to be theory-laden: facts are given, not made), renders the role of the observer invisible or irrelevant. Rather than acknowledge how culture and ideology inevitably filter how we select and interpret facts and data, this view engages in the fantasy of "immaculate perception." Nonetheless, the correspondence theory has long been dominant not only in Anglophone analytic philosophy but in much of the social and natural sciences as well.

Coherence Theory of Truth

The coherence theory of truth views it as part of a logical system of interconnected notions (Walker 1989). The truth of individual propositions can only be assessed when they are judged as part of a broader web of meanings, i.e., how well they cohere with other propositions. Logical consistency is key here. As Walker (1985, p. 2) argues, "The coherence theory is not the theory that coherence is a likely guide to truth, but rather the view that coherence is all there is to truth, all that truth amounts to." Individual words, for example, are only true or false when they acquire meaning as part of a linguistic framework. This notion of truth has roots in rationalist Enlightenment philosophers such as Baruch Spinoza, Immanuel Kant, and Gottfried Leibniz, as well as Georg Hegel's holistic worldview. Grounded in an idealist view of reality, the coherence argument holds that we cannot ascertain the truth of propositions by appeal to the facts, but only to other propositions. Worldviews that include contradictions and inconsistencies are thus incoherent, and false. However, consistency itself is not evidence of truth: Bertrand Russell pointed out that *every* statement can be made to seem coherent by appealing to other statements. As Young (2018) exemplifies this notion,

> The proposition (1) "Jane Austen was hanged for murder" coheres with some set of propositions. (2) "Jane Austen died in her bed" coheres with another set of propositions. No one supposes that the first of these propositions is true, in spite of the fact that it coheres with a set of propositions.

The coherence view has often been used to justify metaphysical arguments; as these have fallen out of favor, the coherence view has accordingly declined in popularity. Bertrand Russell noted that this view of truth does not preclude many, conflicting interpretations of what is true: there can be several, equally coherent but incompatible belief systems.

Pragmatist Theory of Truth

The pragmatist theory of truth owes much to the works of Charles Peirce, John Dewey, and William James (1907). This view holds that "truth" is determined and confirmed by its utility an effectiveness in application, i.e., from its consequences: truth is that which is useful in solving problems or making assertions (Cormier 2000). Truth is the product of inquiry, which is prompted by doubt (Haack 1976). Unlike the correspondence theory, which view truth as eternal and static, pragmatism acknowledges different truths that result from different interests and experiences. Truth must be consistent with experience, and beliefs that are not true are overthrown by subsequent experience. In this sense, pragmatism is a form of radical empiricism. The difference is that pragmatism emphasizes the utility of truth in achieving practical outcomes; truth is a function of practical significance. As James (1907, p. 2) put it, "the 'true' is only the expedient in our way of thinking, just as the 'right' is only the expedient in our way of behaving." James therefore argued that religious experiences were "true" in that they served the interests of the believer. In contrast, atheist Bertrand Russell held that "the fact that a belief has a good moral effect upon a man is no evidence whatsoever in favour of its truth" (quoted in Hick 1990, p. 236).

Charles Peirce (1931) wrote "The opinion which is fated to be ultimately agreed to by all who investigate, is what we mean by the truth, and the object represented in this opinion is the real." This line of thought gleefully straddles the boundary between intellectual thought and the world of action, removing ideas from some abstract Platonic realm and resituating them in the context of everyday life.

Pragmatism and later conceptions, such as the consensus and coherence views, fall under the umbrella of what is often called constructivist perspectives on truth, which start with the proposition that knowledge is produced socially. Truth in this view is not reflective of some transcendental reality, but is created to advance interests; they are made, not given. The origins of this line of thought are often credited to the Italian Renaissance philosopher Giambattista Vicco, who argued that history is not some objective reading of reality but is always produced to serve interests in the present: in his words, *verum ipsum factum*, "truth itself is constructed." He is also credited with the famous line "What is true is precisely what is made." In the 19th century, constructivist interpretations of truth were advanced by Hegel and Marx; the latter, in particular, held that all knowledge serves class interests, and that truth was an epiphenomenal reflection of the material bases of production and life. Constructivism was vital in holding up truth as a social product, not some timeless essence suspended in an ahistorical void. However, constructivism lacks consensus about who precisely constructs truth and how: is it the product of the scientific community? Several varieties of constructivism vie with one another: relational, radical, and critical interpretations. (This topic is explored in more depth later).

Consensus Theory of Truth

The consensus theory of truth owes much to the German philosopher Jürgen Habermas, often regarded as the last defender of the Enlightenment. Habermas (1991) famously argued that communications are central to the social process of truth construction, through which individuals and communities of interest partake in the public, discursive interpretation of reality (cf. Calhoun 1992). Habermas's "ideal speech situation" consisting of unfettered discourse is central to the "public sphere" in which social life is reproduced and through which truth is constructed in the absence of barriers to communication. As Shafick (2021) puts it "The free flow of information is often conceived as productive of a democratic public sphere in which truth is rationally negotiated between the diverse truth claims available." Truth in this reading is inseparable from lived experience, intent, and social practice, a marked departure from the correspondence theory of truth. In this reading, all participants in a debate would theoretically have equal rights and abilities to make their views known and to challenge any other view; when all power relations have been removed from the freedom to engage in discourse, the only criteria for resolving contesting claims is their truth value. And, importantly, "the participants in an ideal speech situation [must] be motivated solely by the desire to reach a consensus about the truth of statements and the validity of norms" (Bernstein 1995, p. 50). Truth in the consensus approach is what we agree upon in the context of unfettered debate.

It should be noted that these definitions often overlap and share some elements in common. Because truth is a social construction, as a body of knowledge that reflects what we think is real about the world, it is a constantly evolving set of beliefs. What is "true" at one moment in history ("god is real"; "the earth is flat") may be seen as wrong-headed at another.

The Enlightenment, Empiricism, and Positivism

Modernist notions of truth lie in the Renaissance of the 16th and 17th centuries, when humanism, exploration, and scientific discoveries began to shift the notion from the received word of god to propositions with a basis in facts and logic. As Inglis and Robertson (2006, p. 93) state,

> Renaissance practices and attitudes of self-fashioning suggest an openness to endless possibilities, including learning from those living in other parts of the world, respecting their cultural otherness, and including certain aspects of their thinking and lifestyles within one's own sense of self and social existence.

By the late 15th century, the shackles of the Church were being steadily challenged by a growing body of secular thought. Central to this transformation was humanism, a loose collection of ideas that revolved around the notion that people, not god, lay at the center of the world (Johnson 2007). (The term "humanism" was a 19th century invention). Greatly enabled by the printing press (Eisenstein 1979), humanism acquired growing legions of followers, notably in Italy and later in much of Western Europe. The Dutch scholar Erasmus, for example, became a leading proponent. Humanism succeeded beyond its founders' wildest expectations, and throughout the Renaissance and Enlightenment gradually became the core of modern Western culture. Above and beyond the great intellectual flowering of art and science that it enabled, including the revival of classical learning, humanism also encouraged a tolerance for difference. Scholars and intellectuals such as Francesco Petrarch (1304–1374) played a central role in this process, and he was followed by a long list of like-minded others. So too did the observations and discoveries of scientists such as Galileo; indeed, astronomy and the Copernican revolution were vital to the emerging, secular world order (Crombie 1980).

The Enlightenment, which unfolded in the 17th and 18th centuries, offered a vast array of new ideas and discoveries (Porter 1990; Pocock 2008). Often called the "Age of Reason," it witnessed a sustained decline in the "generators of delusion like faith, dogma, revelation, authority, charism, mysticism, divination, visions, gut feelings, or the hermeneutic parsing of sacred texts" (Pinker 2018, p. 8). In the wake of the printing press and rapidly growing rates of literacy, it led countless people to free themselves from the shackles of superstitious ignorance. Rising standards of living led to the emergence of numerous writers, scholars, scientists, and other intellectuals, and a corresponding flowering of scientific and social thought. For example, famous Enlightenment scholars included Voltaire, Rousseau, Montesquieu, Diderot, Isaac Newton, Gottfried Leibniz, Michel de Montaigne, Adam Smith, John Locke, David Hume, Thomas Hobbes, Edward Gibbon, Alexander Pope, Immanuel Kant, Georg Hegel, Karl Marx, Franco Venturi, James Hutton, Edmund Burke, Samuel Johnson, and Friedrich Schiller. Others would add Benjamin Franklin, Thomas Paine, and Thomas Jefferson. Modern scientific disciplines, including biology, physics, chemistry, and geology, were all products of the Enlightenment. Books declined rapidly in price and rose in volume, as did newspapers and encyclopedias. Universities, academies, salons, and coffeehouses played major roles. An increasingly secular body of knowledge about both the natural and social worlds, countless scientific discoveries and breakthroughs, and rising productivity opened the door to notions like progress. In breaking the chains of religious dogma and popularizing science, the Enlightenment marked the most important intellectual transformation in the history of humanity. As several observers have put, the Enlightenment marked the beginning of a long process of emancipation from ignorance (Porter 2000). Ultimately this transformation gave birth to modernity itself. It must be noted, however, that the Enlightenment was not a simple trajectory of growing freedom; it also saw colonialism and the birth of racism (Bouie 2018). As Withers (2007) points out, this process was geographically uneven; there was not one, but several Enlightenments, each unfolding in a different context. Despite its manifold variations, the Enlightenment constituted a major breakthrough in human knowledge and scientific understanding.

It is all too easy to overlook the enormous social repercussions of these changes. As a response to the persistence, even resurgence, of science denialism, Steven Pinker's (2018) book *Enlightenment Now* offers a robust defense of Enlightenment values. As Pinker puts it (p. 4):

> We take its gifts for granted: newborns who live more than eight decades, markets overflowing with food, clean water that appears with the flick of a finger and waste that disappears with another, pills that erase a painful infection, sons who are not sent off to war, daughters who can walk the streets in safety, critics of the powerful who are not jailed or shot, the world's knowledge and culture available in a shirt pocket.

Pinker is right: capitalism, modernity, and science have made the world healthier, wealthier, safer, and happier than ever before (see also Deutsch 2011). Global poverty is down; famines have declined greatly; malnutrition has decreased; violence from war is on the wane; even accidents have lost much of their potency. Conversely, literacy and educational levels are on the rise. Never have so many people in human history lived so well. Despite all the horrors of colonialism, war, racism, sexism, and environmental destruction – all exacerbated by neoliberalism – modernity, grounded in truth, has made more people better off than at any point in human history.

The Enlightenment was simultaneously a social and intellectual transformation associated with the historical emergence of capitalism, the triumph of market-based social systems. The explosion of cartography, printing, the scientific method, and the celebration of objectivity formed the foundations of a worldview that became dominant in the West and indeed eventually across much of the globe (Wallerstein 1980; Wood 2002).

Philosophically, its first great product was empiricism, the view that all knowledge is grounded in experience and evidence (Marr 2003; Sober 2008). Francis Bacon, John Locke, David Hume, and others contributed to the growth of this worldview. It is difficult to overstate the significance of this transformation. Empiricism was radical in its day, helping to undermine the authority of the church by appealing to facts and data rather than divine revelation (Riskin 2002). Renaissance philosopher and statesman Francis Bacon (1561–1626) declared that experience freed human knowledge from the limitations imposed by traditional philosophy (Renaldo 1976). He argued that traditional philosophy, structured by the syllogisms of Aristotle, could not adequately describe the nature of the physical universe. Rather, he advocated for induction and the careful observation of events in the world. Knowledge should be based on perceptual experience, and facts are true without recourse to theory. The view presumes a sharp distinction between facts and values, observer and observed. Bacon was also central to the inception of what, over time, would become modern science; he is sometimes called the father of the scientific method (Gaukroger 2001). Although empiricism today has been derided because it does not value theory, it certainly played a progressive role in the formation of modern science and knowledge.

Intimately associated with the rise of empiricism and modern science was the Cartesian cogito (Hintikka 1962). The notion was proposed by Rene Descartes in Meditation Two: Of Meditations, Objections, and Replies, in which he famously concluded *"Cogito, Ergo Sum," or* "I think, therefore I exist." This became the model of human behavior that underpinned the philosophy of the natural and social sciences until the late 20th century. The cogito is an all-knowing observer suspended out of space and time who sees the world objectively, without bias or prejudice. It presumes a sharp distinction between mind and body (what one wag termed "minds in vats"), and implicitly equates mind with rationality while the body is the site of emotions and irrationality. The idea became the foundational principle that science was, or at least should be, objective and value-free. Its view of knowledge is highly individualistic and renders invisible the idea that knowledge is socially and collectively produced. Moreover, the Cartesian subject emerged hand-in-hand with Cartesian notions of absolute space as given and pre-social. With the emergence of post-positivist philosophies in the late 20th century, the notion has been widely criticized for its dismissal of subjectivity and false assumption of objectivity (Pompa 1984), what Haraway (1991) calls the "god-trick" of seeing from nowhere. In addition, as feminists have pointed out, the Cartesian subject is implicitly white and male (Broad 2017).

With roots in British empiricism, positivism began to take shape in the 19th century, when August Comte coined the term (a positive v. a normative view of reality). Unlike empiricism, which minimizes the role of theory, positivism held theoretical principles in high regard. The Vienna Circle of the 1920s and early 1930s drew upon symbolic to logic to formalize logical positivism as a coherent body of thought, explicitly articulating its principles. Like empiricism, it relied on a sharp dichotomy between viewer and viewed, subject and object. Positivism rejected "values" as unscientific, upholding the goal of an objective view of the world. In this reading, all knowledge claims are based on logical consistency and empirical verifiability; if either condition is violated, the claim to knowledge is spurious. Ultimately, this train of thought gave rise to the deductive-nomological view of knowledge, in which science is endlessly law-searching in nature. Knowledge, and truth, are garnered through careful observation, deduction, hypothesis testing, reproducible results, and the discovery of regularities. The world is seen to be inherently ordered, not chaotic, and the job of science is to uncover the laws at work in both the natural and social worlds: science brings order out of chaos. Quantitative methods and predictability are held up as the hallmarks of science. (In Karl Popper's famous revision of positivist principles, it is not verifiability but falsifiability that defines scientific knowledge).

In *Geographical Imaginations*, Derek Gregory (1994) identifies this perspective as an historically-specific "scopic regime," which, since the Renaissance and particularly the Enlightenment, has centered on a detached Cartesian observer with an ostensibly objective "view from nowhere," leading to a worldview that he calls the "world-as-exhibition." Donna Haraway (1991) famously called this notion the god-trick, but it forms the foundation of positivist epistemology. This notion confers the power to know and define the world – both social and natural – on an invisible, rational, implicitly male, decontextualized, all-knowing observer, the Cartesian cogito.

In addition to its views of knowledge and the knower, this worldview also relied upon a particular notion of space. Specifically, like the isotropic plains of location theory and regional science, traditional practitioners of GIS invariably invoke an absolute, Cartesian view of spatiality as given, not produced, a homogenous surface devoid of social origins. Absolute space has a long lineage in Western history that can be traced back to classical Greece, including Plato, Aristotle, and Greek geometry. Euclidean geometry, grounded in the assumption of one, uniform, continuous space, dominated the mathematics of spatial representation for the next two millennia. Thus, Ó Tuathail (1996, p. 70) asserts that "Greek geography, geometry, and cartography are all suffused with the teleological dream of displaying space as a simultaneous, synchronic totality." Absolute space was greatly advanced in popularity, utility and sophistication by René Descartes, who, among other things, proposed a mechanical view of the world centered on a disembodied, rational mind without distinct social or spatial roots or location. However, "positivism is based on the primacy of data, that is, information that is directly detectable through the senses. Positivist epistemology is, then, logically grounded in the materiality of people's bodies. Yet, positivism denies the presence of these bodies in making its claims to validity" (Sprague and Kobrynowicz 1999, p. 28).

In Renaissance Europe, Cartesian views of space were instrumental in the development of geometry, cartography, land surveying, civil engineering and architecture (Cosgrove 2012). The Cartesian/Euclidean notion of space – infinite, absolute, and homogenous – was replicated throughout the Renaissance and the Enlightenment, forming the basis for Newtonian physics and the theory of gravity. Such a perspective was highly instrumental to the emerging logics of globalized commodity production and consumption. For European navigators, for example, smoothing space by reducing it to distance rendered the oceans navigable, ordering the multitude of world's places in a single, unified, coherent and panopticonic understanding of the world. Similarly, Isaac Newton, greatly influenced by the recent popularity of the clock, viewed space as an abstract, absolute entity that existed independently of its measurement, that is, its existence was absolute, real regardless of whatever it contained or how it was measured. In all of these cases, space was robbed of substantive social context to become an ordered, uniform system of abstract linear coordinates.

Needless to say, positivism also attracted its share of critics. Some took aim at the notion that objectivity is possible, a view that denies the inescapable role of the observer and the unavoidable subjectivity that it entails (the so-called "myth of immaculate perception"). In adopting the god's-eye perspective, positivism fomented a false sense of objectivity. Moreover, it runs the risk of hypocrisy: attempting to be objective and value-free is itself a value. Scientific principles are themselves normative, not positive.

The strict separation of facts and values is also problematic: all data are filtered through theory, which determines what is relevant and what is not to understanding a given problem. What if facts are not as simply as we usually think they are? Indeed, as Bruno Latour (1993) argued in his work on the sociology of science, facts themselves are created, that is, made, not given. Based on his observations of scientists working in laboratories, Latour concluded that when they amass a sufficient number of observations, a consensus arises that they revolve around a "truth": in this way a fact is born. Such a view does not deny the importance of facts, but it does undermine their taken-for-granted nature.

If facts are social constructions, then they too have a history. Poovey (1998) wonderfully illustrates that facts are a form of "systematic knowledge that is derived from the theoretical interpretation of observed particulars," that is, numbers, and traces the rise of quantitative facts to the rise of mercantilist capitalism, in which counting and numbers became matters of great social import. In this reading, facts were born of the Italian Renaissance bankers and traders and the need for accurate double-entry accounting. Similarly, Shapiro (2000) brilliantly traces the birth of the fact to the English legal tradition in the 16th century. Facts became central to British empiricism, natural science, the emerging news media, and the impartial application of the law (e.g., witnesses and their credibility; jurors were seen as "judges of the fact").

Finally, positivism is incapable of understanding science as a social product; because it cannot appropriate for itself the necessary conceptual tools that embed knowledge in its social contexts, it risks forever being unable to be critical about the world; it may describe social reality, but not show how to make it better.

As a response to these criticisms, a variety of post-positivist perspectives on truth and knowledge took hold over the years.

One of the most trenchant critiques of the Enlightenment came from the Frankfurt School. Horkheimer and Adorno's (1944/2004) enormously influential volume *Dialectic of Enlightenment* positioned the Enlightenment within the context of emerging capitalism and the commodification of knowledge. While they celebrate the Enlightenment's challenge to metaphysics, they depart from conventional liberal readings of the event as part of the historical march of progress. Instead, they offer a critical reading. Their key point is that given the dynamics of commodification, Enlightenment truths are inevitably destined to decay, to become perverted, to be used as weapons of mass deception. In this bleak reading, reason is condemned to devour itself. As they put it (p. xvi), "the retreat from enlightenment into mythology is not to be sought so much in the nationalist, pagan and other modern mythologies manufactured precisely in order to contrive such a reversal, but in the Enlightenment when paralysed by fear of truth." Reason and unreason, truth and falsehood, are thus inescapably and dialectically intertwined. Worse, the "culture industries" facilitate the colonization of reason.

The Problem of Pseudo-Science

> It is far better to grasp the universe as it really is than to persist in delusion,
> however satisfying and reassuring.
> Carl Sagan

If science is grounded in truth and verifiability, then pseudo-science is its awful sister. Unfortunately, the boundaries of what constitutes valid science, and therefore accepted truth, are often unclear. The rise of modern science during the Enlightenment was grounded in empiricist and positivist notions of truth (Chapter 2). Pseudo-science has vastly different epistemological underpinnings. Pseudo-science has a long and ignominious history as old as science itself. Examples include alchemy, social Darwinism, eugenics, numerology, dowsing, cryptozoology (e.g., Big Foot), dianetics, hypnosis, extraterrestrials, graphology (handwriting analysis), and feng shui. Health-related fields are an exceptionally ripe hunting ground for pseudo-science: phrenology, aromatherapy, reflexology, rolfing, reiki, naturopathy, homeopathy, iridology, faith healing, ear candling, cupping, vitalism, and urine therapy. Others are more explicitly geographical, such as the flat Earth thesis, Atlantis, and the Bermuda Triangle.

Pseudo-science flourishes because the public is scientifically illiterate. As Sidky (2018) notes,

At the start of the twenty-first century, over 40 percent of Americans did not know that the Earth orbits the sun in a year-long cycle. ... Another 52 percent did not know that dinosaurs died before the appearance of humans, and 45 percent were unaware that the world is older than 10,000 years. It is unnecessary to mention the equally alarming numbers of people who believe in ghosts, space aliens, paranormal monsters, devil possession, angels, demons, miracles, and so forth.

Pseudo-science often superficially appears to be like science, especially to those with little or no scientific training. But what exactly are the boundaries between the two? The problem is compounded when the borders between science and pseudo-science are blurry, such as with herbal medicines or psychoanalysis. Pseudo-science is not the same as science denial, although the two are often related. As Hansson (2008), notes, "Science denialism usually proceeds by producing false controversies with legitimate science, i.e. claims that there is a scientific controversy when there is in fact none." Rather, it is more an example of what Frankfurt (2005) calls bullshit, falsehoods that are uttered to further the interests of the bullshitter. Bullshit is not necessarily lying, but often just a careless disregard towards the truth. As Ladyman (2013, pp. 52–53) argues,

> As a first approximation, we may say that pseudoscience is to science as science fraud is to bullshit. ... This is only a first approximation because we usually assume that bullshitters know what they are doing whereas ... many pseudoscientists are apparently genuinely seeking the truth. Just because one's first-order representations are that one is sincerely seeking truth, it may be argued that, in a deeper sense, one does not care about it because one does not heed to the evidence. A certain amount of self-deception on the part of its advocates explains how pseudoscience is often disconnected from a search for the truth, even though its adherents think otherwise.

Science denialism is typically spread by those whose beliefs are in conflict with real science. It often attempts to cast doubt on scientists as biased and mistake-prone, and is typically accompanied by claims that no scientific theory can ever be proven true. On the latter point they are correct.

Karl Popper (1963) famously distinguished between science and pseudo-science on the grounds of falsifiability: scientific propositions can be shown to be false, whereas metaphysical and pseudo-scientific ones cannot. Popper declared falsifiability to be both necessary and sufficient to demarcate the boundaries of science. However, this seemingly simple solution falls short. As Lakatos (1978, p. 23) asks:

> Is, then, Popper's falsifiability criterion the solution to the problem of demarcating science from pseudoscience? No. For Popper's criterion ignores the remarkable tenacity of scientific theories. Scientists have thick skins. They do not abandon a theory merely because facts contradict it.

In short, Popper's view does not address the social embeddedness of science. He ignores the possibility that a pseudo-scientific claim can be refuted. For these and other reasons, philosophers have rejected Popper's thesis as simplistic (Agassi 1991; Hansson 2006).

Hansson (2008) explores the question of demarcation between science and pseudo-science in detail. There is no single standard that differentiates one from the other. Many argue that pseudo-science fails the most basic of scientific (i.e., positivist) principles, that is, reproducible results. Pseudo-science cannot be incorporated into the existing networks of sciences. It has low standards of evidence and uses impossibly high standards in attempting to discredit real science. Pseudo-science typically uses cherry-picked examples to buttress its claims, appeals to authority, and disregards information that refutes it. It relies heavily on anecdotes rather than systematically gathered data. It often makes vague and unsubstantiated claims. Its portrayal of the causal mechanisms at work is typically unclear. Pseudo-science lacks predictability and makes no progress over time.

Despite its manifest philosophical failures, pseudo-science lives on. For example, drawing on a long tradition of pseudo-scientific eugenics, Herrnstein and Murray (1994) argued in *The Bell Curve* that genetics allegedly explained the intellectual inferiority of African-Americans and hence their generally lower socio-economic status. The book received enormous attention and was widely condemned for its poor methodology as well as its racism (e.g., Kincheloe et al. 1997; Heckman 1995). Another example is "conversion therapy," an attempt by conservatives to get gay and lesbian people to change their sexual orientation, which was, after a brief moment of notoriety, exposed as scientifically fraudulent (Cianciotto and Cahill 2007). Yet other examples abound: vaccines cause autism; astrology; creationism and intelligent design; UFOs; climate change denial.

Hollywood is arguable the world's largest producer of pseudo-science. Indeed, given the film industry's inability or unwillingness to take science seriously, what passes for science on the big screen is at best a simulacrum, at worst outright falsehoods posing as science. The issue here is not science fiction or honestly presented fantasy, which make no claim to represent the world accurately, but depictions of science that violate the established norms of science. Thus, Hollywood has inaccurately depicted sharks (Cermark 2021), climate change (e.g., *The Day After Tomorrow*), geology (e.g., *The Core*), dinosaur DNA (e.g., *Jurassic Park*), and disasters (Keane 2006). Neither is Hollywood accurate about history, with distorted representations of Egyptian mummies (e.g., *The Mummy*), the American revolution (e.g., *The Patriot*), and slavery (e.g., *Amistad*). Thus, D-day is reduced to *Saving Private Ryan* and history becomes The History Channel. The dream factories that produce the world's films aptly illustrate Baudrillard's (1984) notion of a simulacrum, in which representations become more real than what they represent. Movies blur the boundaries between fantasy and reality, giving many viewers a false sense of knowledgeability. Thus, for many people, "I saw it in a movie" becomes the equivalent of truth.

Pseudo-science is the fake news of the scientific world. It persists not because it is debunked intellectually but because it offers simplistic answers to complex problems, enables charlatans, comforts those clinging to religion (e. g., creationism), or legitimates conservative social agendas (eugenics, conversion therapy). It has been used as a weapon against immigrants (e. g., early IQ tests) and an instrument of corporate deception (e. g., regarding tobacco and smoking).

Marxism and Truth

Grounded in dialectical historical materialism, Marxism offered a theory of truth that both intersected with and challenged notions inherited from the Enlightenment. Marx wove together elements of French utopian socialism, German idealism (Hegel), and British political economy to form an enormously persuasive and influential ideology that had major social impacts in the late 19th and 20th centuries. Marxism, of course, is not a single philosophy, and has many variants and species that have changed historically; structural Marxism, Western cultural Marxism (a la the Frankfurt School), and feminist Marxism are some examples. But running throughout all of these is the notion that only Marxism, of whatever type, can accurately analyze social predicaments and offer a path forward. Marx wrote about many things, and Marxism as a philosophical and analytical tradition are concerned with many different topics, but it is the issue of ideology and truth that is of most concern here.

Grounded in the Enlightenment, Marx, and Marxists, viewed Marxism as the science of society. Marxism thus inherited many Enlightenment assumptions, such as the notion that the world is fundamentally ordered, progress is possible, if not inevitable, and that objectivity is both possible and desirable. In this way Marxism shared much in common with its Enlightenment cousin, positivism.

Marx's adamant materialism held that it is the real world of work, labor, and power that drives ideas, not vice-versa (in contrast to a long tradition of German idealism), that is, of an economic base sustaining a cultural superstructure. Some critics claim that his materialism led him to pay scant attention to issues of consciousness, ideology, and lived experience. His great innovation in this respect was to tie ideas, and truth, to the notion of class: "The ruling ideas of each age have ever been the ideas of its ruling class, i. e., the class which is the ruling material force of society is at the same time its ruling intellectual force" (Marx and Engels 1976, p. 59). In short, ideas that gain currency and legitimacy tend to be those that serve the interests of the ruling class, justifies its dominance, and/or renders it invisible. Prevalent ideologies and discourses of each age tend to naturalize it, show it to be inevitable and unchangeable, and thus represent inequality and injustice as inescapable. Marx reserved his most scathing comments for religion, which he famously dismissed as the "opiate of the masses." Often dominant ideologies portray particular ideas as not falling into the service of the ruling class but serving society as a whole. This issue is particularly important when the ruling class exerts control over the means of production of ideas, whether they be the church, the media, or educational systems, that is, the cultural superstructure.

Conventionally, Marxism held that "ideology" concealed reality, a set of bourgeois truths: it was, in short, "false consciousness" (Pines 1993; Torrance 1995; Parekh 2015). Such a view posits that ideology is inevitably set in contradiction with science, that is, with Marxism. The problem with this notion is that, obviously, Marxism too is an ideology, even if it purports to be a science. Indeed, the arrogance of proclaiming to possess the one "true" reading of the social world proved to be a major weakness in Marxism, leading it to be slow to respond to critiques, include new perspectives, and adjust to the ever-changing nature of capitalism. Marxism's view of culture, consciousness, ideology, everyday life, and social reproduction were never particularly sophisticated or convincing, despite a multitude of attempts to graft these onto it. Marxism also developed a well-earned reputation for letting theory run roughshod over the data. Georg Lukács, for example, once argued "Truly orthodox dialectical Marxists paid little attention to the so-called facts" (quoted in López 2020, p. 50).

Marxism continued to play a highly important role in subsequent analyses of ideology, including Lukács, Gramsci, the Frankfurt School, and Althusser. Gramsci's works on ideology helped to expose the resilience of capitalism and its hold over everyday life, holding that ideology kept people in a state of voluntary servitude. Western Marxists in particular questioned the primacy of the economic base over the cultural superstructure and upheld the autonomy of the cultural and the political as independent spheres in their own right. Marx's dialectics helped to establish the notion of truth as relational and context-bound. Most importantly, Marxism exposed the intimate links among truth, power, class, and politics. Marx, of course, was not the first to undertake this task – Nietzsche, at least, beat him to it. But Marxist thought was far more influential than Nietzsche's ever was. Moreover, Marx historicized knowledge and truth, showing they cannot be understood outside of their particular social contexts.

The Relativization of Truth

I'm for truth, no matter who tells it.
Malcolm X

The accepted notion of "truth" that exists whether we recognize it or not received its first challenge from Friedrich Nietzsche (1844–1900). Nietzsche was a complicated figure whose worldview exhibited numerous facets, from the *ubermensch* to his Social Darwinism, contempt for morals, ultra-individualism, and militant atheism, but it is his perspectivism that concerns us here. In declaring god is dead, he announced the end the god's-eye view, i.e., that of any overarching, value-free view of the world. In short, he rejected objective truth and the correspondence theory of truth (Cox 1999; Remhof 2015). For Nietzsche, knowledge is conditional, dependent on the viewer, situated, and partial. This notion challenged the long-held (and still widespread) notion that knowledge is a reproduction of reality. Essentially, he held that "there are no facts, only interpretations," making him an early predecessor of post-truth (Gemes 2018). The old distinction between facts and values, observed and observer, collapses. The grounds for deciding one view is better than another are shaky, and often lodged in social values rather than scientific evidence. Nietzsche is thus credited with the notion of perspectivism, the notion that all views are a view from somewhere, that truth – and knowledge more broadly – are always reflective of the knower. Nietzsche thus uncouples truth and objectivity and injects relativism into the heart of concerns about truth. This view in some ways borrows from and extends the Continental tradition of faith in reason, a common element of many idealist philosophers.

Moreover, one's knowledge and perspective are inextricably bound to one's social position, interests, and power relations. As he put it in his famous book *Daybreak* (1888/1997), "All things are subject to interpretation; whichever interpretation prevails is a function of power and not truth." In *Beyond Good and Evil*, Nietzsche discusses the "will to truth": "It is our needs that interpret the world; our drives ... Every drive is a kind of wish to rule; each one has its perspective that it would like to compel all the other drives to accept as a norm." This notion then leads him to frame truth as a set of stories serving interests rather than knowledge linked to facts:

> What then is truth? A movable host of metaphors, metonymies, and anthropomorphisms: in short, a sum of human relations which have been poetically and rhetorically intensified, transferred, and embellished, and which, after long usage, seem to a people to be fixed, canonical, and binding. Truths are illusions which we have forgotten are illusions – they are metaphors that have become worn out and have been drained of sensuous force.

In this reading, truth is not synonymous with facts or data, but how well it fits into an existing framework, i. e., how well it serves an interest, a view with hints of the coherence and pragmatist versions of truth. One might say that Nietzsche's view of truth is that it is life-affirming, that is serves the end goals of living and the will to power. Truth is thus the justification of might; in doing so, Nietzsche irrevocably sutured truth to power, a view that greatly influenced Foucault and others.

Geographers have generally been loath to invoke Nietzsche (but see the special issue of *ACME* in 2010). Guelke (2003) pointed out that the popularity of postmodernism in geography owed much to Nietzsche, whose anti-humanism he views as having contaminated the current reincarnation of perspectivism. Günzel (2003), among others, tackles Nietzsche's geophilosophy, advocating a Deleuze-Guatarrian view of landscapes in *Thus Spake Zarathustra*. Jacobs (2010) links him to the discipline's concerns with morality and place-based knowledge, the long-standing tension between universal explanations and local knowledge. (Notably she examines the Australian government's apology to aboriginal peoples, although in Nietzsche's worldview the powerful never apologize, or need to do so).

Ludwig Wittgenstein, the famed Austrian philosopher, also played a role in the relativization of truth. He started as an analytic philosopher wedded to the correspondence theory, as embodied in the *Tractatus*, in which he argued that the logical structure of language provides the limits of meaning and philosophy. Thus, he famously stated "What we cannot speak of, we must pass over in silence." Later, Wittgenstein came to abandon his earlier position in favor of a more linguistically-oriented notion, language-games, or communities of understanding, that emphasized the utility of words within everyday life, as elucidated in *Philosophical Investigations* (Ellenbogen 2003). In this later view, meanings are defined pragmatically, not logically, and can only be understood within their social context. Meaning is derived from actions, not thought, that is, by being engaged with the world. Wittgenstein was important in solidifying the notion that truths, and all knowledge, could not be separated from their expression in language.

The relativization of truth in the sciences received a tremendous push with the publication of Thomas Kuhn's famous and enormously influential volume, *The Structure of Scientific Revolutions* in 1962. Rather than some inevitable march of progress, Kuhn posited that scientists formed communities of scholars with shared values and assumptions, or paradigms. As he put it (1962/2012, p. x), paradigms are "universally recognized scientific achievements that for a time provide model problems and solutions to a community of practitioners." Paradigms are thus constellations of theories that define problems and solutions. For windows of time, paradigms defined what he called "normal science." Normal science is not particularly innovative or revolutionary, following accepted guidelines. It is best exemplified in textbooks. During periods in which anomalies presented great difficulties, this community was thrown into crisis, and the search for a new paradigm began. In Kuhn's (1962/2012, p. 90) words,

> Confronted with anomaly or with crisis, scientists take a different attitude toward existing paradigms, and the nature of their research changes accordingly. The proliferation of competing articulations, the willingness to try anything, the expression of explicit discontent, the recourse to philosophy and to debate over fundamentals, all these are symptoms of a transition from normal to extraordinary research.

The inability of an existing paradigm to solve certain predicaments, mysteries, and problems led to the search for a new one; new paradigms explained issues and answered questions better than did old ones. The most famous of such shifts was that from Newtonian to Einsteinian physics in the early 20th century. The notion of paradigms was soon exported to many other fields of knowledge, including the social sciences (Barnes 1982).

Kuhn, a physicist, initiated the notion that scientists indeed had values and began to undermine the assumption of objectivity. As he argued (p. 157),

> But paradigm debates are not really about relative problem-solving ability, though for good reasons they are usually couched in those terms. Instead, the issue is which paradigm should in future guide research on problems many of which neither competitor can yet claim to resolve completely. A decision between alternate ways of practicing science is called for, and in the circumstances that decision must be based less on past achievement than on future promise. ... A decision of that kind can only be made on faith.

Rather than simply a set of abstract ideas and a cumulative progression over time, science is viewed as the product of communities of scholars who are all too human. It injected issues of cognition into scientific discovery and positioned science within an historical time frame. It forced a reconsideration that there is such a thing as transhistorical standards for truth: rather than a given body of knowledge that is valid eternally, scientific truths are transient and subject to change. While Kuhn's project was clearly path-breaking, one might argue that he failed to socialize the production of knowledge, viewing epistemological transitions in idealist terms in which one set of ideas follows another rather than reflecting changing social priorities in which new forms of knowledge are called forth to address new types of problems. In a sense, Kuhn did not go far enough, i.e., into a full-fledged constructivist critique of science.

Kuhn's work should be situated within the broader context of an emerging group of critics of positivism and empiricism. Prominent among them was the iconoclast Paul Feyerabend (1975), who promoted an anarchist view of knowledge in which "anything goes." In this reading, science should not be privileged; it is only one of many ways of interpreting the world, not the one and only way of creating knowledge. This was a radical relativism that far surpassed that of Kuhn. Even more provocatively, Feyerabend claimed that sscience has advanced despite the practice of the scientific method rather than because of it. Others in this line of thought included Stephen Toulmin (1958) and Imre Lakatos (1970), who challenged not only the prevailing ethos of scientific standards but scientism itself, the notion that science is the most (or even only) valid form of knowledge. As Sorell (1994, p. 35) put it, "Scientism is a matter of putting too high a value on natural science in comparison with other branches of learning or culture." Such works promoted a methodological pluralism and, increasingly, an epistemological one. They challenged the dichotomy between facts and theories and posited there is no rational way of choosing among competing theories. They helped to discredit the inevitability of the scientific method and the façade of objectivity. Critics called such a view anarchist or Dadaist, or even enemy of science.

Finally, it should be noted that the relativization of truth reached new heights with phenomenology, the study of lived experience (Sokolowski 2000; Engelland 2020). Phenomenology has a long and distinguished history that stretches back to medieval hermeneutics. In the 19th century, German philosopher Edmund Husserl famously likened the search for truth to peeling an onion, pulling back the tenacious layers of mystification that surround human experience to find its "essence": we may never discover a final "truth," but the process is what counts. Husserl's student, Martin Heidegger, was also fascinated by truth: the task of phenomenological description was to provide a platform for an interpretive understanding of being. Of all the approaches to truth, phenomenology takes most seriously the nature of perception and interpretation. There is an objective world, but we only know it subjectively; we cannot escape from the world of human meanings. Subjectivity is thus not a barrier to truth, but the only means of understanding it. This body work made a powerful case for a radical perspectivalism, taking Nietzsche to the level of the individual. In so doing, it foregrounded human intentionality, experience, meanings, and languages, blurring the subject/object division. Phenomenology was important in asserting that truth is always truth *for someone*, that is, truth does not hang in some void but is always embodied, put to use, made to work. Truth that resides in dusty library books is no truth at all.

However, if phenomenology was great at interrogating lived experience, its epistemological account of truth was less fruitful. It runs the risk of endless relativism, of lacking the capacity to differentiate some truths from others. If we all live in our own subjective worlds, can truth be shared intersubjectively? Where phenomenology fails is in its inability to portray truth in social, not simply individual, terms. In a sense, phenomenology represents the relativization of truth taken too far, to extremes that deny it the ability to harness truth to historical context, power, and social life.

In the wake of Kuhn's *Structure*, social constructivism began to take hold, particularly in the social sciences. Constructivism is a broad term, and there are many variants of it, and it has been applied in different ways in different disciplines. The notion became particularly widespread in educational circles, many of whom were influenced by Brazilian educator and author Paulo Freire. However, even in the sciences constructivism began to take hold (Kukla 2013). Constructivism may be defined as the view that knowledge is socially (not simply individually produced), and thus is inseparable from the circumstances of its making (Watzlawick 1984; Gillett 1998; Kratochwil 2008). In contrast to objectivism, which denies the role of perception, constructivism emphasizes that the world is only known subjectively. This view does not deny the existence of a reality but holds that knowledge of that reality is always and inevitably mediated through human perceptions, ideologies, and interests. Constructivism thus calls attention to the importance of interpretations, language, representations, lived experience, and the inseparability of the knower and known. Knowledge is thus historically situated and always contingent, and the criteria for valid knowledge shift over time and space. The most radical forms of constructivism reduce the world to discourse, an idealist error: as Sprague and Kobrynowicz (1999, p. 27) argue, "If positivism is the epistemology of fact, radical constructivism is an epistemology of fiction." Because much, but not all, of knowledge addresses the relevant problems of the day, forms of knowledge that address pressing predicaments rise to the fore of political agendas, while those that do not take a back seat. Finally, constructivism holds that knowledge does not simply passively mirror the world but enters into its making: discourses are constitutive as well as reflective of the world.

Foucault and the Social Construction of Truth

If Kuhn initiated the project of socializing knowledge and paved the way for constructivism, it was Michel Foucault who decisively led it into the domain of social constructivism. It is difficult to overestimate Foucault's impact on philosophy and the social sciences; he was arguably the most influential philosopher of the twentieth century, with enormous effects on multiple disciplines. Foucault's studies ran wide and deep, and concerned a large number of topics: the emergence of modernity; the role of the state and governmentality; discipline, surveillance, and panopticons; sexuality; biopolitics; and discourse and the production of human subjects. He was regaled or vilified, depending on one's position, as a structuralist, Marxist, and post-structuralist. For our purposes, it is Foucault's epistemology that is important.

In contrast to prevailing (notably Marxist) notions of power as exclusively a top-down phenomenon, Foucault offered a view of power from the bottom-up, that is, power as it was manifested in daily practices. He thus resituated politics from the abstract level of the state to the sphere of everyday life. Power relations thus do not simply hinder or constrain behavior, but are productive of it, enabling some behaviors and not others. Particularly with the rise of the Western bureaucratic state, power has become extensive rather than intensive in nature, i. e., found more in the self-subjugation of subjects rather than the heavy, visible hand of state oppression. The modern Western subject and the rise of bureaucratic surveillant societies are thus two sides of one coin, and emerged hand-in-hand.

Central to his life's work were the intersections of power and knowledge. Foucault offered a powerful notion of truth grounded in historical reality, i. e., truth as a social construction. For Foucault, knowledge, and thus truth, are inseparable from power. He famously stated (1980, p. 131):

> Truth is a thing of this world: it is produced only by virtue of multiple forms of constraint. And it induces regular effects of power. Each society has its regime of truth, its "general politics" of truth: that is, the types of discourse which it accepts and makes function as true; the mechanisms and instances which enable one to distinguish true and false statements, the means by which each is sanctioned; the techniques and procedures accorded value in the acquisition of truth; the status of those who are charged with saying what counts as true.

Power in this conception is not simply imposed from above, but woven into the fabric of everyday life. As Foucault (1977, p. 27) states, "no power can be exercised without extraction, appropriation, distribution or retention of knowledge'; therefore 'power and knowledge imply one another." Power as ideology is a way of producing subjects, of disciplining them, including their bodies via the microphysics of biopolitics (e. g., schools, hospitals, asylums). Foucault's suturing of truth and power deeply shaped his views of mental illness in *Madness and Civilization* (1965), the history of power in *The Archaeology of Knowledge* (1969), and the production of ideas in *The Order of Things* (1966). Social science and institutions are thus forms of power that naturalize some versions of reality and marginalize others. Thus, Foucault socialized the notion of truth, noting that what is held to be truth varies historically (and geographically). Every claim to truth is a claim to power, linked to an interest; the claim to universal truth is a claim to universal power. If for Habermas truth is the product of reasoned debate unfettered by power, for Foucault it is all about power and the ability to produce subjects that imbibe discourse as truth (Nielsen 1997).

Central to Foucault's project were discourses, power/knowledge constellations that integrated ideas, ideologies, and philosophies, or as he called them, "epistemes." A discourse ore episteme is a structured set of meanings, a way of knowing, or set of rules of knowledge construction. Examples include science, religion, nationalism, gender, racism, the market, and globalization. These differentiate truth from falsehoods at varying historical moments. Foucault (1980, p. 197) argues:

> I would define the episteme retrospectively as the strategic apparatus which permits of separating out from among all the statements which are possible those that will be acceptable within, I won't say a scientific theory, but a field of scientificity, and which it is possible to say are true or false. The episteme is the 'apparatus' which makes possible the separation, not of the true from the false, but of what may from what may not be characterised as scientific.

Critically, discourses don't just mirror the world; people are produced through discourses, which define the contours of socialization, the boundaries of what is considered normal, important, and proper. Foucault thus denied the existence of the autonomous, independent subject, and for this reason is widely considered to be anti-humanist in his outlook.

To excavate the truths that each era constructs for itself, Foucault advocated the strategies of "archaeology" and "genealogy." By archaeology, Foucault attempted to differentiate his approach from conventional history and its longitudinal emphasis. Rather, he was interested in all the elements that contributed to the hegemony of discourses at particular moments in time. Truth in this reading becomes historically-specific. "Each society has its regime of truth, its 'general politics' of truth; that is the types of discourse it accepts and makes to function as true" (Foucault 1980, p. 131). Archaeology is a form of historical analysis that defines the rules of what may be conceived and expressed in different contexts. In contrast, genealogies, which are based on archaeologies, focus on how people adopt particular epistemes, the deep origins of the taken-for-granted, and the breadth and power of discourse; it is a deconstruction of truths. Thus, rather than see the history of thought as a continuous line, Foucault emphasized its disjunctures and inconstancy.

In a famous essay *What is Enlightenment?* that appeared in 1984, Foucault thoroughly historicized the Enlightenment, which means uncovering the social conditions in which it arose, its multiplicity of expressions, the political interests to which it was linked, and the power relations that accompanied the rise of modern Western knowledge. He was adamant that the Enlightenment be viewed as set of diverse practices:

> We must never forget that the Enlightenment is an event, or a set of events and complex historical processes, that is located at a certain point in the development of European societies. As such, it includes elements of social transformation, types of political institution, forms of knowledge, projects of rationalisation of knowledge and practices, technological mutations that are very difficult to sum up in a word (Foucault 1997, p. 121).

Foucault challenged the notion that science and rationality led inevitably to moral progress. Viewed this way, that is, skeptically, the Enlightenment must be viewed as something more than simply the long arc of truth and rationality, a favorite myth of liberal intellectual history.

In viewing the rise of modern, Western society this way, Foucault took the constructivist approach to knowledge to denaturalize the Enlightenment and expose its historical contingency. Such a move undermines implicit, Whiggish notions of history as some teleological inevitability. Moreover, Foucault decisively historicized any and all notions of truth and knowledge, and demonstrated their close linkages to power relations. In doing so, he opened the door to the massive relativization of truth that unfolded in the late twentieth century in the forms of postmodernism and poststructuralism.

Feminism and Truth

Feminism arose from women's secondary status in patriarchal societies. Feminism views the world through the lens of gender, much as Marxism did with class. Social reality, including how we know the world, is gendered, shot through with the multiple assumptions that are deeply woven into gender as a social and political construction. Not surprisingly, feminists have added depth and complexity to epistemology and the study of truth. Feminism, of course, is not one, unified body of thought but a series of intertwined perspectives, which are often at odds with one another. There are, for example, feminist Marxists and feminist postmodernists. Some versions (e.g., ecofeminism) risk essentializing women, arguing that "women's ways of knowing" emanate from their roles in social reproduction. However, feminism has made decisive contributions concerning the relations between knowledge and power, upholding the view that knowledge and truths are partial, situated, and embodied. It has helped to foment respect for marginalized subject positions whose social status often led to them not being taken seriously. As with much of critical social theory, feminism is a means to give voice to those whose voices have not been heard.

This body of work elevated gender from an ontological category to an epistemological one concerned with how knowledge is produced, by whom, and for whom. It reveals the Cartesian observer as implicitly male in a worldview that equates rationality with masculinity, a view that automatically reduces women to the level of the irrational. Barbour (2018, pp. 211–212) holds that:

> Central to many feminist perspectives has been an argument that the epistemological project to articulate neutral, objective and transcendent knowledge has privileged the understandings of dominant Western white men. ... Thus, the feminist challenge to Western epistemology

has been to reveal the constructed nature and male bias of "knowledge", to recreate "knowledges" to include multiple perspectives, and to validate women as knowers.

Accordingly, the beliefs, practices, and views of women, and other marginalized groups, have often been ignored in Western philosophy and science. Like other relational approaches to philosophy, feminism views knowledge as a social, not simply intellectual, product, and its production inevitably reflects different historical and geographical contexts.

Feminist scientists and philosophers have issued powerful indictments of masculinist approaches to knowledge (Rose 1994). Sandra Harding (1986, 1991), for example, raised insightful concerns about the nature of scientific knowledge, what questions are asked, what agendas are set, and the taken-for-granted notion that science is a masculinist act of penetrating nature and unlocking "her" secrets, calling into question its deeply androcentric and phallocratic character. Of course, acknowledging that science is gendered is to view it as a social process, not simply a set of ideas. Her work raised the issue of "strong objectivity," asking what kinds of knowledge are objective (or not), and for whom. In this reading, scientific research cannot be separated from daily life, from the context and ideology of the researcher; the gap between observer and observed disappears.

Similarly, Donna Haraway (1985, 1988) advocated for situated knowledges, in which different perspectives are applied to different issues and contexts, allowing a diversity of viewpoints to flower. By emphasizing the contingent nature of all truth claims, these works redefined the notion of objectivity, moving it away from its traditional preoccupation with being value-free to mean views that acknowledge their own subject positions and the contingent nature of all claims to truth. She argues (1988, p. 590), for example, that viewed this way, "science becomes the paradigmatic model, not of closure, but of that which is contestable and contested." By translating across different perspectives and connecting ever-changing situated views of the world, we can construct a provisional agreement, or truth.

This line of thought led to methodological advances such as standpoint theory (Hartsock 1984; Hekman 1997), which takes seriously personal knowledge in the analysis of inter-subjective discourses, an experiential approach to knowledge and truth. Sprague and Kobrynowicz (1999, p. 27) note that "Standpoint theorists begin by rejecting positivism's pretentions of creating a view from nowhere in favor of the postulate that each subject is specific, located in a particular time and place. But this in turn raises the hoary question of whose standpoint matters the most. Hartsock held that good social theory is one that enables social justice, i.e., one that exposes inequalities and points the way to overcoming them. Thus standpoint theory assigns epistemic priority is to people of color and other oppressed groups.

Feminist epistemology, while diverse, nonetheless offers a consensus of sorts (Potter 2006): that an epistemic agent's life context is relevant to the views and knowledge that they produce; that knowledge, and thus truth, is collectively, not individually produced; all knowledge is partial, situated, reflexive, and embodied; and that the conditions of knowledge are vital to understanding how and what kinds of knowledge are produced, and for whom.

Feminism had powerful and constructive impacts on geography, long a field dominated by men (Hanson 1992). Feminists played a constructive role in injecting gender into urban geography, challenging the public/private dichotomy, studies of commuting, and household divisions of labor. They raised the issue of the gaze and who it belongs to, a notion that stretches from Foucault to studies in tourism. Feminists invented and put to use a variety of qualitative methodologies long overlooked by male geographers, emphasizing positionality and breaking down the power relations between researcher and subject. They elevated the art of listening and cultivating empathy. A spatialized feminist epistemology was particularly advanced by Gillian Rose (1993), who argued that to assume that one knows is to assert authority, which codes others as objects. Geography done this way thus secures the primacy of the gaze of white men; women are reduced to a passive landscape to be gazed upon. The "gaze" was subsequently generalized to other contexts, such as the tourist gaze. To know the Other is to understand him/her on one's own terms.

Post-modernism and Truth

With roots that echo Nietzsche's perspectivism and the coherence theory of truth, postmodernism erupted in the social sciences in the 1980s and 1990s. Post-modernism is a loose collection of beliefs with many variations. The term "post-modern" is unfortunate; it connotes what the perspective is not rather than what it is. It was coined by Francois Lyotard, whose hugely influential book *The Postmodern Condition* (1984) posited that the modern world had fragmented into hyperspecialized communities with limited mutual intelligibility. Lyotard proposed an "incredulity towards meta-narratives," a sustained suspicion of all grand theories and epistemologies (e.g., positivism, Marxism) as holdovers of the Enlightenment, empty promises that offered sweeping views but always fell victim to their own arrogance and overreach. In the place of these grand narratives, Lyotard pointed to the proliferation of less ambitious, non-totalizing explanations (*petits récits*). His view held that our perspectives on reality have become so divergent that it is no longer meaningful to seek "the truth."

Post-modernism is often offered up as part of a series of "posts" that engulfed the world in the late 20th century: post-industrial, post-Fordist, post-capitalist, post-structuralist, post-human, and, yes, post-truth. None of these labels describe what they are, only what they are not. Yet their collective presence testifies to the multiplicity of perspectives, the decay and abandonment of long-standing worldviews, and the search for new epistemologies in the midst of intense and rapid social change. By the late 20th century, post-modernism had become influential in architecture, literary theory, philosophy, and the social sciences.

Following Foucault, postmodernists agree that knowledge, and thus truth, is historically constructed and inevitably linked to power. All ways of viewing the world, including the sciences, reflect particular constellations of cultural values, particularly modern, Western ones that became triumphant globally on the heels of colonialism. Far from consisting of a set of eternal truths, modernity is a claim to universal power. Post-modernism is thus resolutely relativistic, viewing knowledge as contingent and contextual (Best 1991). In this respect it owes much to the pioneering works of Richard Rorty (1987), who argued for retiring the notion of truth in favor of an infinite adjustment of beliefs. This view also firmly agrees with Donna Haraway's (1988) notion that there is no god-trick, no privileged perspective that sees the world "as it really is," only a series of partial, situated worldviews in collision with one another. For Rorty, for example, knowledge should not be conceived as a mirror of reality – the classic Enlightenment view – but rather as a conversation of multiple voices, an aural rather than optic image. The discussion is a more apt metaphor for how knowledge is created than is the mirror, a challenge to Western occularcentrism. This line of thought displaces seeing as the privileged way of knowing with hearing and listening, a move that foregrounds the partial nature of all worldviews and their embodiment in subjects grounded in time and space.

In keeping with the linguistic turn that entranced many social theorists – the view that language and representation are inescapable and profoundly shape how we view the world – post-modernism places a heavy emphasis on issues of language and discourse. Everything is a discourse because there is no way of viewing the world outside of it. Language is not simply a mirror of the world because we live in it, all the time. As with Roland Barthes's notion of intertextuality, this view notes that every sign or signifier inevitably refers to other signs and signifiers, an endless process of referentiality. Thus, in the words of Derrida, *il n'y a pas de hors-texte*, "there is no outside-text" (often misinterpreted as "there is nothing outside of the text"). To resolve this, Derrida proposed that we define concepts not in relation to the external world, but through their differences with other concepts.

Post-modernism perhaps finds its most explicit statement in the deconstruction of Jacques Derrida, in which all truths are held to be social constructions, partial, and reflect social interests. While he wrote on many topics, Derrida (1967/2016) is best known for his work on deconstruction, a reinterpretation of the old medieval custom of hermeneutics. Deconstruction reverses the old Platonic hierarchy that privileges essences over appearances; rather, all we have to work with are the appearances of things, a notion with shades of Humean empiricism. Deconstruction holds that meanings are lodged in the realm of appearances. Derrida attacked the Western tradition of logocentrism – the long-standing view that language is indicative of an external reality – arguing that signs and symbols had become distinct from what they represent. In doing so, he rejected the tradition of binaries that are often used to frame difference (e. g., good/evil, presence/absence). To deconstruct, say, a text or a landscape, is to examine the origins of ideas, to pull out their multiple meanings and play them against one another, to show there is no essential core, and to reveal the historical assumptions behind it. Rather than uncover "truth," deconstruction aims to open up the possibilities of infinite meanings. It invites us to read between the lines and examine absences as much as presences. To deconstruct is to expose the contradictions inherent in every text, to rob them of their fixed meanings, and to show that fixed, determinate meanings are impossible. Deconstruction, in showing there is no fixed, given order, played a major role in the development of post-structuralism.

Post-modernism also popularized the notion that power and knowledge are intimately linked, a view that draws heavily on Foucault. This view was found, for example, in debates over "Great Books" in universities – whose literature should be taught? Who decides what constitutes the canon? On what grounds? Is the only valuable literature written by dead white men? The notion soon expanded into multiculturalism, which had important impacts on curricula and teaching in higher education. More broadly, it shifted the focus of much inquiry from the social core – those with power and prestige – to the periphery, to groups long marginalized in politics and academia, whose voices have long been silenced. Influenced by Marxism, social history had initiated such a move much earlier to hold up the everyday lives of the poor and powerless as worthy of attention. This focus on the subaltern soon spread beyond class to encompass gender, ethnicity, and sexuality, all of which are bound together in complex webs of intersectionality. The life experiences of people such as women, ethnic minorities, gays and lesbians, and the handicapped were held to be valuable sources of insight offering different ways of knowing. Post-modernism thus inculcated a habit of listening to the dispossessed, of being respectful of difference, to take seriously the views of those with whom we do not share much in common socially or culturally. In short, social distance matters not just ontologically, that is, as a matter of politics, but epistemologically, i. e., as a way of knowing.

Post-modernism achieved wide acclaim, and ridicule, when it challenged one of the central Enlightenment notions: that the world is fundamentally ordered. The purpose of science, in this view, is to reveal the laws that make reality intelligible. Yet perhaps this notion is itself flawed. Lyotard (1984), for example, questioned the utility of grand metanarratives that purported to show how reality is structured. Rather, he argued, such discourses tend to hide as much as they reveal. What if the universe is not fundamentally structured in ways that we can interpret? When we look for order, and truth, we find it, but the same can be said for disorder and falsehood. What makes one more evident than the other? What if our languages so oversimplify reality that they mask its fundamental disorder and chaos? Perhaps the world is more complex than our languages allow us to admit. As Michael Mann (1986, p. 4) elegantly put it, "Societies are much messier than our theories of them." In this sense, post-modernism is post-foundational, i.e., it is freed from any grounding in basic, essential, and unchangeable principles.

What, then, is "true" in a post-modern world? There is no easy answer to this question. Post-modernism accepts that there are a variety of truths, each of which has differential sway over varying patches of time and space. There is no right or wrong answer, only narratives. Professions of truth are inevitably reflections of the ideology of the party making them; all knowledge claims are assertions of authority. Truths are always context-dependent, and reflect the truth-producer's social status, including ethnicity and gender. Because nothing exists independent of the discourse that gives rise to it, understanding reality outside of our linguistic webs is impossible. However, by questioning the notion of objective truth, post-modernism also corroded the very notion of truth itself.

Post-modernism's difficulties became apparent when its critique extended beyond the social sciences and humanities to include the natural sciences. Many critiques drew upon Paul Feyerabend's (1975) influential *Against Method*, which asserted that in the cultural construction of knowledge, research methodologies are simply ornamentations to justify truths arrived by irrational means. Social constructivists gave rise to "science studies" to show that science, too, was a set of discourses that served political ends (Koertge 1998). In the process, objective truth was thrown out the window as hopelessly old-fashioned. Sidky (2018) holds that "postmodernists transformed the reasonable position that 'facts do not speak for themselves' into the absurd conclusion that 'there are no facts,' and that no knowledge of the empirical world is possible, which is a gross *non sequitur*." Feminists chimed in that science was a masculinist attempt at "prying the secrets loose" from mother nature (Merchant 1990), and Sandra Harding (1986) claimed that Newton's famous *Principia Mathematica* was a "rape manual." The attempt produced a predictable backlash. Gross and Levett (1997), issued a call to arms, holding that postmodern critiques of science were put forth by people who knew nothing about it. Alan Sokal (1996) published a famous tongue-in-cheek satire in *Social Text* that used post-modernism's tenets against it, deliberately spouting nonsense that the journal's editors failed to catch; he later expanded his critique (Sokal and Bricmont 1998; Sokal 2008). The fall-out was enormous, causing widespread embarrassment among social theorists (Sidky 2018). Postmodernism was often equated with left-wing irrationality (Stove 2001). Even Bruno Latour (2004, p. 227), founder of science and technology studies, lamented the antiscientific turn, noting that

> Entire Ph.D. programs are still running to make sure that good American kids are learning the hard way that facts are made up, that there is no such thing as natural, unmediated, unbiased access to truth … while dangerous extremists are using the very same argument of social construction to destroy hard-won evidence that could save our lives (see also Kofman 2018).

Post-modernism runs the risk of endless relativism (Iannone 2017), one in which there are few, if any, criteria that define good knowledge from bad, or reality from fiction. In its most extreme versions, post-modernism collapses into nihilism, i.e., that there is no truth whatsoever, only fictions that we tell one another. As philosopher Daniel Dennett lamented, "what the postmodernists did was truly evil. They are responsible for the intellectual fad that made it respectable to be cynical about truth and facts" (quoted in Cawalladr 2017). In this way, post-modernism played a very real role in the rise of the post-truth society (Calcutt 2016; Boler and Davis 2018). Not surprisingly, the insights offered by post-modernism were eventually co-opted by right-wing political forces to serve their own ends, including science denial.

Blurring the boundaries between fiction and reality also calls to mind Baudrillard's (1983) famous notion of the simulacrum. Simulacra are representations or imitations that never had an original referent, or whose referent has vanished: a copy without an original. An Irish bar filled with four-leaf clovers becomes more Irish than Ireland itself; the History Channel becomes more real than history does itself. In each case there is a substitution of signs of the real for the real itself. In a postmodern world defined by information-intensive capitalism, the boundaries between image and reality, representation and the represented, image and reality, blur and become vague, even meaningless. Under the relentless pressure of consumerism, use values evaporate into exchange values: the real world of the laborer, of sweat and pain, is obscured, and only advertisements are real. Simulacra have both epistemological and ontological effects. As Baudrillard (1981/1994, p. 79) argues in *Simulacra and Simulation*, "We live in a world where there is more and more information, and less and less meaning." The world of signs represents reality so well that it threatens to replace it (Hagerty 2004). Unmoored from the real world, simulacra have *become* reality, or even better, hyperreality. Baudrillard offers Disneyland as a prime example of hyperreality, where the gap between the real and the imaginary disappears. Although offered as an imaginary kingdom, hyperreality takes on a life of its own, as a lived reality, infantilizing everyone in the process. Even more broadly, in *America* (1986) he imagines the U.S. as a kind of Disneyland writ large, a country that has lost its origins, is mired in consumerism, and lacks a clear identity.

Simulacra are deeply spatial. For example, Jorge Luis Borges wrote about cartographers who create a life-size map so detailed that it obscures what it was meant to represent (Tally 2018). As the map slowly dissolves, Borges (1983) argues the representation is more real than the reality: "Henceforth, it is the map that precedes the territory—precession of simulacra—it is the map that engenders the territory and if we were to revive the fable today, it would be the territory whose shreds are slowly rotting across the map."

Perhaps more than any other single phenomenon, television exemplifies the post-modern blurring of image and reality. Television became the first medium to stitch together the world as a collage of simultaneous sights and sounds divorced from their historical or geographical context. As Baudrillard (1986) notes, "There is nothing more mysterious than a TV set left on in an empty room." Television proved to be more than up to the challenge of providing viewers with massive amounts of rapid, discontinuous information. As an enormous body of work has demonstrated, television powerfully structures everyday understandings by providing unrealistic role models, gender and ethnic stereotypes, promoting immediate gratification, short attention spans, and a "sound bite" mentality that encourages passive, not active learning, detracting from reading, schoolwork, and exercise. For Esslin (1982), television comprises a banal, anti-intellectual and mentally debilitating world that robs viewers of their critical powers of intellect and cultivated values of ephemerality and superficiality. Television may be regarded as a distinctively postmodern medium by virtue of how it challenges modern emphases on linear rationality, contextual coherence, continuity of narrative, detached comprehensiveness, and objectivity. What it does do above all else is entertain (Postman 1982). It offers a surreal post-literate universe that floods the viewer with massive volumes of unstructured information, one in which local context is trivialized, the continuity of narratives is broken into incoherent, and the boundaries between fact and fiction are blurred to the point of nonexistence. Perhaps no medium has done more to make hyperreality more real than reality itself.

Geography's encounters with post-modernism were complex and stimulating. Some, such as David Harvey (1989), rejected the notion altogether as the "window dressing" of late capitalism. For Harvey and other Marxists, post-modern landscapes are only the most recent manifestation of capitalism, particularly the post-industrial, post-Fordist version that took shape in the late 20th century. Unlike its predecessor, post-modern capitalism is typified by globalization and flexible accumulation, the microelectronics revolution, and, with advanced telecommunications, intense time-space compression. In Harvey's words (1989, p. 293), "We have, in short, witnessed another fierce round in that process of annihilation of space through time that has always lain at the center of capitalism's dynamic." Similarly, Jameson (1984) holds that in the post-modern era, space has abolished time, but simultaneously, space has become so warped and distorted as to defy conventional interpretation. Thus, his famous essay concerning the disorienting effects he feels in the Bonaventure Hotel in Los Angeles posits that "this latest mutation in space – postmodern hyperspace – has finally succeeded in transcending the capacities of the individual human body to locate itself, to organize its immediate surroundings perceptually, and cognitively to map its position in a mappable external world" (p. 82–3).

Other geographers were more sympathetic to post-modernism. For Ed Soja (1989, 1993), it offered a valuable means of counteracting the persistent historicism inherited from the Enlightenment, the view that privileges history over geography, and time over space. History was long viewed as the study of change, the dynamic, while geography became relegated to the static and inert. Soja holds that post-modernism allows for the reinsertion of space into social theory, a notion that by now has become commonplace. Time and space become central to social explanation, and thus the construction of truths. When and where events transpire matters greatly to how they transpire. Geographers' successes in asserting the role of space led to a "spatial turn" across the social sciences (Warf and Arias 2008), in which an array of disciplines took up spatiality in their own terms.

Post-structuralist Truths

Post-structuralism was in many ways post-modernism's successor. With roots in earlier constructivist approaches, post-structuralism overlaps with post-modernism in many ways (e. g., the respect for language), but also escapes some of its endless relativism. Like post-modernism, it has distinctively French roots (e. g., Lyotard, Foucault, Derrida, Latour) that can be traced to the 1960s.

Poststructuralism simultaneously borrowed from postmodernism and rejected elements of it. Like post-modernism, post-structuralism is anti-foundational and skeptical of universal claims to truth (Belsey 2002; Williams 2005; Harrison 2006). Like post-modernism, it is sensitive to multiplicity and difference and is anti-essentialist. Like other perspectives, it views truth relationally and as a social construction. Like post-modernism, post-structuralism challenges familiar but simplistic dualities (e. g., subject/object, theory/practice). As Dillet (2017, p. 522) writes, "If there is one thing all poststructuralists agree on, it is invention and creativity, that theory should be an experience in thought and practice beyond the confinement of readymade categories." However, unlike post-modernism, post-structuralism avoids collapsing into epistemological nihilism. As Daly (2008, p. 59) maintains, post-structuralism

> tends in a materialist direction in so far as it affirms an essential gap between the external world and the way we interpret that world. No discourse is capable of eliminating the gap or of establishing absolute closure; otherwise there would be a complete identity between discourse and object.

Post-structuralism is also more assertively political than is post-modernism: truth here is a social product tied to political ends. There may be multiple truths, but all reflect contending interests. There may be no overarching, universal truths, but neither are we condemned to the solipsism of post-modernism and phenomenology. Truths in the post-structuralist view are stories constructed to advance political purposes, weapons in the battles of ideologies and ideas. And unlike the post-truth perspective, post-structuralism holds that there *are* truths, even if they are partial, relational, embodied, contextualized, and situated in time and space. Relativism is to be celebrated as a reflection of the context-dependent nature of knowledge.

Central to post-structuralism is a concern with discourse, a notion it inherited from Foucault (Belsey 2002). Discourses are power/knowledge constellations always tied to interests and that advance particular agendas, creating identities and forming subjects. In response to criticisms that post-structuralism exaggerates the influence of language, "Post-structuralists responded by claiming that no objects were outside the systems of representation, and that any claim to know them in an unmediated way was no more than an exercise of power whereby one theoretical stance was privileged above all others as both accurate and truthful" (Woodward et al. 2009, p. 396). Some discourses, notably those that imply support for the ruling class, tend to be hegemonic (e. g., nationalism, religion, metaphysics), but many others are counter-hegemonic (e. g., Marxism, cosmopolitanism). But if post-modernism made the classic idealist error of collapsing the world into discourse, poststructuralism offered a vision of society as ensembles, networks, and assemblages that link material practices and ideologies.

Post-structuralism is sometimes blamed for the rise of a post-truth world. Such a view, however, is "based on a shallow caricature of the theory and an exaggerated estimation of 2 of its effects" (Perrin 2017). Post-structuralism does not ask us to reject all facts and data. Rather than yearn for an impossible objectivity, it invites us to interrogate the political roots and consequences of discourses and knowledge claims. Rather than a single truth put forth by an all-knowing observer, post-structuralism points to contending, situated, partial and embodied truths.

Post-structuralism had enormous impacts on the discipline of geography (Murdoch 2005; Woodward et al. 2009). It solidified the transition from absolute to relational space, from geometry to topology. Geographies became seen as fields of differences, of situated social networks. Central to this view was the body of work by Deleuze and Guattari (2000), whose view of society as interlinked rhizomes was hugely influential. Spatiality was transformed into networks, flows, and linkages; places were not things, but processes, held together by social relations. Rhizomes, in turn, helped to encourage the adoption of actor-network theory of Latour (2007), which militantly jettisoned long-standing dichotomies such as individual/society, mind/body, local/global, and nature/culture. Overcoming the last dichotomy led to controversial notions such as non-human actors and a more-than-human world.

Post-truth as Epistemology and Ontology

> Living in the post-truth world means never having to acknowledge facts.
> Rabin-Hart (2016, p. 156)

The term "post-truth" was coined by Steve Tesich in 1992 in a highly influential article published in *The Nation* discussing lies by presidential administrations, and why they often succeed. Truth, he held, had become irrelevant to American politics. When confronted with the uncomfortable facts of the Watergate scandal, most Americans became disdainful of the truth. The Iran-contra scandal of the 1980s followed a similar path: "President Reagan perceived correctly that the public really didn't want to know the truth. So he lied to us, but he didn't have to work hard at it." Tesich concluded that the public prefers pleasant platitudes to the harsh reality of truth. The post-truth condition arises from the public's unwillingness to know the truth, which it frequently equates with bad news. In essence, the public chooses to live in a post-truth world at the expense of democracy. He offers a damning indictment of American society:

> We are rapidly becoming prototypes of a people that totalitarian monsters could only drool about in their dreams. All the dictators up to now have had to work hard at suppressing the truth. We, by our actions, are saying that this is no longer necessary, that we have acquired a spiritual mechanism that can denude truth of any significance. In a very fundamental way we, as a free people, have freely decided that we want to live in some post-truth world.

In 2016, the Oxford Dictionary named "post-truth" the word of the year, rocketing it to public attention. Oxford defined the term as "Relating to or denoting circumstances in which objective facts are less influential in shaping public opinion than appeals to emotion and personal belief." Post-truth means that truth is wholly subjective. The term is often associated with frequent and persistent assertions made without proof or evidence. In the post-truth world, feelings and opinions hold as much weight as does data (Prado 2018). Sismondo (2017) asserts earthily that "post-truth era is one in which bullshit is highly valued." Thus, in an age of "weaponized lies," critical thinking skills to combat post-truth have become essential (Levitin 2017).

The notion of post-truth led to a massive outpouring of works on the subject (Keyes 2004; Manjoo 2008; Fuller 2018; McIntyre 2018), with varying explanations for the rise of a post-truth world. Davis (2018) notes that post-truth has become ubiquitous: he adopts a broad definition, including lying, obfuscation, bullshit, deception, nonsense, and gibberish. He points to "the central curiosity of bullshit – why so much of it exists even when it is transparently drivel." This type of fake news commonly confuses young and old alike, every ethnicity and gender, and sometimes even well-educated people. He links the growth of post-truth deception to short time horizons and opportunism (e. g., cashing in on lies) and mass complacency in the face of such lies that gives rise to a culture of mendacity. For the authors in Prado (2018), post-truth reflects the rise of a new, extreme form of relativism that relocates the grounds for truth from evidence to personal opinion. As D'Ancona (2017, p. 84) writes, "When healthy pluralism is supplanted by unhealthy relativism, the cultural assumption is that all opinions are equally valid." Once truth becomes entirely personalized, those who espouse post-truth cannot be held accountable for their falsehoods. For McIntyre (2018), post-truth is the result of the decline of traditional forms of media, the growth of social media, and postmodernism. Whereas once households subscribed to more than one newspaper on average, today the internet allows for news consumers to inhabit information silos and receive little or no news that contradicts their values and assumptions. For Fuller (2018), the exclusionary "protection racket" of universities and professional bodies attempts to exert a monopoly over what is true and what is not; in this reading, post-truth is part of a wider revolt against expertise. In this sense, Fuller mimics the post-truth assertion that experts are an evil cartel rather than a source of verifiable and valuable information. Rather than excluding people, he argues, universities should seek to disseminate knowledge as a public good.

Post-truth is simultaneously a social and intellectual phenomenon. For Braun (2019, p. 432),

> Post-truth is first and foremost an ordering device, a concept that serves as a means to create order in a complicated world and make sense of what is going on. ... It merges a broad range of observations and experiences into a new universalizing meta-narrative that draws a distinction between then and now, right and wrong, truth and power.

Similarly, McIntyre (2018, p. 11) writes that "post-truth is not so much a claim that truth *does not exist* as that *facts are subordinate to our political point of view*" (italics in original). In this sense, post-truth amounts to a political strategy, an ideological weapon to convince audiences to believe something whether there is evidence for it or not.

If television was the defining technology of post-modernism, making reality and entertainment coterminous, its post-structural counterpart is the internet. Indeed, the internet and post-truth arose in tandem. The internet tells us a great deal except how to filter out erroneous information. As D'Ancona (2017, p. 53–58) puts it, "The Web is the definitive vector of Post-Truth precisely because it is indifferent to falsehood, honesty, and the difference between the two. ... If digital technology is the hardware, Post-Truth has proven to be a mighty software." Long gone are the early days of the Internet, when it was heralded as an emancipatory machine that would overcome ignorance. Rather, it has given rise to a wide range of views and assertions, many lacking empirical grounding and often outright false. A torrential outpouring on social media has undermined the traditional hierarchical structure of the media, making way for a cacophonous free-for-all. Forgas and Baumeister (2019, p. 5) nicely sum up the relationship between the internet and truth:

> One important recent influence promoting gullibility is the advent of Internet-based communication. Until recently, it was the privileged class of experts, truth-seekers, and truth-tellers who following the Enlightenment were institutionally established in our social systems and whose job it was to discover and communicate truth. They have no lost their privileged position and information monopoly, and it seems truth in public life is also at risk.

Cyberspace abolishes the boundaries between the respectable and the fringe. Search algorithms are indifferent to the truth. In the multiple realities promulgated online, people can select the one they prefer, as if from a buffet.

For many writers, post-truth emerges from the psychology of information processing in the age of digital information. Although everyone suffers from cognitive dissonance to one degree or another, the proliferation of information sources allows more people to avoid confronting their opinions with inconvenient data. Post-truth thus reinforces the self-worth of individuals regardless of the facts. This phenomenon has long been known in psychology, which has produced a voluminous literature on confirmation biases, a notion that goes back to a seminal paper by Peter Wason (1960). Confirmation bias is the means by which we interpret information so that it confirms our pre-existing beliefs. For Strong (2017, p. 140), "Confirmation bias is defined as the unconscious but pervasive human propensity to filter out information that contradicts an existing belief and instead retain only information that confirms that belief."

Confirmation biases are accentuated by availability biases, in which judgments are made in light of the ease of obtaining information (Tversky and Kahneman 1973). Availability bias often leads individuals to exaggerate the relevance and importance of sensational events and underplay the importance of ordinary ones. It also allows them to avoid cognitive dissonance and to distrust news sources with which they are not familiar. Similarly, other researchers point to motivated reasoning, the notion that what we hope to be true shapes our perceptions of what is actually true. The idea reflects the famous line by Upton Sinclair: "it is difficult to get a man to believe something when his salary depends on him not believing it." Yet another variation is the "backfire effect," in which people confronted with evidence that undermines their political opinions reject the facts and double down on their beliefs. Finally, the perception of reality, and thus truth, is affected by the Dunning-Kruger effect, a.k.a. the "too stupid to know they're stupid" bias, which points to widespread overconfidence among many holding firm beliefs. In essence, self-love obfuscates our weaknesses. The Dunning-Kruger effect reveals that the greatest inflation of people's self-assessment is found among the lowest performers in workplaces.

Manjoo (2008) argues that media fragmentation has given rise to innumerable echo chambers that reinforce members' views, indulging biases and pre-existing beliefs. Biased assimilation of information leads people to interpret new information that accords with their existing prejudices. Compounding the problems is intense political partisanship, which has distorted our collective notions of what is "real" and what is not. As he puts it (p. 4), "the limitless choices we now enjoy over the information we get about our world has loosened our grip on what is – and isn't – true." Media fragmentation allows us to engage in selective exposure to information, steering clear of that which contradicts our beliefs. As he notes (p. 107), reality "splits when people selectively expose themselves to different facts, or when they interpret the same evidence in divergent ways." Selective exposure is thus complemented by selective perception. News outlets often slant their coverage to fit their audience's beliefs because it gives the appearance of being accurate. These blinders occur just when political opinions have become highly polarized, a reflection of the inequalities unleashed by neoliberalism and the rise of identity politics. As a result, popular trust in the institutions of democracy has been on the decline for years. Such explanations are useful as far as they go, but they ignore the deep structural origins of post-truth, the political interests involved in promoting it, and its ties to neoliberalism.

Post-truth is often taken to mean a society in which large numbers of people fail to respect science, data, evidence, or facts. In this sense, post-truth reflects the anxieties of the current historical moment, the widespread distrust in government and the media. It reflects a culture saturated with promotionalism and commercialization, the extension of market values into all spheres of society. As Harsin (2018) puts it, "the idea is not that lay citizens see the world falsely through the ideology of ruling-class thinkers, but that "popular" conceptions of reality have become confusing or suspicious because of the saturation of reality representation with games of expertly researched and thus exclusive strategic deception." Keyes (2004) heralds this as the age of mass dishonesty. Intense political polarization and hyperspecialized news ecosystems destroy the credibility of any society-wide truth tellers. The post-truth world is thus also a post-trust society. Thus Fukuyama (2016) noted the rise of post-truth reflected partisan political divisions. Indeed, it is no accident that the world over post-truth has grown in tandem with authoritarian regimes and right-wing populism.

Search algorithms create information bubbles in which other opinions, real or not, are dismissed out of hand. Without countervailing opinions, many people lose perspective. A crisis in journalism, including budget cuts and reduced staff, has accelerated this trend. In the digital age, the volume of falsehoods produced is too large to fact-check. As a result, the assumption of truth gives way to a series of believable fictions.

The rise of post-truth society is often associated with what the Rand Corporation termed sardonically "truth decay" (Kavanagh and Rich 2018), the waning influence of facts and data on public life, particularly in politics. Most analyses of this issue attribute its rise to social polarization, the growth of social media, and the cognitive biases brought about by filter bubbles and search algorithms. Pariser (2011) coined the term "filter bubbles" to refer to selective reading on social media and resultant political polarization. Often included are growing mistrust in the media and government, including a widespread distrust of expertise that cultivates a climate in which any opinion is as good as any other (Nichols 2017). The explosion of opinions online has increased their volume substantially more than the growth of facts. An overloaded educational system cannot train students to recognize the difference between the two. The consequences of truth decay are severe, including an erosion of civil discourse and the disengagement of many individuals from public life. Meaningful debate becomes difficult, if not impossible. A disengaged public is ineffective in keeping tabs on corrupt and lying politicians. Lack of trust in the media and experts leads many people to make calamitous decisions, such as refusing vaccines.

One of the most intense forces propelling the emergence of a post-truth world is the intense political polarization found in many countries, some of which may be attributed to the passions ignited by decades of neoliberal austerity programs. Social media is thus a major venue – arguably the major venue – through which fake news spreads and polarization is generated (Centola 2020; Yerlikaya 2020). Isolated in our echo chambers, truth becomes what serves us politically, regardless of the facts. As Sayer (2017, p. 93) argues, "The communities of the like-minded in which most of us live, and the echo-chambers of the social media through which many of us communicate, nurture a culture in which strength of shared feeling is treated as a proxy – and ends up as a substitute – for truth." Similarly, MacIntyre (2018, p. 11) notes that "one gets the sense that post-truth is not so much a claim that truth does not exist as that *facts are subordinate to our political point of view*" (emphasis in original). Social media has accelerated confirmation biases and deeply embedded tribal thinking, such as tendency toward "homophilous sorting," the impulse to congregate with the like-minded, a tendency greatly enabled by the Internet (Farrell 2012). The likelihood of believing what others tell us depends greatly on the level of trust one has, as individuals treat some sources of evidence more than others: typically, people will trust evidence from those who hold similar beliefs and distrust it from those whose beliefs are markedly different (O'Connor and Weatherall 2019; Mercier 2020). In highly polarized political climates, one side's truth automatically becomes the other's falsehood. This line of thought is good as far as it goes, but it ignores the fact that post-truth has been weaponized almost exclusively by one political side, extreme conservatives. Right-wing movements use fake news to promote a variety of causes, particularly during periods of political strife. Tandoc et al. (2018, p. 149) stated that "fake news needs the nourishment of troubled times in order to take root. Social tumult and divisions facilitate our willingness to believe news that confirms our enmity toward another group. It is in this context that fake news finds its audience."

These explanations are useful in emphasizing that the rise of a post-truth culture did not simply happen by accident, but was manufactured. Much as the rise of post-modernism and post-structuralism can be traced to the hegemony of globalized, neoliberal capitalism, so too does the emergence of a post-truth world reflect the pervasive digitalization of everyday life and renewed challenges to a social order long dominated by white males.

Chapter Conclusion

What can we conclude from this meandering journey through the various philosophies and histories of truth? "Truth," it turns out, is no simple thing. There is no single definition of truth, no universally agreed-upon criteria for what is true and what is false. Mere appeal to the "facts" no longer suffices, if it ever did, a serious flaw in empiricist and positivist views of truth. Facts themselves are social constructions, often slippery ones, and never speak for themselves; they must be interpreted in order to form truth(s). It is not the facts that produce truth, but our interpretation of them. Interpretation inevitably involves subjectivity. Thus, objectivity has been challenged, if not jettisoned completely. Unlike Platonic views of knowledge that refuse to come to terms with its social origins, and consequences, contemporary views point to how knowledge is created, by whom, and for what purposes. That said, the Enlightenment project of universal truths has collapsed, and been exposed as a social project deeply tied to the hegemony of capitalism and white males.

The relativization of truth has a surprisingly long history, going back to Nietzsche, often heralded as the grandfather of post-structuralism and, ultimately, post-truth. But it is of no help to contrast post-truth with some mythologized previous golden era in which honesty reigned supreme: such a world never existed.

Nor can post-truth be blamed on its epistemological ancestors, post-modernism and post-structuralism. Whereas post-modernism and post-structuralism held to the notion of multiple, contending truths, a post-truth vision denies the very existence of truth. In feminist standpoint theory and poststructuralism, opinions that hold to the truth may be respected, even if one vehemently disagrees with them; in post-truth, truth is jettisoned altogether. Thus, post-truth involves a radical relativization of truth. Truth simply becomes a matter of perspective. When the decline in objectivity becomes normalized, emotions and affect rise to the fore (Boler and Davis 2019). As waves of fake news and fake science (e.g., climate change denial, anti-vaccination discourses, creationism) wash over the country, it has suffered a decline into a post-truth abyss. In the process, the very notion of objectivity has come under question, as has the Enlightenment notion of reason. As conservative philosopher Roger Scruton (2017) puts it, rather earthily, "Somehow the boundaries between true and false, sense and nonsense, opinion and reality, thought and bullshit have been erased, and no one really knows how to reinstate them."

We are left with the inescapable conclusion that there is more than one kind of truth, and that truths are historically and geographically contingent. If one accepts a constructivist perspective, truths vary in time and space, and their meanings are closely intertwined with social relations and the distribution of power. Truth is a social construct, a set of stories we tell ourselves about the world to make sense of it. What we hold to be true cannot be detached from our languages, discourses, and interests in the world.

The evolution of truth over the last century has been a long slide from the apex of Enlightenment obsession with objectivity into a marked relativism, a shift initiated by Nietzsche's perspectivalism and accelerated by social constructivism of various forms. Subsequent theorists emphasized the social origins, and consequences, of truth. In knocking truth off of its pedestal of objectivity, Marxism weaponized truth as an instrument of class struggle. Kuhn upended the notion of a continual progression to ever-greater truths, holding that one paradigm replaces another. Foucault forever sutured truth and power: every claim to truth is a claim to authority. Feminists showed knowledge to be gendered, and in contrast to objectivity, offered situated knowledge. Truth is thus partial and embodied. If one accepts discourse as pervasive, then meanings are always unstable, and vary across time and space.

Postmodernism created a slippery slope that risks epistemic nihilism. Poststructuralism rescued truth from this abyss, upholding the centrality of discourse and representation. If for Nietzsche, Marxists, and Foucault truth is produced through power, then for feminists, postmodernists, and poststructuralists truth is produced at the margins, by those lacking power, whose everyday experiences reflect structural inequalities: speaking truth to power. The notion of objective, overarching truths has long been discarded; instead, we are left with a multiplicity of partial truths, embodied in people, situated in time and space.

Post-truth, then, is the latest chapter in a long evolution of epistemology. Some might argue that it is the culmination of the long slide into relativized notions of truth. Others maintain that it represents the triumph of epistemological nihilism, the death of truth itself. These contradictions serve as a reminder that post-truth means different things under different circumstances. Lying, mendacity, obfuscation, and fake news are not new: what is new is the ability of large numbers of actors to generate nonsense digitally. Post-truth in some respects reflects the unfortunate intersections between neoliberal capitalism and its intensified competition on the one hand and microelectronics revolution and the internet on the other.

Each of these viewpoints has markedly affected geography; different epistemologies gave rise to varying types of spatialities. Grounded in the correspondence theory of truth, positivism had enormous impacts in the mid-twentieth century, leading to an infatuation with models and quantitative methods. Marxism raised uneven spatial development to the level of a moral problem. Feminist geographers complicated longstanding masculinist dichotomies, such as public and private. Phenomenology helped to show that truth is embodied, often in the highly personal terms of everyday life. Poststructuralists cemented the rule of relational space and relational identity in the discipline, viewing space and truth as relational. Yet post-truth, which has just begun to receive attention, has not had its geographies subject to serious examination. That is the task of the following chapters.

Chapter 3
The Historical Geography of Fake News and Post-Truth

> The truth is, truth has never been high on the agenda of Homo sapiens.
> Yuval Noah Harari

Post-truth geographies emerge from a depressingly long history of attempts to lie, deceive, and misinform people throughout the ages. From fake news to information warfare, betrayal of the truth has frequently been used by various parties to weaponize information to obtain their objectives. Just as the production of knowledge and truth developed unevenly over time, so too is there an historical geography of the creation of falsehoods and deception. If the previous chapter dwelled upon the varied epistemological dimensions and implications of different meanings of truth, this one explores the historical ontologies of one variant, post-truth. It is concerned with the ways in which lies, falsehoods, propaganda, conspiracy theories, fake news, and disinformation have been produced over time and space.

This chapter proceeds in nine steps. First, it asks what constitutes fake news, and defines it. Second, it describes the evolution of fake news over time, which has a remarkably long and colorful history. Third, it turns to yellow journalism, which spouted copious quantities of fake news in the late 19th and early 20th centuries. Fourth, it focuses on fake news and immigration; migrants have long been disproportionately the objects of lies and slander. Fifth, it traces the contours of military propaganda: deceit has long been a central part of warfare. Sixth, it examines civilian counterpart of military propaganda, false advertising. Eighth, it notes the explosion of fake news with the rise of the internet. The chapter conclusion draws together some major themes.

What is Fake News?

Fake news seems to be everywhere. Corporations, governments, dictators, political parties, and malignant actors on social media seem to have generated a tsunami of false stories, spreading deceit and mistrust among vast numbers of people across the globe (Ball 2017; Levenson 2017). The growth of fake news has generated an enormous outpouring of scholarly attention (e.g., McNair 2017; Cooke 2018).

Fake news refers to stories that are intentionally and verifiably false, typically with a political objective in mind (Gelfert 2018; Tandoc et al. 2018). It is produced

https://doi.org/10.1515/9783110749847-004

with the explicit intention to deceive and designed to imitate legitimate media. Fake news usually consists of fabricated stories that mimic reliable media outlets. These include conspiracy theories, sensationalistic reporting, hoaxes, fabricated "facts," and rumors of varying degrees of outlandishness (Ball 2017; Levinson 2017). As Bodner et al. (2020) note, "conspiracy theories reflect reality back to us in heightened, twisted forms, and they direct blame, in profitable and often hateful ways." In this sense, fake news does not simply report the news, it creates it. Unlike real news, which necessitates reporters and field work, fake news can be invented costlessly. The point is not to inform an audience, but to inflame them. To be maximally effective, fake news typically contains a seed of truth, then builds on it with gross exaggeration, generating layer upon layer of falsehood until it bears little connection to reality. Indeed, the point of fake news is often to disrupt the notion of a shared reality. Producers of fake news may or may not believe that the audience accepts it as true. Because it typically fits in with people's existing cognitive frameworks, it is difficult to identify and correct. Fake news is mostly likely to be believed when it confirms the worldview of the recipient. Fake news thus flies directly in the face of long-standing journalistic values of objectivity and detachment. Media outlets often employ fact-checkers, but they are often overwhelmed by the sheer volume of lies and fake stories.

Fake news differs from parodies of news or satire, such as the newspaper *The Onion*, i. e., political satire that is written for humorous purposes but does not claim to be factually accurate. The purpose of satire is to entertain and ridicule, not to inform. Satire does not purport to be true, but is more of a practical joke. Marche (2017) holds that "political satire is the opposite of fake news. Satirists rip away the pretenses of journalism to reveal what they believe to be true. Fake news sites use the pretenses of journalism to spread what they know to be false." Likewise, propaganda is fake news deliberately twisted to serve a political end. Its goal is to demonstrate authority over the truth, the facts be damned. "Propagandists may fabricate facts, be selective with facts, or present opinions as facts" (Safieddine 2020, p. 8). In contrast, fake news purports to be real, is produced to mislead readers intentionally, and can be shown to be false empirically. It is used to create divisions and foment moral outrage. However, Mercier (2020) argues that people are not as gullible as commonly thought, and that most campaigns of mass deception have failed.

Coady (2020) objects to the term fake news on the grounds that it is overly ambiguous, comparable to earlier, politically charged terms like "heresy" or "conspiracy theory." There are indeed wide variations in how the term is defined and interpreted. Nonetheless, the term has gained wide popularity. Donald Trump falsely claimed that he invented the term, which he uses to mean any news with which he disagrees.

Fake news is closely associated with the notion of a post-truth or post-factual world, in which reason, logic, and evidence are deemed unimportant or irrelevant. As Gabler (2016) writes, the purpose of fake news is "to destroy truth altogether, to set us adrift in a world of belief without facts, a world in which there is no defense against lies." In this sense, it runs directly counter to Enlightenment values that emphasize rationality and objectivity. Indeed, fake news is the foremost symptom of the post-truth age (D'Ancona 2017; Fuller 2018). While fake news is sometimes found in media reports about health and other issues, it is in the political domain that it finds its fullest expression (Rabin-Hayt and Media Matters 2016). Unfortunately, fake news has most often been deployed to mislead the public, arouse xenophobic sentiments, and attack democracy (Giusti and Piras 2020).

The Early History of Fake News

> We are at war and have been for thousands and thousands of years. You must arm yourselves
> with knowledge and truth. Because we do battle with ignorance, deception and lies.
> Gavin Nacimiento

Unfortunately, fake news has a long and inglorious history (Soll 2016; Gorbach 2018). Fake news has several motivations, including revenge, but the most important drivers are political opportunism and making money. Traditionally fake news circulated only in a few, narrow channels; the newspaper opened one-to-many possibilities of dissemination, while the internet created many-to-many opportunities.

Before the age of printing, the use of gossip and slander to malign political opponents was common. During the Roman civil war between Octavian and Mark Antony (30 – 32 BC), the former smeared his rival by printing coins with short slogans portraying him as a drunken womanizer who wanted to be buried in the Egyptian pyramids, a sort of metallic tweet (Posetti and Matthews 2018). Antony, upon hearing that Cleopatra had died, stabbed himself in the stomach, only to learn that the rumor of her death was false. In the sixth century, the historian of Byzantium, Procopius of Caesarea, smeared the recently deceased emperor Justinian with fake news in a treatise called *Secret History* in an attempt to curry favor with his successor (Burkhardt 2017).

Religious fraud was a form of fake news for centuries during the medieval era and Renaissance, including miracles, relics of saints, and pieces of the "one true" cross (Chidester 2003; Will 2013). These were designed to attract the attention, and donations, of gullible pilgrims. The Holy Grail, the chalice allegedly used by Christ at the Last Supper, was a popular medieval fiction constructed by medieval authors in the 12th century. The Shroud of Turin, purporting to be the burial shroud of Jesus and bearing his image, was found by radiocarbon dating to have been made between 1260 and 1390. The trade in relics was so prevalent that it earned the scorn of Erasmus in the 16th century. (For atheists, of course, all religion is fake news).

In 1475, a Franciscan friar in Trent, Italy, Bernardino da Feltre, gave sermons claiming that a missing baby boy had been murdered by Jews on Easter Sunday, leading 15 of them to be burned at the stake (Soll 2016). The Pope, Sixtus IV, tried to squash the rumors to no avail. The event inspired similar actions in other cities. The papacy intervened and tried to stop the stories but failed to do so. Fake stories about child-murdering and blood-drinking Jews became a staple of European anti-Semitism. In the 20th century, the Nazis relied on the same trope to demonize Jews.

During the Renaissance, as printing and literacy spread, fake news proliferated. For example, the art of anonymous lampooning, *pasquino*, became a form of biting political parody. The satirist Pietro Aretino used sonnets and pamphlets to blackmail wealthy people and tried to manipulate the pontifical election of 1522 by writing wicked sonnets about all the candidates (except the favorite of his Medici patrons) and pasting them for the public to admire on the bust of a figure known as Pasquino near the Piazza Navona in Rome. The "pasquinade" then developed into a common genre of diffusing nasty news, most of it fake, about public figures (Darnton 2017).

In the 17th century, the pasquinade was gradually replaced by the canard, printed broadsides that circulated the streets of Paris. One famous one cited a story about a monster being shipped from Chile to Spain, while others took aim at Marie Antoinette and likely played a role in the pathological hatred that led to her execution during the French Revolution. Around the same time, many Venetians were tricked by purportedly leaked Venetian government correspondence known as *relazioni*; as these were gradually revealed to be false, many citizens gave up on the idea that their government would provide reliable news.

The 18th century was something of a golden age for post-truth. In 1704, George Psalmanazar, born and raised in France, claimed to be from Formosa (Taiwan); after publishing a book of fantastical tales about the Orient, he was invited to teach Formosan at Oxford University (Keevak 2004). In 1710, Jonathan Swift complained about fake news in "The Art of Political Lying," in which he said "Falsehood flies, and truth comes limping after it, so that when men come to be undeceived, it is too late; the jest is over, and the tale hath had its effect" (quoted in Burkhardt 2017). Using the pseudonym Isaac Bickerstaff, Swift predicted the death of astrologer John Partridge, insisting he was dead even though Partridge was very much alive; the hoax was an attempt to embarrass naïve believers of astrology. In New York, a fire in 1741 burned down the governor's mansion. Fake news spread blaming African Americans for the event, leading to the arrests and imprisonment of 150 Black men, 20 of whom were executed (Lepore 2006). In 1755 news of the Lisbon earthquake carried rumors the disaster was a form of divine retribution against sinners. Fake news pamphlets called *relações de sucessos* emerged in the wake of the disaster claiming that survivors owed their lives to an apparition of the Virgin Mary. In response, Voltaire denounced religious explanations for natural disasters, making him perhaps the first critic of fake news.

In early America, even reputable figures such as Benjamin Franklin deliberately blurred the lines between fact and fiction. His essay "Witch Trial at Mount Holly," published in 1730, reported dancing sheep and Psalm-singing hogs to ridicule superstitions about witchcraft (Gorbach 2018). In 1782, Franklin created a counterfeit issue of the newspaper *Boston Independent Chronicle* that falsely depicted Native Americans scalping colonists in the service of King George (Watson 2018).

Racism has a long history of post-truth. In *Stamped from the Beginning*, Kendi (2016) argues that racist ideas proliferated as post-truths from 15th century Europe through colonialism into the current context by people who claimed to be following God's will, nature's design, or science. Black people have been subjected to decades of grotesque stereotypes in the service of White dominance. In the late 19th century, Social Darwinism was widely popular post-truth used to naturalize racial inequalities. Meija et al. (2018) argue that the entire history of post-truth can be read through a racialized lens, an "investment in whiteness." Racist post-truth continues to subjugate ethnic minorities in education, the labor market, housing, finance, the media, and other domains. This line of thought serves as a warning against treating the phenomenon in purely epistemological terms.

As newspapers proliferated in the age of printing, so too did distrust of them. Even Thomas Jefferson argued that "Nothing can now be believed which is seen in a newspaper. Truth itself becomes suspicious by being put into that polluted vehicle" (quoted in Gorbach 2018) and that "The most truthful part of a newspaper is the advertisements." In the 19th century, the era of the penny press (one cent per paper), newspapers used fake news to boost circulation (Conboy 2002). Cheap newspapers such as these specialized in gossip and sensationalistic scandals and crimes. Hoaxes about various pseudo-scientific "discoveries" were common in the 19th century. In 1835, Edgar Allan Poe wrote a false newspaper story in the *Southern Literary Messenger* about a man who crossed the Atlantic Ocean in a balloon in three days (Poe 1835). It was intended as a hoax. When neither balloon nor balloonist were discovered, the story was retracted, although it sent the paper's readership to new heights. Poe also wrote several other fake news stories. However, Poe's stories were eclipsed by the Great Moon Hoax of the same year.

On August 25, 1835, the *New York Sun* published the first in a series of six sensational stories about the discovery of life on the moon, the first mass hoax. As Gorbach (2018, p. 249) puts it, "The six-part moon hoax of 1835, which is possibly the most successful ploy in history and certainly among the most legendary, was a straightforward bid for newsstand sales, the pre-digital, print-era version of clickbait." The articles were given the byline of Dr. Andrew Grant, said to be a colleague of a famous contemporary astronomer Sir John Herschel. The stories featured graphic pictures of the discoveries made by Herschel using a telescope that was 24 feet in diameter at his observatory on the Cape of Good Hope, South Africa, including large bi-pedal beavers, bison, unicorns, pyramids, and furry humanoid creatures with batwings (Fig. 3.1). It was complete fantasy, but many readers were fooled and sales spiked. As the story became more outlandish, more people were hooked on it. One month after it was published the *Sun* confessed to the hoax (Zielinksi 2015), but sales of the paper did not suffer after the deception was revealed.

Figure 3.1: *New York Sun* Lithograph of the Great Moon Hoax of 1835.

A few years later, Philadelphia newspapers published false stories that Irish men were stealing Bibles from schools, which led to riots (Soll 2016).

The rise of "respectable" journalism with claims to objective truth was late in coming. In early America, no one expected the media to be objective, but to serve partisan interests. As Schudson (1981) argues in *Discovering the News: A Social History of American Newspapers*, the modern idea of "news" arose during the Jacksonian era. Specifically, he credits the rise of the Associated Press (AP), which was organized by New York newspapers in 1848. Since the AP sold news to papers with a wide variety of political allegiances, it could only succeed by being sufficiently "objective" to be acceptable to all of its clients.

Yellow Journalism

The seminal moment in the birth of modern fake news occurred in the U.S. with the rise of the Hearst newspaper chain. Owned and operated by William Randolph Hearst, the doyen of "yellow journalism" during its apogee, and, to a lesser extent, that of Joseph Pulitzer, Hearst's papers regularly published false and misleading stories (Campbell 2001; Borchard 2018; McQueen 2018); indeed, his name became synonymous with yellow journalism. Hearst's empire included outlets such as *The San Francisco Examiner, New York Journal*, and *New York World*. Hearst and Pulitzer's rivalry is famous, and by the 1890s each drew more than 1.2 million readers.

The term "yellow journalism" originated from a very popular cartoon character, the Yellow Kid, drawn by Richard Outcault that first appeared in the *New York World* from 1895 to 1898 (Fig. 3.2), before its creator was wooed away to Hearst's *New York Journal*. It was then that the term "yellow journalism" became associated with their newspaper rivalry. The style, featuring bold typography, multicolumn headlines and dramatic illustrations, has continued today in the pages of supermarket tabloids where sightings of space aliens and Elvis have become routine.

Hearst's papers in particular also fostered waves of Sinophobia and overt racism directed at immigrants. He repeatedly warned about the coming "Yellow Peril," blamed Chinese for opium use, cited the Tong wars as evidence that Chinese were sneaky and violent, and used the bubonic plague pandemic of 1900 to attack San Francisco's Chinese population (Tchen and Yeats 2014).

The Hearst newspapers reveal how fake news can be used to start a war. Hearst was an enthusiastic backer of U.S. entry into the 1898 Spanish-American War, believing it would boost newspaper sales among the middle class (Carey 2016). He regularly portrayed Cubans as freedom-loving but oppressed by their cruel Spanish colonial overlords. Most notoriously, his shaped public support for the U.S. role in the Spanish-American war of 1898 by exaggerating the Spanish mistreatment of people in Cuba and the Philippines and by claiming that the destruc-

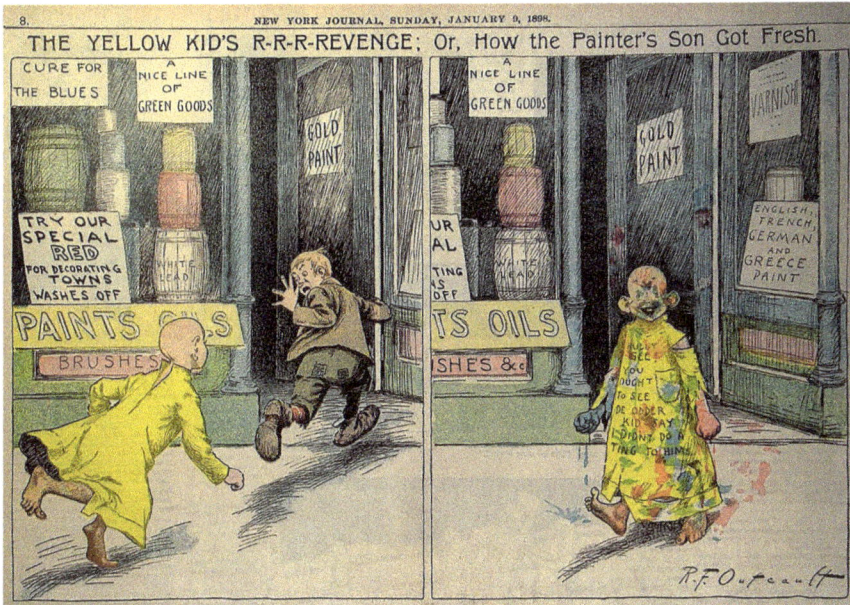

Figure 3.2: The Yellow Kid.

tion of the battleship USS *Maine* was a deliberate act of Spanish aggression (Campbell 2001; Spencer and Spencer 2007). He repeatedly called for U.S. intervention to assist anti-Spanish revolutionaries in Cuba. When told there was no problem there, he famously replied "You supply the pictures, I'll supply the war" (quoted in Harsin 2018). His *New York Journal* notoriously stretched the truth to assist in this effort. After the USS *Maine* was sunk, he ran the headline "The War Ship *Maine* was Split in Two by an Enemy's Secret Infernal Machine," arguing the Spanish had planted a torpedo under the ship. A subsequent investigation revealed the explosion originated inside the ship. As Joseph Wisan said in 1934, "The Spanish-American War would not have occurred had not the appearance of Hearst in New York journalism precipitated a bitter battle for newspaper circulation" (quoted in McIntyre 2018, p. 100). Hearst also called for "benevolent assimilationism" in the Philippines.

Critics of the day savaged purveyors of yellow journalism, notably Hearst, for the sensationalistic and frequently false stories he published (Figure 3.3). As *Washington Post* reporter Ernest L. Meyer put it, "Mr. Hearst in his long and not laudable career has inflamed Americans against Spaniards, Americans against Japanese, Americans against Filipinos, Americans against Russians, and in the pursuit of his incendiary campaign he has printed downright lies, forged documents, faked atrocity stories, inflammatory editorials, sensational cartoons and photographs and other devices by which he abetted his jingoistic ends" (quoted in Seldes 1938).

Figure 3.3: A cartoon by L.M. Glackens from 1910 depicts William Randolph Hearst as a jester tossing yellow sheets of sensationalism toward eager readers.

Fake news circulated over other media outlets as well, such as radio. Father Ronald Arbuthnott Knox gave a radio broadcast called "Broadcasting the Barricades" on BBC claiming that London was being attacked by Communists, that Parliament was under siege, and that Big Ben had been blown up. In 1938, 23-year-old Orson Welles gave an infamous radio broadcast, "The War of the Worlds," about a Martian invasion of New Jersey that terrified millions and led to mass hysteria in the United States. It is perhaps the most famous incident of fake news in history. Those who missed the introduction noting that the story was fictional believed it to be true. Many believed Martians and their war machines were headed toward New York City. The story, by H.G. Wells, was originally published in 1898, but few had read it, and Orson Welles converted it into fake news bulletins. The credibility of the story was enhanced when the radio station failed to pause the story for the customary station identification. Few who produced the show, however, expected to deceive listeners in the way that it did.

Fake News and Politics

The failure of the broadcast media to stand up for truth and knowledge
gives politicians little incentive to tell the truth.
Wren-Lewis (2018, p. 3)

Post-truth if fundamentally political and emotional. It not surprising, therefore, that politics has long been a primary arena of fake news. Politicians lie routinely, which has contributed to the public's generally low opinion of them. As Rose (2017, p. 555) writes "The belief among voters that politicians lie is near ubiquitous in contemporary political systems, and politicians in general are routinely placed at or towards the bottom of indices of trust." In part, this sad state of affairs results from the marriage of convenience between politics and misinformation (Edelman 2001): if information is power, so is misinformation. *Mis*information, or communication of incorrect news without malicious intent, is not synonymous with *dis*information, the deliberate spread of fake news with the purpose of deception.

This phenomenon is not new. Writing in the midst of the Spanish civil war of the 1930s, George Orwell worried about the media's ability to report the truth of political events. Noting that newspapers often simply made up facts, he wrote that the experience

> often gives me the feeling that the very concept of objective truth is fading out of the world. After all, the chances are that those lies, or at any rate similar lies, will pass into history... Yet, after all, *some* kind of history will be written, and after those who actually remember the war are dead, it will be universally accepted. So for all practical purposes the lie will have become the truth (quoted in MacKenzie and Bhatt 2020, p. 217).

Famed philosopher and social critic Hannah Arendt was an astute observer of political truths and lies. She was well attuned to the porous boundary between political truths and falsehood, noting (1968, p. 239) that "Factual truth is no more self-evident than opinion, and this may be among the reasons that opinion holders find it relatively easy to discredit factual truth as just another opinion." In "Lying in Politics," she (1969) argues that truthfulness cannot be counted among the political virtues and that lies have long been deployed to advance political agendas. Unwelcome opinions can be dismissed, but unwelcome facts present a real problem. She wrote:

> The deliberate falsehood deals with *contingent* facts; that is, with matters that carry no inherent truth within themselves, no necessity to be as they are. Factual truths are never compellingly true. The historian knows how vulnerable is the whole texture of facts in which we spend our daily life; it is always in danger of being perforated by single lies or torn to shreds by the organized lying of groups, nations, or classes, or denied and distorted, often carefully

covered up by reams of falsehoods or simply allowed to fall into oblivion. ... Facts need testimony to be remembered and trustworthy witnesses to be established in order to find a secure dwelling place in the domain of human affairs.

To the lying politician, the gains of changing the world through lies exceed the costs of sacrificing honesty. Unencumbered by truth, the lying politician can tailor his/her message to different audiences. Politicians may even believe their own lies: as Arendt (1972, p. 34) notes, "The more successful a liar is, the more people he has convinced, the more likely it is that he will end by believing his own lies." In the age of post-truth, political lies are judged on their affect or emotional appeal. As Lockie (2017) puts it, "What matters is not whether the claims of politicians can be proven true. What matters is whether those listening to those claims would like them to be true – truth being judged not by evidence but by consistency with listeners' existing beliefs and values." In essence, post-truth political lies use the coherence theory of truth.

Political lies may actually be welcomed if they substitute for more violent means of gaining and exerting power. The recipients of lies may welcome them eagerly, a phenomenon of great concern given how many people live under autocratic governments. In *The Origins of Totalitarianism*, Arendt (1951, p. 474) observed that "the ideal subject of totalitarian rule is not the convinced Nazi or the convinced communist, but people for whom the distinction between fact and fiction ... true and false ... no longer exists." Harsin (2018) notes that "As Arendt foresaw, organized, systematic lying, or, more easily proven, deceptions, the bread and butter of consumer capitalism and the communications wing of the state security apparatus, have come also to be the organizing force of mediated political life."

In the U.S., politics has long been plagued by fake news (Cortada and Aspray 2019). The raucous election of 1828 between Andrew Jackson and John Quincy Adams, which featured two political parties and direct votes by citizens, also saw enormous amounts of disinformation circulate in the forms of posters, fliers, and word-of-mouth. During the late 19th century, as the Republican Party drifted from its origins as the party of Black emancipation to become increasingly racist and xenophobic, racist fake news sprouted with increasing frequency (Heckler and Ronquillo 2019). In the wake of Reconstruction, many newspapers published stories that Black people were incapable of self-governance, and needed the guiding hand of Whites. Cartoonist Thomas Nash created cartoons that savagely satirized Black legislators. Whites who supported civil rights were depicted as ignorant carpet-baggers. Similarly, racist fears of Chinese immigrants led to fake news that culminated in the Chinese Exclusion Act of 1882. Racist fake news that Native Americans were to blame for their own poverty led directly to the Dawes Act of 1887, which stripped tribes of their land and reallocated it to individual members, giving unfarmed land to Whites and violating previous treaties (Carlson 1981).

During the Progressive Era in the late 19th and early 20th centuries, liberals opposed fake news, such as that spewed out by Hearst. Others used it to sow misdoubts about the mainstream media such as the Associated Press (AP). The *New York Sun* called the AP a "fake news factory." In 1896, William Jennings Bryan started his own newspaper to express his views because "There seems to be an epidemic of fake news" (quoted in La France 2017). Progressives derided the attempts by the cartels to manipulate public opinion. In 1914, Max Shereover wrote in his book *Fakes in American Journalism* that "A certain state of public mind is often necessary for "the economic masters of this country to flimflam the people" (quoted in Jordan 2018).

One of the most dramatic examples of political fake news unfolded in 1948, when overconfident editors of the *Chicago Daily Tribune* published the erroneous headline "Dewey Defeats Truman" on November 3. Upon his victory, Truman triumphantly held up the newspaper, as captured in an iconic photograph (Fig. 3.4). An observer quoted Truman as saying "That ain't the way I heard it." To its great embarrassment, the *Tribune* retracted its story and published the real results the following day.

Conspiracy theories surrounded the assassinations of President Lincoln in 1865 and President Kennedy in 1963. The assassination of JFK created a gargantuan outpouring of speculations that painted the event from every conceivable perspective, arguing it was, variously, attributable to the Soviet Union, Cuba, the Mafia, white supremacists, the FBI, or the Secret Service. Six decades after the murder conspiracies continue to abound (McAdams 2011). The enduring popularity of conspiracy theories illustrates what Richard Hofstadter (1965/2012) famously called the "paranoid style" in American politics based on suspicion and exaggeration in which vaguely defined villains perpetuate fiendish acts. In this way of looking at the world, disparate events that may have no connection in reality are sown together through a sweeping narrative that requires huge leaps of logic.

Presidents, in turn, have generated fake news when they lie. They often make campaign promises that they cannot possibly keep. They may lie if they think it is in the national interest or to protect its security. Alterman (2004) traces the history of presidential lies from FDR to JFK, Johnson, Nixon, and Reagan. Eisenhower lied about the spy pilot Gary Powers. Kennedy lied about his intentions to invade Cuba. Johnson lied about the Gulf of Tonkin incident, Nixon lied about the secret bombing of Cambodia, and Reagan lied about the Iran-Contra scandal. Reagan claimed to have helped film the Nazi concentration camps and their liberation, when in fact he never left the US during World War II. Clinton lied about sex with Monica Lewinsky. Alterman uses the term "post-truth presidency" to describe the George

Figure 3.4: President Truman holding newspaper falsely announcing his defeat, 1948.

W. Bush administration, which lied about Iraq (weapons of mass destruction, Hussein's ties to Al Qaeda) on the eve of the US invasion in 2003. And of course, Trump lied more than 30,000 times during his term in office.

In the 2004 presidential election, fake news was weaponized against Democratic candidate John Kerry by a group of reactionary veterans ironically calling themselves Swiftboat Veterans for Truth. Although Kerry had a distinguished record of military service and received awards for his efforts during the Vietnam War, Swiftboat Veterans mounted a sustained advertising campaign to paint him as a liar and coward. They were funded by a network of right-wing Texan millionaires. Kerry's fatal error was choosing not to "dignify" the group while they assailed him on national television. The effort succeeded so well that the term "swiftboating" became synonymous with deliberate distortions of political news.

The internet allowed political fake news to be produced by many more actors and to circulate at the speed of light. Digital fake news can generate dissent, discredit politicians, and accentuate political divisions. Because many people obtain their news via social media, they are particularly vulnerable to this kind of tactic, often inhabiting an echo chamber where views inconsistent with their beliefs never appear. Yerlikaya (2020, p. 184) notes that

> It has now become very common to spread fake news and to manipulate voters with fake accounts during election periods. Distorting the personal information of candidates in elections and the character assassination of politicians through false information are also used as an effective method. Another manipulation technique is the sharing of personalized content that will trigger voters emotionally and change their political decisions by conducting voter profile studies.

The trend has led to an erosion of confidence in mainstream news sources. Among the poorly educated and uninformed, political fake news is used to spread an emotional contagion, particularly resentment and anger.

Political fake news occasionally takes the form of rumor bombs (Harsin 2018), intentionally produced and strategically deployed rumors intended to hurt or help particular politicians. Rumors, of course, are a time-honored tool of politics, but the internet let rumors be weaponized to an unprecedented degree. Examples include the fiction that Obama was not born in the U.S., that he is a Muslim, that he banned the Pledge of Allegiance, or that the Pope endorsed Donald Trump. Textual rumors circulating on social media can be complemented by doctored photographs or deepfake videos purporting to show something that did not happen in fact.

In Europe, fake news has plagued electoral politics for years. In France, for example, during the presidential campaign in 2017 the MacronLeaks disinformation network on social media consisted of bots, automated computer scripts disguising themselves as humans (Ferrara 2017). The right-wing National Front falsely claimed that Macron had created a government card that gave Muslim immigrants 40 euros per day (Yerlikaya 2020). In response, Facebook suspended 30,000 automatic accounts for spreading disinformation. Purportedly leaked email embarrassing Macron were later shown to be the result of a Russian disinformation campaign. Fortunately, however, fake news websites reach a much smaller share of the population than do mainstream media outlets (Fletcher et al. 2018). In Poland, the ruling party, Prawo I Sprawiedliwość (Law and Justice), routinely disseminates falsehoods about gays and that refugees spread disease (Traub 2016). Many European countries have much stricter laws against the dissemination of fake news for political purposes than does the U.S., and there is a welter of fact-checking and debunking organizations there.

Waisbord (2018) makes the intriguing argument that the explosion of fake news is the result of the collapse of the old order of journalism, in which a few large media companies acted as gate-keepers. Rather, the internet has lowered barriers to entry and allowed the proliferation of innumerable voices, including corporations and governments waging information warfare. Journalism in many ways has lost its authority as the only real source of valid news. In the wake of this transformation, a huge array of falsehoods has proliferated.

Fake News and Immigration

Immigrants, because they come from different countries and cultures, have long been the targets of racism, xenophobia, and fake news (Cullloty and Suiter 2021). Immigrants are the most visible "Other," and have been blamed for taking jobs, crime, and diseases. Often the broader goal is simply to undermine multiculturalism (Nortio et al. 2021).

Between 1870 and 1930, more than 30 million immigrants entered the United States. Most came from Southern and Eastern Europe; as a result, there arose numerous attempts to preserve Anglo-Saxon dominance, including pseudo-sciences such as eugenics and social Darwinism and the first, highly flawed IQ tests. American xenophobia has historically been coupled with fake news (Lee 2019). Nativism has a long institutional history, including the American Party and the Know-Nothings of the 1850s, Immigration Restriction League of the early 20th century, and Tea Party of the 2010s. Throughout the 19th century, lies were told about various immigrant groups to the U.S., such as the Irish. Driven by poverty and famine, the Irish were the first Catholics to arrive in large numbers in the country. They were, accordingly, often accused of being agents of the Pope. The anti-immigrant Know Nothing Party (1850–1860) fostered waves of fake news about the Irish, such as the notions that they hated freedom, the flag, the president, the media, and freedom of speech (Tyler 1992).

Fake news about immigrants and disease has a particularly repulsive history. During a 1748 yellow fever outbreak in Philadelphia, John Lining, then port physician of Charleston, published a pamphlet in which he had noted that "There is something very singular in the constitution of the Negroes, which renders them not liable to this fever" (quoted in Hogarth 2019); belief in the immunity of African-Americans to the disease persisted into the 20th century. This argument notion played into a long-standing trope that white bodies were pure, clean, and civilized whereas "others" were construed as dirty or impure (Brown 2011). Between 1895 and 1910, false assertions that Chinese and Japanese carried trachoma were used to deny entry to numerous immigrants; similar allegations were levied against East European Jewish immigrants (Markel 2000), part of the emerging discourse of the "yellow peril." Likewise, a bubonic plague outbreak in San Francisco in 1900 was blamed on the Chinese, largely due to the energetic lies of the Hearst newspapers. In 2003, a minor outbreak of SARS (Severe Acute Respiratory Syndrome) on the east coast of the U.S. was blamed on Asians; "In Boston and New

York City false rumors of infection proliferated faster than the virus itself" (Schram 2003). In 2005, Lou Dobbs, a prominent Fox News television commentator, claimed that unscreened illegal immigrants from Latin America were bringing the biblical disease leprosy to America (van den Heuvel 2007). Fox News has pushed populist narratives of minorities carrying disease on many of its programs, with host Tomi Lahren claiming that Mexican immigrants are bringing diseases such as tuberculosis, chickenpox, and hepatitis (Da Silva, 2018). In 2015, Donald Trump claimed that "tremendous infectious disease is pouring across the border. The United States has become a dumping ground for Mexico and, in fact, for many other parts of the world" (Saul 2015). Finally, with the outbreak of covid-19, Trump frequently used the term "kung flu" to underscore its Chinese origins. Indeed, fake news about the covid pandemic led to a surge of anti-Asian violence (Wright and Duong 2021).

European fake news about immigration typically supports the continent's far right's racist vision of immigrants (Ellinas 2010). It frequently uses social media to normalize racist and xenophobic attitudes, generating an affective politics of hostility and hate. For example, Swedish racists have used Facebook to target Somali immigrants (Ekman 2019). British reactionaries foment opposition to Romanian immigrants (Cheregi 2015). Often produced as a tool of spreading Russian propaganda, this type of disinformation often focuses on alleged crimes by immigrants, particularly rape. Muslim immigrants are often painted as jihadists. Some anti-immigrant propaganda is directed against the European Union, such as allegations that the EU encourages immigration as part of a broader strategy to eliminate nation-states (Juhász and Szicherle 2017). The right-wing Alternative for Germany (AfD) used social media bots to great effect to spread lies about immigrants and refugees. Other examples include false accusations that the Merkel Administration in Germany knew of the impending flood of immigrants in 2015 and that George Soros was behind the refugee crisis.

Military Propaganda and Fake News

> Truth is the first casualty in war.
> Ethel Annakin, 1915

Fake news has been widely used during periods of war, which have frequently generated misleading coverage (Cunningham 2002; Taylor 1995). Mass media have been central to the propagation of propaganda. Propaganda may be defined as the "deliberate, systematic attempt to shape perceptions, manipulate cognitions, and direct behavior to achieve a response that furthers the desired intent of the propagandist" (Jowett and O'Donnell 2014, p. 7).

Information warfare is a time-honored tactic used by many militaries throughout history. Unlike information targeted at domestic audiences, information warfare is aimed at opposing states. The bluntest forms involve disabling an enemy's communication systems (e.g., cutting submarine cables) or jamming radio broadcasts. The boundaries between military and civic propaganda are often blurry. The use of misinformation and propaganda to confuse or distract opponents has a long history. (The word "propaganda" was coined by the Vatican in the 17th century to combat Protestants; it originally meant to sway the unconverted). As Taylor (1995, p. 14) notes, "propaganda tells people *what* to think whereas education *teaches* people *how* to think" (italics in the original). It may sow fear, panic, or dissent among the civilian population, lower morale, undermine discipline, threaten political legitimacy, or spread doubts, confusion, and mistrust. Misinformation can push a counter-narrative that challenges explanations advanced by the state or media. Fake news is often used by partisans to delegitimize news that contradicts their prejudices. It often exaggerates the strength of one side and the weaknesses of the other; it typically paints one side as noble and moral and the other side as barbaric. Propaganda goes as far back as the stelae erected in ancient Babylonia boasting of a king's ruthlessness. Over the years, other examples include monumental statues, ruses, triumphal parades, and the planting of rumors. The emergence of printing during the Renaissance saw military propaganda become more prevalent and widespread. With rising literacy rates, militaries could use posters, pamphlets, and leaflets, plant stories in newspapers, spread caricatures and cartoons of rulers, rewrite history, and spread stories about atrocities committed by the other side. The press became the favored way for governments to manipulate public opinion. Maps too were used to spread lies (Monmonier 1996). Censorship flourished in response.

The spread of military disinformation has been a vital part of contemporary warfare since at least the 18th century. Benjamin Franklin was adept at manipulating the French press to tell stories about the British, claiming, for example that they let the injured die without care. His efforts helped to undermine support for the war in Britain.

Throughout the 19th century, as newspapers became abundant and cheap, military propaganda flourished. The invention of the telegraph and photography added greatly to this effort, as did the rise of public educational systems and rising literacy rates. The British used propaganda to great effect to tout their successes throughout the empire. British defeats at the hands of the Zulus were dismissed as the result of being overwhelmed by sheer numbers. In the U.S. during the

Civil War, northern propagandists portrayed the Confederacy as traitors, while their Southern counterparts depicted the Union as the product of immigrants.

World War I saw propaganda become markedly more sophisticated in nature, a process that Nazi Germany took to new heights. Relying on the newly created secret Bureau of War Propaganda, the British media published fake news about "Germans impaling babies with bayonets, sexually assaulting nuns, enslaving and murdering priests, cutting off the hands of children, using civilians as human shields, turning cadavers into soap and margarine, crucifying soldiers, and cutting the breasts off nurses" (Higdon 2020). British and American newspapers regularly published images of the Beastly Hun and the Prussian Ogre (Fig. 3.5). They had a field day with the sinking of the *Lusitania* in 1915. The British press employed authors such as Arthur Conan Doyle, H.G. Wells, and Rudyard Kipling in these efforts. British propagandists also used balloons to spread leaflets over the Western front. Famed French historian Marc Bloch (1921/2013) lamented the spread of "false news" and how it led to a culture that disdained accuracy, truth, and facts. The Americans, too, used propaganda, such as that produced by the Committee on Public Information. As Taylor (1995, p. 184) notes, "The Kaiser was portrayed as a devil in a spiked helmet, German soldiers as violators of innocent women (nurses and nuns being favourite targets of their lust) and child murderers." American advertising firms, which had recently perfected the art of mass marketing, joined the effort, as did Hollywood, which produced a series of spy films.

In the newly established Soviet Union, propaganda became a state-sponsored art form. With limited literacy rates, the Bolsheviks relied on posters, radio, and cinema. The state newspaper, *Pravda* ("truth"), became well known for its openly propagandistic methods, somewhat like Fox News in the 21st century. As the editor of *Pravda* stated in 1978, 'Our aim is propaganda, the propaganda of the party and the state. We do not hide this" (quoted in Taylor 1995, p. 264). With the establishment of the Third International, or Comintern, in 1919, the USSR began to export propaganda abroad, such as with organizations like the World Peace Council, which echoed the Kremlin's line. Soviet actors distinguished between *aktivnyye meropriyatiya* (active measures) and *dezinformatsiya* (disinformation) (Prier 2017). The KGB and Soviet diplomats surreptitiously mounted disinformation projects around the world, providing fabricated documents and forgeries and planting newspaper stories and rumors. These were largely aimed at audiences in the developing world. Examples include stories that the CIA tried to assassinate the Pope, that the U.S. supported the Balkanization of India, and that the Americans planned coups d'état in several states (Kux 1985). Simultaneously the Soviets attempted to seal off their residents from foreign broadcasts, typically by jamming signals. Soviet attempts to contain the influx of foreign information began to

Figure 3.5: U.S. Anti-German Poster by Harry Ryle Hopps, 1917.

decay in the 1980s as new communications technologies penetrated the state's defenses.

World War II marked perhaps the greatest propaganda battle of all time. German complaints about the *luegenpresse* (lying press) arose during the revolution of 1848, and persisted on and off through World War I (Cortada and Aspray 2019). Hitler's Germany used the term *luegenpresse* to intimidate the media and convince Germans to accept Nazi fake news. Under Paul Josef Goebbels, the Ministry for Propaganda and Enlightenment, founded in 1933, produced a steady avalanche of fake news. Goebbels was famous for his mastery of radio and the cinema for these purposes. A famous line attributed to him was "If you tell a lie big enough and keep repeating it, people will eventually come to believe it." He emphasized the importance of repetition in a struggle against bourgeois individuality. The willingness of the audience to swallow lies was also important. Thus, Goebbels said that "propaganda works best when those who are being manipulated are confident they are acting on their own free will" (quoted in McIntyre 2018, p. 114). Nazi propaganda films tended to be expressive and emotive rather than informative. Some suggested that Britain had been taken over by Jews. One famous film, *Theresienstadt*, made to show to the Red Cross in 1944, portrayed life in the concentration camps as happy and joyful, perhaps the most horrific example of fake news ever made. Under Goebbels, the Ministry's influence spread throughout every corner of German life. Under the Nazis, Germans, particularly the youth, were indoctrinated to the extreme. All Nazi propaganda pointed to the inevitability of German victory.

Japanese propaganda, or "thought war," was carried out by the official news agency, Domei. The famous broadcaster Tokyo Rose spoke to homesick American troops. The Japanese also sent pornographic postcards to Australian troops suggesting that their wives were committing adultery back home (Taylor 1995). Prisoners of war made broadcasts falsely claiming that they were being treated well.

Americans, too, engaged in a propaganda effort. The U.S. government set up the Office of War Information in 1942, which worked hand-in-hand with Hollywood to turn out movies favorable to the Allied cause. Near the end of the war, the Americans unleashed the Monroe bomb, which could drop 80,000 leaflets at a time over German cities urging them to surrender.

One of the most pernicious examples of fake news is denial that the Holocaust ever happened, in the process trivializing the murder of six million Jews (Wistrich 2012). As Primo Levi once said, "The very enormity of genocide nudges us toward incredulity, toward denial and refusal." This form of historical revisionism, spread by neo-Nazis and their sympathizers (and occasionally by Islamicist groups), became a concern in many liberal democracies in the late 20th century. Various forms of denialism exist, from outright rejection of the facts to attempts to minimize the number of victims and play down the horrific violence that it exemplified; some types even excuse the genocide as justified. Examples include *The Hoax of the Twentieth Century* by Arthur Butz and *Did Six Million Really Die?* by Richard Harwood. The internet allowed a whole new spate of denialism to arise. The reaction against it was so strong that 14 European states criminalized denial of the Holocaust as an attempt to rehabilitate Nazism. The issue prompted extended debates about the limits of free speech and academic freedom, as well as numerous lawsuits. The most famous of these took place in London in 2000, when historian David Irving sued the American academic Deborah Lipstadt, author of *Denying the Holocaust: The Growing Assault on Truth and Memory*, on the grounds that she impugned his professional reputation. After large amounts of professional testimony, the judge agreed with Lipstadt, Irving was soundly defeated, and forced to pay a hefty fine. The judge ruled that his falsification of the historical record was deliberate. Other cases went up before the European Court of Human Rights. Denialism is universally regarded as a hate crime. Countries such as Australia, France, Canada, and Germany have successfully prosecuted deniers, but their jurisdictions end at their borders. In response, Whine (2008, p. 59) notes, "denial and racist sites have relocated to jurisdictions where no supervisory regime exists or where there are no legal sanctions." In short, denialism and attempts to skirt it suppression have a distinct political geography.

During the Cold War, both superpowers used propaganda to advance their aims. The U.S. military enlisted Radio Free Europe and Hollywood in this cause. The emergence of television also offered a new medium to disseminate propaganda. Both sides used lies and disinformation extensively (Snyder 1997). Both sides represented the struggle in simplistic, good v. bad terms. Both spread propaganda among the newly independent countries of Africa and Asia. As Taylor (1995, p. 259) puts it,

> When the Soviets and Americans viewed one another, they tended to see the dark side of their own characteristics which they reflected back at their view of the other. This isn't a recipe for genuine mutual understanding, but it is conducive to an effective domestic propaganda campaign feeding off paranoia.

Central to the Soviet effort was Agitprop (the Administration of Agitation and Propaganda), established in 1947. In response, the U.S. passed the Smith-Mundt Act in 1948, which shifted the country's information services into high gear; nominally this was "cultural diplomacy," but in fact amounted to propaganda. President Truman launched a "Campaign for Truth" in 1950 following the outbreak of the Korean War, and launched Voice of America the same year.

Anti-Soviet propaganda shaped daily life domestically as well, such as with the House of Representatives' Un-American Activities Committee (HUAC), founded in 1938 to detect Nazis but used extensively after the war against liberals in the name of anti-Communism and culminating in Senator Joseph McCarthy's (R-WI) witch hunts. McCarthy (R-WI) repeatedly used fake news to further his aims (Schrecker 1999). He repeatedly and falsely alleged that communists were lodged in the federal government, notably the State Department (Michaels 2017). Many reputable news sources reported sympathetically about government roundups of alleged communist sympathizers, helping to feed the moral frenzy of the Second Red Scare. McCarthy's lies never sent a single "subversive" to jail, but they did destroy careers and set the stage for future Republican conspiracy-mongering (Menand 2020). At times they even led to staged events: A fake communist takeover of Mosinee, Wisconsin, in the 1950s organized by the American Legion left many people worrying about a Soviet victory in the Cold War (Fried 1998).

The Vietnam War marked a new era in American duplicity. Hollywood endorsed the effort with films such as *The Green Berets* (1968), starring John Wayne, followed later by *Rambo*. In 1964, American news media repeated false White House claims that a U.S. destroyer had been attacked by the North Vietnamese in the Gulf of Tonkin; President Johnson used the incident to request that Congress authorize the use of force there, leading to an escalation of the conflict. However, continued proclamations that the war was being won were belied by the corpses of soldiers returning in body bags. The first "television war" likewise showed the horrors in living rooms, including images of victims of napalm bombing and prisoners being executed. The war signaled new levels of public distrust in the American government.

"If there was a central font of fallacy, it was the war in Iraq, which, like the war in Vietnam, split wide the gulf between reality and perception" says Manjoo (2008, p. 190). In 1991, during the first U.S. invasion of Iraq, the Pentagon deployed a public relations firm, Hill and Knowlton, to produce an interview with an alleged nurse who claimed to have seen Iraqi soldiers steal incubators from a Kuwaiti hospital, leaving 312 infants to die. The war was the most extensively covered to date, with satellites, the internet, and new cable channels such as CNN and MSNBC giving it round-the-clock coverage. Indeed, Baudrillard (1995) famously argued that the Gulf War did not event take place, by which he meant that it was a carefully scripted, hyperreal media event as much as a real conflict on the ground. Conversely, Hussein's own Information Minister, Muhammed Saeed al-Sahhaf, aka "Baghdad Bob," was known for his ludicrously inaccurate press conferences, such as denying that U.S. tanks were in Baghdad even as they rolled behind him during an interview.

After the terrorist attacks of September 11, 2001, U.S. propaganda reached new heights (Snow and Taylor 2006). The "war on terror" seamlessly merged public relations and psychological warfare. The Bush Administration created the Office of Strategic Influence to deceive foreign leaders, as Secretary of Defense Donald Rumsfeld admitted. The U.S. government is constitutionally prohibited from waging psychological warfare against its own people, but free to do so abroad, and did. Thus, Operation "Iraqi Freedom," the invasion of that country in 2003, was based largely on fake news, such as the myth that Saddam Hussein cooperated with Al Qaeda and was thus linked to the events of 9/11. Shortly before the U.S. invasion, President George W. Bush alleged that Saddam Hussein possessed weapons of mass destruction (WMD), one of the greatest examples of fake news in the 21st century. The pretext for the war was central to the contemporary politics of lying. What Kellner (2007) calls Bushspeak consisted of repeated brazen, shameless lies, exaggerations, and falsehoods. London's *Evening Standard* published a headline screaming that Iraq could launch WMD within 45 minutes. Secretary of State Colin Powell even described Iraq's WMD to the United Nations, although later it was shown that none existed. A year after the invasion, one-third of Americans believed that WMD had been found, even though that was not the case (Lewandowski et al. 2005). The *New York Times* even apologized for its erroneous reporting on the topic. The complicity of the media in spreading the fake news led to a crisis popularly known as "weapons of mass deception."

The 9/11 attacks spawned a universe of conspiracy theories comparable to those surrounding the assassination of JFK (Stempel et al. 2007; Soukup 2008). These form another example of Hofstadter's (1965/2012) paranoid style of politics. So-called 9/11 "truthers" argue, among other things, that high level government officials knew of the attacks beforehand and approved of them, that the explosions that brought down the World Trade Center buildings were the result of controlled demolitions, that the Pentagon was hit by a missile rather than a jet, and that the North American Aerospace Defense Command (NORAD) issued a stand down order in advance of the attacks. The motivations alleged to be behind the attack include justifications for the invasion of Afghanistan and the re-election of George W. Bush.

With the rise of the internet, information warfare has become an integral part of cyberwar, including social media (Ventre 2012). Cyberwar has many dimensions, such as the use of electronic networks to cripple an opponent's infrastructure or financial systems, but it also includes the deliberate spread of disinformation through the internet and social media. As the most recent chapter in the long history of psychological warfare, fake news can be weaponized to create divisions and distractions, sow doubt, and lower morale. For these reasons, internet trolling has become a kind of warfare. The actors involved may or may not be sponsored by the state, blurring the lines between civilian and military parties. This strategy often uses bots to force social media algorithms to recognize a given topic as trending, helping to spread propaganda, rumors, and fake news. As Raganathan (2022, p. 20) states, "The algorithm-enabled content enables repetition and creation of an 'illusory truth.'"

Corporations and Fake News

Because businesses have long been active manipulators of information, corporations have long used fake news to promote products, squash unfavorable rumors, or deal with public relations crises.

Corporations have frequently deployed false and misleading claims to promote their products and increase demand (Zgheib 2017). Egregious claims about the benefits of some products, particularly foods and medicines, drew mounting concern starting in the late 19th century (Fig. 3.6). Television and the internet allowed false advertising to proliferate with abandon. False advertising may include failure to disclose, disparagement of rival products, or claims based on flawed research. At a minimum it is unethical; at its worst it is dangerous. Typically, false advertising greatly exaggerates the ostensible benefits of products: Kellogg's, for example, paid $5 million for wrongly claiming that its Rice Krispies enhanced children's immune systems and that its Mini-Wheats increased intelligence. Volkswagen, Hyundai, and Kia incurred large penalties for making false claims about their emissions levels. Airborne Herbal Supplements claimed it could prevent the common cold. Dannon claimed its Activa yogurt expedited the digestion process; it didn't. The British supermarket chain Tesco, caught putting horse meat in its beef products, claimed the entire industry did so. New Balance claimed its shoes helped wearers burn more calories. Extenze said it can extend penis length. Lumos Labs claimed that its Luminosity prevented dementia. Splenda said it was "made from sugar" even though it was not. L'Oreal Cosmetics claimed its skincare products were "clinically proven" to "boost genes." Wrigley claimed its Eclipse gum killed germs. "Georgia" peaches grown in California are another example, as is "champaign" that is not from France.

False advertising is illegal because it denies consumers the right to know what they are purchasing. Advertisements are false when the advertiser has no reasonable basis to claim the representation is true or when they contain false, deceptive or misleading statements. A statement or representation in an advertisement may also be false or fraudulent even when it constitutes a half-truth. Examples include hidden fees, misuse of terms (e. g., "organic" or "natural"), misleading illustrations, and bait-and-switch (advertising one product but selling another).

A Woman's Face Is Her Fortune.

DR.SIMM'S ARSENIC COMPLEXION WAFERS

After a few days' use will permanently remove all Blotches, Moles, Pimples and Freckles, producing an Entrancingly Beautiful Complexion that shames the use of powders and creams. Warranted perfectly harmless. Sold by all leading druggists at $1 per box of 100 wafers.

Dr. Simms' Safe Periodical Wafers are sure and reliable for all female irregularities. Price $2 per box. Sent by mail (secure) on receipt of price. Warranted to contain no "Tansy" for "Pennyroyal."

THUMLER & Co., 83 Chambers St;, New York. H. M. Parchen & Co.. Sole Agents, Helena.

Figure 3.6: An 1889 Advertisement for "Arsenic Complexion Wafers" in the *Helena Independent.*

In 1914, as part of Progressive Era reforms, the Federal Trade Commission Act, which states that false advertising is a form of unfair and deceptive commerce, went into effect. The Federal Trade Commission has regulatory power to end false claims. The penalties for firms that are convicted of false advertising can be very steep.

Corporations may also be the targets of fake news (Jahng 2021). Starbucks has been falsely accused of putting feces in its coffee; a right-wing troll started the false rumor that the company would give free coffee to undocumented immigrants on "Dreamer Day." The CEO of Pepsi was falsely quoted as saying that supporters of Donald Trump should "take their business elsewhere." Coca Cola was falsely reported to have recalled bottles of Dasani water because it was infected with "clear parasites." Indian restaurants in Britain were accused of selling human meat. Tesla was the victim of a faked video showing one of its driverless cars crashing into a robot; the film was produced by RT, a Russian television company funded by the Kremlin. Some operators use fake news to inflate share prices and sell their stocks to earn quick profits, spreading rumors of impending takeovers or product break-throughs. Worried that fake news might hurt their share prices, some companies pay third parties to trawl social media (Atkinson 2019). Some investment firms use algorithms to scour press releases to inform their decisions (Ferraro and Chipman 2019). Finally, some firms resort to legal recourse to combat defamation.

More insidious than false advertising is corporate information warfare. Given the lax rules governing lobbying and campaign spending, and the enormous re-sources corporations have at their disposal, their means to effectuate this strategy are formidable. Corporate information warfare involves attempts to influence pub-lic policy and opinion through a variety of means, including setting up bogus think tanks that tout a pro-corporate agenda (Barros and Taylor 2020). One example is the Heartland Institute, located in Chicago, which promotes denial of anthropogen-ic climate change and other conservative causes. Others include the highly influen-tial Heritage Foundation, the Hoover Institution, the George C. Marshall Institute, the American Enterprise Institute, and the Discovery Institute in Seattle, which promotes intelligent design. Many are funded by the fossil fuel industry; other re-ceive funds from the Coors company or right-wing billionaires such as Richard Mellon Scaife. These outfits often publish newsletters, magazines, and journals, many of which constitute a simulacrum of science.

Corporations have a long and unsavory history of using "experts" to manipu-late the news. The Heritage Foundation, for example, receives funding from Gen-eral Motors, Chase Manhattan, and ExxonMobil. The Heartland Institute receives funds from Philip Morris. Beyond the defense of profits for large firms, defenders of this approach tend to hold radical libertarian views in which *any* government action is automatically deemed one for the worse. Using scientists who capitalized on popular awe of their field, firms hid behind a veneer of pseudo-science to jus-tify their aims, with untold long-term consequences of health and the environ-ment. Corporations often use conservative scientists, particularly physicists, with distinguished pedigrees to promote these views, people who think *any* type of gov-ernment regulation is illegitimate. Often they speak on subjects about which they have no expertise, such as physicists railing against news that tobacco was linked to cancer. Others were adamantly opposed to environmental regulations such as the Clean Air and Clean Water Acts and the Endangered Species Act. Corporate anti-science often led to political attacks on the Environmental Protection Agency. Besides questioning the science involved, environmental restrictions were painted as anti-democratic. Although the scientists involved found themselves increasingly at odds with the scientific community, their voices were amplified by the conservative news universe. As a result, market fundamentalism was married to disdain for mainstream science.

Corporate information warfare began in the 1950s as tobacco companies mobilized against the newly emerging links between smoking and lung cancer. In their famed and influential volume *Merchants of Doubt* (2011), Oreskes and Conway detail how tobacco companies (specifically, the Tobacco Research Industry Committee, or TRIC) misused scientists to sow confusion about the health effects of smoking. TRIC took out ads in many newspapers denying any link between smoking and cancer. As Oreskes and Conway put it (p. 16), "The industry's position was that there was 'no proof' that tobacco was bad, and they fostered that position by manufacturing a 'debate'." Tobacco firms insisted that secondhand smoke posed no danger, insisting it was a routine risk like crossing the street or driving a car. The point was to sow confusion and undermine scientific research, to create the appearance of a debate when there was none.

TRIC's campaign became the blueprint for other science-denying strategies. Other firms used similar strategies to deny the consequences of DDT, acid rain, nuclear winter, the destruction of the ozone layer, gun safety, and climate change, or to promote Ronald Reagan's "Star Wars" fantasy. The George C. Marshall Institute in particular played an especially aggressive role in minimizing the risks and opposing regulation in each and every one of these issues. In essence, scientific issues became highly politicized. Corporate denial of climate change existed long before that cause became a pillar of the post-truth conservative movement (Chapter 4). Exxon, for example, knew by the 1970s that burning fossil fuels was changing the planet's climate. "Exxon knew the truth, but spent decades funding research to create confusion and public uncertainty about the very existence of climate change" (Rabin-Havt 2016, p. 36).

Another form of corporate information warfare, and a vital pillar of post-truth media, is the use of paid pundits and alleged experts to espouse views favorable to companies without revealing their ties to their clients. These pundits inject their views promoting firms into media broadcasts but fail to disclose their sources. Large public relations, marketing, and advertising firms produce short, prepackaged video news releases (VNRs) by the thousands each year (Harmon and White 2001; Broaddus et al. 2011), which are then frequently downloaded by local news stations eager for content and shown on television or websites. Others are posted on YouTube or social media. VNRs look like real news stories but are in fact advertisements in disguise. This practice essentially mainlines promotional videos into newsrooms, a demonstration of complicity or negligence; for this reason, VNRs are often dismissed as "infoganda." For example, WalMart released a

"Great For You" food labelling initiative VNR; Wendy's announced its nutrition app via a VNR; Towers Perrin, a human resources consulting firm, released a VNR about employees and job satisfaction touting its work; Quest Diagnostics produced a two-minute infomercial about sick children; and Siemens used Medialink, the world's largest producers of VNRs, to create one about the wonders of its process automation systems. Government agencies such as the Defense Department engage in this practice as well. The Bush administration released one of jubilant Iraqis tearing down a statue of Saddam Hussein in 2003 (Barstow and Stein 2005), an event that was staged. Rarely, if ever, are the sources of VNRs revealed. Manjoo (2008, p. 200) notes that these are powerful because "we're much more likely to believe and to remember a message if we see it as part of a newscast than if we see essentially the same thing in a commercial." Because most people get their news from local televisions stations, such videos have enormous effects shaping public opinion.

Yet other types of corporate propaganda include "astroturf" campaigns designed to give the appearance of a groundswell of public support (Lyon and Maxwell 2004). The tactic is particularly favored by lobbying firms seeking to influence legislation under construction. These may include newspaper advertisements, phone bank operations, online videos, letter-writing campaigns, and manufactured rallies in cities. For example, in 1992, when the Environmental Protection Agency issued a warning about secondhand smoke, the tobacco industry turned to a public relations company, APCO Worldwide, to initiate an astroturf campaign that aimed to sow doubt about the findings by linking them to other supposed frauds such as climate change. The tobacco industry founded the National Smokers' Alliance in 1993 to oppose anti-smoking legislation in Congress. In 2018, the Louisiana-based energy company Entergy was fined for using paid actors to speak up at city council meetings in favor of a controversial power plant under development. People for the West! characterizes itself as a "grassroots campaign supporting western communities," but 96% of its funding comes from mining and petroleum firms. Consumer Alliance is a nonprofit firm dedicated to preventing lower prices for prescription drugs for Medicare recipients – entirely funded by the pharmaceutical industry. The Koch Brothers funded an astroturf campaign against wind farms in New England. In many ways the Tea Party was an astroturf campaign due to its heavy funding from two Koch-financed groups, FreedomWorks and Americans for Prosperity. Astroturf campaigns are thus simulacra of true populist political movements. They are designed to take advantage of the bandwagon effect, the notion that many people will support something if they think large numbers of others do too.

The point of corporate fake news was to sow doubt, downplay the risks of products, keep controversies going, chill dissenting views, and promote a counter-narrative. It creates distractions and sets up "straw man" versions of progressive positions that can be easily demolished by conservatives. Corporate fake news often impugns the behavior of scientists and accuses them of rushing to judgment. The media often gave voice to these views in the guise of giving weight to both sides, when in fact, in the scientific world, there is only one side (e.g., regarding tobacco or climate change). Corporations often hire paid "experts" to produce fake research, which is then converted into talking points and repeated on television. They hire 20 lobbyists for every member of Congress. As Rabin-Havt (2016, p. 4) puts it, "our democracy has been hacked, manipulated by political practitioners who recognize that as long as there is no truth, there can be no progress." In short, corporate information warfare merged anti-scientific positions with reactionary political thought.

Modern Day Tabloids

> A lie doesn't become truth, wrong doesn't become right, and evil doesn't become good, just because it's accepted by a majority.
> Booker T. Washington

The journalistic equivalent of junk food, tabloids have a long history and are found today in many countries of the world. Their origins may be traced to the scandal sheets popular in the 18th and 19th centuries. Typically, such outlets cater to naïve, gullible, and poorly educated readers (Bastos 2016), deliberately blurring the boundaries between news and entertainment (i.e., infotainment), invariably at the expense of the former. Such papers are frequently sold at supermarket checkout counters, feature screaming headlines in large print, and emphasize the lurid, spectacular, and metaphysical. Salacious gossip about celebrities, sensational crime stories, and astrology occupies a large share of their pages. Typically they cater to readers' worst instincts and occasionally publish outright lies; they are not above doctoring photographs and paying sources. Prominent examples include the *National Enquirer* in the U.S. and in Britain, *The Sun* and *News of the World*. In many respects these represent the most recent incarnation of early 20th century yellow journalism. With the rise of the internet, most moved from paper to online versions.

Tabloids tend to be conservative politically, often vehemently so. Take, for example, the *National Enquirer*, the largest American tabloid. Founded in 1926 in New York by William Griffin, a protégé of Hearst, it grew to become a popular and widely read gossip magazine. In the 1930s and 1940s, it consistently pro-fascist messages favoring isolationism earned it federal charges of sedition. In the 1950s it became increasingly sensationalistic, and pioneered the model of being sold in supermarket checkouts. At its peak it had more than six million readers Its reputation for inaccuracy, falsehoods, and even blackmail haunted it for decades. The tabloid has been sued numerous times by celebrities for slander and defamation. In 2016, as an enthusiastic backer of Donald Trump, the tabloid published stories insinuating that the father of Senator Ted Cruz (R-TX) was involved in the assassination of J.F. Kennedy. When Karen McDougal alleged she had an extramarital affair with Trump, the tabloid paid her $150,000 for the rights to the story and then buried it.

Another spectacular tabloid example is *Weekly World News*, an online tabloid that is filled with farcical, breathless stories of the bizarre, grotesque, and improbable. It ran in print from 1979 to 2007 and has existed only online since then. Weekly World News, published in Florida, was renowned for its outlandish cover stories featuring aliens, monsters, and Elvis Presley. A particularly notorious figure was Bat Boy, a half-human, half-bat creature that appeared on its pages routinely and became something of a folk hero. It also featured apocalyptic forecasts and absurd stories about politicians past and present. At its peak in the 1980s it reached roughly 1.2 million readers per week (Heller 2014). The outlet claimed to publish the truth, even if its stories were routinely weird, but its stories are routinely so unrealistic that it is impossible to view it as anything but comedic satire. It never retracted a story until 2004, when it began stating that "the reader should suspend disbelief for the sake of enjoyment."

Around the world, many tabloids are owned by right-wing media mogul Rupert Murdoch. Examples include *News of the World* and *The Sun* in Britain, *Star* and the *New York Post* in the U.S., and the *Herald Sun* in Australia. Murdoch's News Corporation owns 800 outlets across the globe, including the *New York Post*, television stations such as Fox News, and 20th Century Fox. His outlets routinely support conservative politicians, including the Conservative Party in the UK and Donald Trump (McKnight 2010). News Corporation has donated heavily to many right-wing organizations and political figures, and the *Post* regularly reports news tilted to the far right.

Britain, too, has popular and raucous tabloids, such as *The Sun, Daily Mail*, and *Daily Express.* These too tend to be politically conservative, frequently supporting the Tories with unabashed enthusiasm. The most sensationalistic, such as *The Sun* and *The Daily Mirror*, are often called "red tops" due to the color used for banner headlines. Like their American counterparts, their readers tend to be older and poorly educated. The more conservative ones were instrumental in zealously supporting Brexit by spreading fake news in advance of the vote to leave (Bennhold 2017).

Fake News and the Internet

> A lie will go around the world while the truth is pulling its boots on.
> Mark Twain

During the digital era, with the explosive use of the internet and social media, fake news has proliferated with abandon (Barclay 2018). In essence, the internet greatly reduced the role of the traditional media as the gatekeepers of information. As *New York Times* CEO Mark Thompson noted, "Whatever its other cultural and social merits, our digital ecosystem seems to have evolved into a near-perfect environment for fake news to thrive" (quoted in Uberti 2016). The low entry costs associated with digital information have allowed an enormous number of voices to arise on various webpages, blogs, applications (e. g., Facebook), and video channels (e. g., Youtube), all augmented by highly sophisticated algorithms and bots designed to amplify emotions (Lazer et al. 2018). Social media sites provided an alternative to mass media and allowed both real news and fake news to multiply exponentially. The reluctance of the public to pay for reliable news also played a part.

Fake news web sites appeared almost immediately after the birth of the internet. One of the first was MartinLutherKing.org, created by the white supremacist group StormFront to discredit Dr. King's accomplishments. Over time, hyperpartisan web pages, Facebook accounts, and Twitter feeds have slowly generated a post-truth information ecosystem. Homogeneous media ecosystems greatly reduce the opportunity to encounter opposing views or information and amplify confirmation biases. As a result, rumors and unfounded allegations circulate at the speed of light, giving new meaning to the old adage that "a lie can travel halfway around the world while the truth is putting on its shoes." The sheer scale and rapidity with which disinformation circulates today renders traditional models of news diffusion meaningless. Numerous websites exist only for the purpose of producing demonstrably false "clickbait," which maximizes advertising revenues. The proliferation of bots, trolls, and blogs also contributes to the diffusion of false stories.

Fake news includes graphics as well as text. Traditionally, the photograph became almost universally accepted as an accurate, unbiased, straightforward mirror of the world, one with the power to capture the fidelity of visual experience, to re-present the past faithfully (Sontag 1977). Nonetheless, almost immediately the capacity of photographers to manipulate and retouch images began to undermine the taken-for-granted capacity of the camera to reflect reality objectively (Fineman 2012).

While the editing of photos and videos certainly long predates the internet, digital technology has taken the practice to new heights (or lows). Adobe's Photoshop appeared in 1988 and, because it offered unprecedented abilities to manipulate images, gave rise to an entire image-remaking industry (Jones 2013). Although it was initially used mostly in the media that covered the fashion industry, its applications soon spilled out into other contexts. Such software undermines the long-held assumption that photography offers an unadulterated access to objective reality. Manjoo (2004) writes:

> There was a time when photographs were synonymous with truth – when you could be sure that what you saw in a picture actually occurred. In today's Photoshop world, all that has changed. Pictures are endlessly pliable. Photographs (and even videos) are now merely as good as words – approximations of reality at best, subtle (or outright) distortions of truth at worst.

The recent rise of "deepfake" videos, which appear quite real but are in fact digitized fantasies, only amplifies this problem. Deepfakes require enormous amounts of data and neural networks to operate (Negi et al. 2021). Within computer science, a vast literature has emerged to detect them, setting off a cat-and-mouse game between deepfake producers and their critics. Deepfake videos originated in 2017 when the pornography industry posted artificial-intelligence generated videos of actresses in the act. Deepfakes have been used to digitally "undress" women on social media and to steal millions of dollars from companies by imitating executives' voices on the phone. They have been used for blackmail and cyberbullying, and lead people to become suspicious of surveillance footage. They were soon applied to the political sphere. One famous deepfake, for example, showed Democratic Speaker of the House Nancy Pelosi appearing to be drunk and slurring her words (Hodge 2021). The proliferation of deepfake videos threatens to unleash a whole new form of information warfare (Chesney and Citron 2019). They can be used to make it appear that politicians said things that they did not, create fraudulent evidence in corporate transactions, and bamboozle the public. Highly realistic, sensationalistic fake videos can incite violence, discredit leaders, tip an election, and aid in the recruitment of terrorists. This phenomenon casts doubt that we can trust our eyes in searching for truth, bringing new relevance to the old quip by Chico (not Groucho) Marx, "Who are you going to believe, me or your own lying eyes?" Europol (2022), the European Agency for Law Enforcement, wrote that "The increasing volume of deepfakes could lead to a situation where "citizens no longer have a shared reality, or could create societal confusion about which information sources are reliable; a situation sometimes referred to as 'information apocalypse' or 'reality apathy.'"

Digital fake news has flourished during a period of intense ideological polarization. As Spohr (2017) points out, filter bubbles and selective exposure to social media are highly effective in minimizing the chances that readers will come across news that does not fit their political framework. In the U.S., the classic division is between conservative viewers of Fox News on the one hand and liberals who watch CNN or listen to NPR on the other. There is little overlap between the two. In social media, the widespread use of filter bubbles, or algorithms that customize users' online experiences, by Facebook and similar outlets limits the range of news outlets from which readers can choose. Some chatbots even use artificial intelligence, such as ChatGPT, for this purpose (Hsu and Thompson 2023). Most users are not aware that such programs are at work, and only consume news that aligns with their preconceptions, never coming across views that are inconsistent with their prejudices. Even facts that bluntly contradict their worldview may be ignored. When never confronted with a differing perspective, many people may not even know that such alternative views exist, let alone that they have any merit. This selective exposure, or what psychologists call confirmation bias, plays a major role in fomenting hyperpartisanship. This division goes far to explain why these two political groups live in markedly different realities, frequently interpreting the same event in very different ways. Political groups often inhabit echo chambers that segregate them ideologically from those with differing values and opinions. In the process, the possibilities of open, respectful democratic debate are minimized.

The proliferation of fake news has occurred precisely as the public's trust in government and the media has steadily declined, particularly among conservatives. Combined with a suspicion about expertise in general, the alleged preserve of liberal "elites" who look down on working people, fake news and distrust of the media foster an environment in which "anything goes," that any view is as good as any other. These observations are a sobering antidote to early, utopian expectations that the Internet would expose people to the other side of the political divide. Moreover, they underscore the notion that the ways in which people process information are "first and foremost pragmatic, survival mechanisms and only secondarily truth detection strategies" (Friedrich, 1993, p. 298).

Unfortunately, fake news is often lucrative. Indeed, like information, disinformation has become commodified. Across the world a shadow industry of "disinfo-for-hire" has arisen. As Fisher (2021) notes,

> New technology enables nearly anyone to get involved. Programs batch generate fake accounts with hard-to-trace profile photos. Instant metrics help to hone effective messaging. So does access to users' personal data, which is easily purchased in bulk.

Examples include British anti-vaccine sites, pro-Beijing activists critical of the Hong Kong democracy movement, Russian influence peddlers, and Bangladeshi content farms that produce and sell false information for anyone who will pay. Other examples abound:

Creators of fake news found that they could capture so much interest that they could make money off fake news through automated advertising that rewards high traffic to their sites. A man running a string of fake news sites from the Los Angeles suburbs told NPR he made between $10,000 and $30,000 a month. A computer science student in the former Soviet republic of Georgia told the *New York Times* that creating a new website and filling it with both real stories and fake news that flattered Trump was a "gold mine" (Drobnic Holan 2016).

Chapter Conclusion

> All truth passes through three stages. First, it is ridiculed. Second, it is violently opposed.
> Third, it is accepted as being self-evident.
> Arthur Schopenhauer

Whatever definition of truth one subscribes to, fake news is never good news. Fake news is the primary and most effective weapon in the arsenal of post-truth. It is invariably used to sow dissent, create doubt and confusion, undermine morale, and deceive people. As the examples cited here indicate, fake news has been deployed in geopolitics, such as when Hearst used yellow journalism to start the Spanish-American War. It has been used in political campaigns, hoaxes, and to promote conspiracy theories. Fake news has misled the public about immigrants, falsely blaming them for unemployment, crime, and disease, among other pathologies. Fake news is routinely disseminated by militaries to undermine adversaries. Corporations use fake news to minimize the damage of exposes, such as those concerning tobacco and climate change, for green washing, and in false advertising. Tabloids appeal to an under-educated segment of the public because they sell emotion and affect, but not the truth.

The weaponization of truth in the age of the internet both reflects and intensifies political polarization. Polarization, in turns, leads people to silo themselves in echo chambers, reading and listening only to like-minded members of the same tribe. Thus, "The world of post-truth politics is the pathetic result of a political culture where ideological victory, not progress, is the ultimate goal," writes Rabin-Havt (2016, p. 21).

Chapter 4
Right-wing Post-truth Geographies

> Those who can make you believe in absurdities can make you commit atrocities.
>
> Voltaire

Although there are occasional liberal and left-wing versions of post-truth, such as some vaccine denialists, the phenomenon is primarily the product of political conservatives and reactionaries, used to make unappealing policies and ideas more popular by deceiving the public or dressing them up in the rhetoric of banality. This pattern is in keeping with the predominant neoliberal ethos of the times: autocratic leaders who use fake news as a weapon; religious conservatives opposed to science; and populist movements that manipulate truth for political gain.

This chapter explores right-wing post-truth, and its geographical dimensions, in several steps. It begins with comments about anti-intellectualism, which flies in the face of Enlightenment values of curiosity, exploration, and scientific inquiry. Second, it focuses on science denial, including examples such as refusal to admit human evolution, the efficacy of AIDS vaccines, and flat-earth theory. Third, it turns to climate change denial, the most dangerous form of post-truth geographies, and how it was embraced by the Republican Party. Fourth, it examines the right-wing mediasphere and the lies it promotes, including Rush Limbaugh, Fox News, and a host of websites that have created an enormous reactionary echo chamber. Fifth, it looks at right-wing conspiracy theories. Sixth, it describes how conservatives used fake news in the 2016 and 2020 U.S. presidential elections. Seventh, it turns to Donald Trump, the poster boy of post-truth, and how his innumerable lies generated false geographies. Eighth, it delves into the world of covid denialism, which has caused the unnecessary deaths of hundreds of thousands. Ninth, it takes up the case of Brexit and how Britain's departure from the European Union was predicated on falsehoods, a clear case of post-truth geopolitics. The conclusion summarizes the major findings.

Anti-Intellectualism and its Aftermath

> When stupidity is considered patriotism, it is unsafe to be intelligent.
>
> Isaac Asimov

Deep and pervasive within the forces that have given rise to a post-truth world is its beating heart, anti-intellectualism. Anti-intellectualism is not the same as igno-

https://doi.org/10.1515/9783110749847-005

rance, but an indifference toward learning and new ideas, intolerance for novelty and diversity, a mistrust of intellectuals and experts, a devaluation of education, and a dismissal of the liberal arts as useless or dangerous. Those opposed to ideas and critical thinking tend to be ignorant and gullible, easily misled, prone to metaphysics, irrationality, and conspiracy theories, unable to master complex topics, and possess exaggerated self-confidence. They are the ones most at home in a post-truth age. Anti-intellectualism is a common tool used by self-described populists against "elites," typically meaning the well-educated. Totalitarian regimes are notoriously intolerant of intellectuals, often imprisoning and executing them.

Anti-intellectualism has varying roots, some of which are religious, and takes a variety of forms, including rejection of teachers and writers, lack of respect for science and scientists, and the equation of "experts" and expertise with "the elite." If intellectuals are often heralded as creators and protectors of "the truth" (surely a vastly overstated claim), then attacks against them fuel the conservative post-truth movement.

Anti-intellectualism has a long and vulgar history in the United States. Richard Hofstadter (1963/2012) famously wrote about the topic in his hugely influential magnum opus, *Anti-Intellectualism in American Life*, a reaction to the 1950s hysteria of Senator Joe McCarthy (R-WI), who led attacks against writers, scholars, and professors. Hofstadter argued that anti-intellectualism was at the front of middle-class revolts against political elites. He distinguished three types of anti-intellectualism: religious anti-rationalism, populist anti-elitism, and unreflective instrumentalism (Rigney 1991). Thus, while anti-intellectualism does not constitute a unified whole, throughout its various species "resentment and suspicion of the life of the mind and of those who are considered to represent it" (Hofstadter 1963/2012, p. 7) were a defining feature of American life. Thus, "There has always been in our national experience a type of mind which elevates hatred to a kind of creed; for this mind, group hatreds take a place in politics similar to the class struggle in some other modern societies." Reactionaries, he argued, often exhibited "a categorical folkish dislike of the educated classes and of anything respectable, established, pedigreed, or cultivated." Lim (2008) charts the growth of anti-intellectualism in presidential rhetoric, a long slow decline in accuracy that reached a nadir under George W. Bush, only to be pushed even lower by Donald Trump. Indeed, the rise of Trump may be said to hail the formal beginning of the post-truth era (Wilber 2017).

Anti-intellectualism occurs across the political spectrum to varying degrees. Leftist anti-intellectuals have often demonstrated intolerance for dissenting ideas, a phenomenon that has become markedly more widespread in an age of extreme political correctness. And there have been, to be sure, numerous insightful, conservative intellectuals: Edmund Burke; William F. Buckley, Jr.; Thomas Sowell;

George Will; Milton Friedman; Friedrich Hayek; and many others. Their ideas enriched political debate and often influenced public policy. Many were influential within the GOP: indeed, at one time, the Republican Party called itself the "party of ideas." But in the 21st century, conservative intellectualism has withered in the face of right-wing populism. Today, anti-intellectualism is a phenomenon largely confined to the political right (Mooney 2012), where distrust of experts is widespread. As Barker et al. (2021) argue, reactionaries are far more likely than liberals to suffer from "epistemic hubris," the expression of unwarranted factual certitude. They find that anti-intellectualism in the U.S. is unevenly distributed spatially and is more common in "red" (Republican) than "blue" (Democratic) states. Particularly as the economic returns to the college-educated have increased over time, and the costs of university tuition continue to soar ever-higher, the equation of experts with "the elite" (including conservative elites) has grown accordingly. Thus, the majority of Republicans said that colleges are "bad for America" (Riota 2017; Soave 2019). Many conservatives view colleges and universities as bastions of left-wing thought in which liberal professors indoctrinate their helpless students.

Anti-intellectualism has profound political effects. It is closely associated with opposition to established science, distrust of experts as part of a cabal of "liberal elites," and right-wing populism (Motta 2018; Merkley 2020). A core stance of contemporary anti-intellectualism is skepticism about climate change, water fluoridation, nuclear power, and genetically modified organisms (Merkley 2020). Such positions are closely tied to populism, the worldview that posits ordinary citizens in opposition to socially privileged elites, typically taken to mean the well-educated. Anti-intellectualism facilitates social movements opposed to science, including the teaching of evolution and promotion of vaccines. Anti-intellectualism also reinforces the media bubbles in which many conservative live and denies them access to opposing views. It is the undercurrent of many populist movements around the world. It celebrates "strong men" as authoritative leaders and encourages blind, uncritical loyalty. Attacks on critical thinking often represent it as a challenge or threat to history, tradition, religion, and established ways of life.

Donald Trump, for example, openly celebrated his anti-intellectualism (Reyes 2020). His refusal to read – even official daily intelligence briefs – is legendary, as is his unwillingness to consider evidence that does not mesh with his preconceived beliefs (Larison 2019). Rather than read or obtain advice from experts, he prefers to "trust his gut." As he puts it, "I have a gut and my gut tells me more sometimes than anybody else's brain can ever tell me" (Le Miere 2018). Trump exhibited a contempt for science, calling climate change a "Chinese hoax," as well as a distrust of health professionals during the covid pandemic. His disdain for education and intellectuals was central to his personality cult and the political movement built around his persona (Reyes 2020). It is no coincidence that Trump's popularity was highest in rural areas and small towns, where the average levels of education tend to be relatively low.

Another facet of anti-intellectualism is the persistent underfunding of higher education. In the U.S., state legislatures, many members of which lack college educations, have been cutting budgets for public universities for decades, resulting in higher tuition and mounting student debt. With many universities emphasizing science and engineering, budget cuts for the social sciences and humanities are particularly severe. As Braun (2019, p. 434) posits, "Dismantling the institutions of critical societal self-reflection seems a rather pervasive feature of contemporary capitalism and has been going on for decades."

Anti-intellectualism is clearly closely related to the rise of post-truth, particularly in the realm of politics. But, as Braun (2019, p. 433) cautions, "Post-truth is often referred to on one breath with right-wing populism and authoritarianism or autocratic governance. Yet, how exactly they relate to each other is less clear." Nonetheless, by explicating the anti-intellectual dimensions of conservative media and politics, this relationship comes to light.

Anti-intellectualism, like ideas, is a social construction. As Kempner (2019) notes, social theory must address not only the links between power and knowledge, but between power and ignorance as well. Debunking science denialism is a major task for educators and opponents of fake news. She writes "some ignorance is produced and mongered by powerful actors for nefarious reasons ... The 'post-truth movement,' which has scholars enraged with its efforts to undermine so much important knowledge, is simply the latest of these efforts" (p. 2). Indeed, ignorance has become so widespread that a whole field has emerged – "agnotology," the study of the deliberate production of ignorance (Proctor and Schiebinger 2008).

Science Denialism

> The good thing about science is that it's true whether or not you believe in it.
> Neil DeGrasse Tyson

Specter (2009) defines science denialism as "denial writ large—when an entire segment of society, often struggling with the trauma of change, turns away from reality in favor of a more comfortable lie." Science denialism is not the same as science skepticism (Schmid and Betsch 2019), which is a healthy questioning of science, but constitutes an outright rejection of science as truth; it thus may also be viewed as a form of pseudo-science (Hansson 2017). It sacrifices intellectual respectability for intuitive appeal (Boudry et al. 2015). Science denialism does not mean a rejection of all forms of science, but only selected issues, notably evolution, vaccines, the cause of AIDS, and anthropogenic climate change. Science denialism is most common when there is considerable uncertainty about a topic and contradictory evidence. It is often associated with conspiracy theories (McLintic 2019). This unfortunate trend results from a combination of religious fundamentalism, corporate information warfare, a scientifically illiterate public, and opportunistic politicians. Science denialism also reflects the erosion of trust of the scientific community, along with a generalized suspicion of "experts" as members of "the elite." Lack of numeracy is also a factor, which leads to a misinterpretation of statistics and probabilities.

Science denialism has long been evident within right-wing circles (Gauchat 2012; Hansson 2017), where it found root among the deeply religious and those suspicious of the government more generally. To be sure, many conservatives accept scientific facts and principles. But the tendency to reject science in favor of metaphysics is largely the preserve of reactionaries of various forms. As Lewandowsky and Oberauer (2016, p. 217) note,

> Rejection of scientific findings is mostly driven by motivated cognition: People tend to reject findings that threaten their core beliefs or worldview. At present, rejection of scientific findings by the U.S. public is more prevalent on the political right than the left.

Many people reject science if it presents evidence that suggests changes in everyday life, such as stopping smoking, eating less meat, driving less, or getting vaccinated. Other forms of science denial are propelled by corporations and right-wing think tanks, including libertarians who equate public health measures with an infringement of "liberty." Rosenau (2012, p. 567) writes that "By dismissing the knowledge produced by scientific processes and touting ideas that are untestable or have failed such tests, science denial misleads the public about how science works, opening the door to other pseudoscientific beliefs."

Ever since Charles Darwin proposed the idea of evolution in the nineteenth century, attempts to discredit the notion have repeatedly surfaced. Religious observers, particularly Christians, noted with alarm the rise of a theory that challenged the religiously-mandated age of the Earth (6,000) years, pointed to material roots of human beings, undermined Biblical authority, and, worst of all, undermined the notion that humans were in some way special or divinely created. Evolution posed a serious threat to Christian theology, and still does. Opposition to evolution became a defining feature of religious fundamentalism after the 1925 Scopes Trial. Despite the overwhelming evidence in favor of human evolution, and that it is universally accepted in the scientific community, vast numbers of people continue to doubt its validity. Branch (2020) notes that opposition to the teaching of evolution, and the frequent erroneous misrepresentations of evolutionary theory by creationists, constitutes another facet of anti-intellectualism. Evolution denial is particularly intense in the United States, the only wealthy country that remains deeply religious, where it is an article of faith among conservative evangelicals. One in three Americans rejects Darwinian science and believes the world was created a few thousand years ago (D'Ancona 2017, p. 66). Often evolution denial relies on pseudo-scientific explanations such as creationism, which attempts to promote a religious explanation under a scientific guise (Pigliucci 2002). The strength of evolution denial is testimony to the sad status of science education and the formidable political power of religious conservatives. Frequently evolution denial is combined with other forms of denial, such as the biological origins of life on Earth or the Big Bang theory of astronomy.

Denial of the efficacy of vaccines is another important form of science denial. This type of denialism is not confined to the political right. Some liberals embraced the idea, particularly after a very famous and badly done study by British doctor Andrew Wakefield asserted that the measles, mumps and rubella vaccines led to autism in children (Wakefield et al. 1998). The scientific evidence does not support this notion (DeStefano 2007). Wakefield's research was fatally flawed, with an undisclosed conflict of interest and results that could not be replicated. The paper that was later retracted by the medical journal *Lancet*, several of its authors disavowed it, and Wakefield's medical license was revoked. However, the paper caused an enormous uproar and led to persistent vaccine denial myths for decades afterwards. Unrepentant, Wakefield went on to make a movie, *Vaxxed; From Cover-up to Catastrophe.*

The movement against vaccines largely reflects skepticism of the medical community and pharmaceutical companies. As Navin (2013, p. 241) puts it, perhaps too charitably, "Vaccine denialists allocate epistemic authority more democratically than do mainstream medical professionals." Reich (2016) emphasizes that many parents reject vaccines because they think they know more about their child than do doctors, placing the emotional understanding of the unique above the rational understanding of broad trends. In this reading, vaccine denialism occupies an alternative epistemological space to that of immunologists. Vaccine denial reached new lows when former Playboy bunny Jenny McCarthy announced on television that vaccines caused autism and was respected for her views, saying she received her degree from the University of Google, whereas pediatric infectious disease expert Paul Offit received death threats for his scientific work (Specter 2009). Vaccine uptakes declined rapidly in the aftermath of the Wakefield paper, and measles became endemic, again, in the UK. As with everything else, vaccine denial has a geography (Dzwonczyk 2020), with hot and cold spots that reflect the political polarization of vaccine choice. Vaccines skeptics tend to cluster in specific communities where conformity of thinking is prevalent. Vaccine denial is particularly important in the case of covid vaccines, about which more later.

Perhaps the most absurd example of science denialism and post-truth geographies is flat Earth theory. In *The Closing of the Western Mind*, Freeman (2007) notes that while the classical Greeks, such as Eratosthenes, knew full well that the world was round, the triumph of the Christian Church in the waning days of the Roman Empire equated Greek knowledge with heresy: hence, the world must be flat (e.g., according to Cosmas Indicopleustes; see Gould 2011). The Greek tradition of rationality did not die of old age: it was murdered by the Christian Church. By the medieval era, however, the round Earth had once again become popular. In 1849, Samuel Rowbotham argued for a flat Earth, as did Orlando Ferguson in 1893 (Fig. 4.1). The International Flat Earth Research Society, founded in 1956, continues to advocate for the notion, and holds its followers are found "all around the world." Modern flat Earth theories are based on the conspiracy theory that NASA faked the moon landing of 1969. Despite its manifest rejection of astronomy, geology, geography, and other sciences, flat Earth theory continues to be remarkably popular (Strauss 2016; Erlaine 2020). For example, professional basketball players Kyrie Irving and Jaylen Brown have asserted the world is flat.

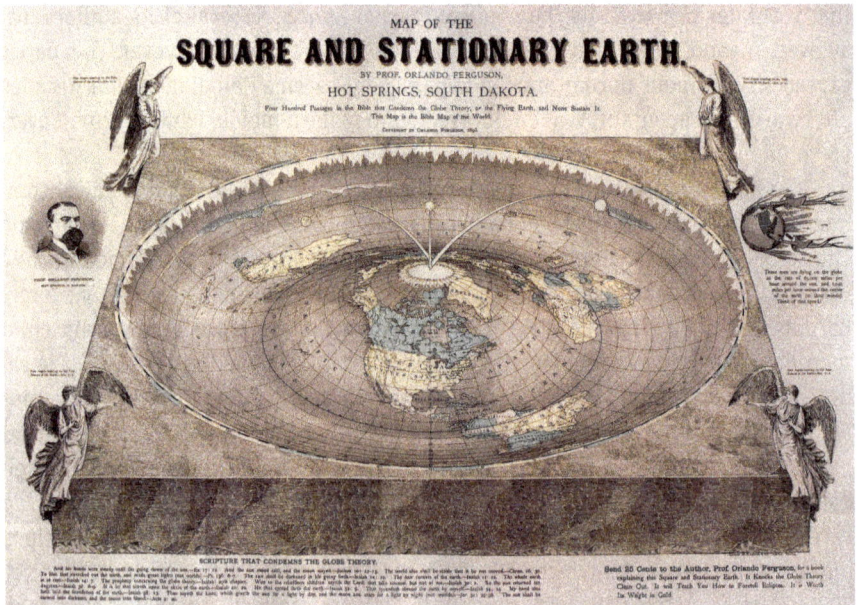

Figure 4.1: Orlando Ferguson's Depiction of a Flat Earth, 1893.

Denial of Climate Change

> Climate change is like my head: it's not visible in every instance,
> but I'm pretty darn sure it's there.
> Kevin Focke

Without doubt the most dangerous and pernicious right-wing post-truth geography is the denial of anthropogenic climate change. McIntyre (2018, p. 27) notes correctly that "Global warming is perhaps the most egregious case of modern science denial." The fact that the world is warming, rapidly, is by now well-established science. Roughly 97 percent of climate scientists agree the issue is real and human-made. The evidence is overwhelming that this change is caused by human beings in the forms of enormous amounts of carbon dioxide and methane that have been released into the atmosphere since the Industrial Revolution began. Climate change is having catastrophic effects on ecosystems around the world, warming the oceans, melting glaciers, causing forest fires, droughts, hurricanes, and wreaking havoc with agriculture. Despite the severity of these changes, a well-organized and well-funded industry of climate change deniers continues to press the notion that climate change is not real, not caused by human beings, and is no great threat (Lopez and Share 2020).

The roots of climate science extend back to the nineteenth century, and periodic warnings appeared throughout the early twentieth. In 1966, Bituminous Coal Research warned that unrestricted burning of coal would lead to irreversible changes. As early as the 1970s, oil companies knew full well that the CO_2 emissions from fossil fuels were doing damage to the atmosphere. ExxonMobil, the most aggressive of the oil giants, well knew that continued use of coal and petroleum would have dire long-term effects (Egan 2015), but nonetheless continued to fund deniers for decades thereafter (Goldenberg 2015). By the 1970s climate modelers had found that rising atmospheric CO_2 levels were warming the earth's environment. In 1980 the National Academy of Sciences undertook its first comprehensive study of the subject. James Hansen, director of the Goddard Institute of Space Studies, announced that global warming was underway. In 1988, the Intergovernmental Panel on Climate Change (IPCC) was created, and it issued its first report in 1990. Climate change data from the 21st century confirm the worst fears and predictions of climate scientists.

Climate change denial arose in tandem with the mounting evidence that climate change was a real and dangerous force. The Reagan Administration systematically downplayed the threat. In 1983, President Reagan's Department of Energy pressured the National Academy of Science to modify its Carbon Dioxide Assessment. Reagan's Secretary of Energy, James Edwards, said climate change posed no threat. After the collapse of communism in the 1990s, the conservative movement became increasingly anti-environmental in outlook. In the unfettered individualism and fetishization of the market that form a key part of neoliberal ideology, *any* action to restrict carbon emissions was viewed as government overreach, a threat to the spread of markets and libertarian notions of liberty. The motivations behind opposition to climate science are thus not simply economic, but also ideological. Opposition to environmental legislation was typically framed as environmental "skepticism" (Dunlap and McCright 2010). Skepticism is not synonymous with denial, although in practice it is difficult to differentiate between the two.

Not surprisingly, opposition to climate change science emanates primarily from the fossil fuel industry, which obviously has the most to lose (Milburn and Conrad 1998; Gelbspan 2005). One example was the formation of a lobbying group, the Global Climate Coalition, which lasted from 1989 to 2001. Following the playbook that they used with tobacco and the movement against chlorofluorocarbons, which damage the ozone layer, corporate interests mounted an organized campaign of denial. Climate change denial was largely spouted by corporate-funded think tanks, including the Heartland Institute, which received millions of dollars from Exxon-Mobil (Dunlap and Jacques 2013). Other corporate funders include the National Coal Association, Peabody Coal, the Western Fuels Association, the American Petroleum Institute, and the Edison Electric Group. Heartland's aggressive denial of climate change was soon imitated by the Heritage Foundation, the American Enterprise Institute, and the George C. Marshall Institute, which closed in 2015. In 1989, the George C. Marshall Institute issued a report attacking climate change, the first of a long series that were repeated by conservative outlets such as the *Wall Street Journal*. The Koch Brothers, who control the largest privately held corporation in the world, used the Koch Family Foundations to support many think tanks that opposed climate change science. Often these forces used "associations" such as the Information Council on the Environment, the Competitive Enterprise Institute, and the CATO Institute to shield their corporate sponsors. In the 1990s, the fossil fuel industrial complex, led by the American Petroleum Institute, attacked the IPCC, trying to undermine its scientific claims. Collectively, these efforts form "one of the largest attempts at mass deception in human history" (Rabin-Havt 2016, p. 44). By 2000, most fossil fuel companies, with the horrid exception of ExxonMobil, had abandoned their attempts to undermine climate science.

American think tanks that denied climate science soon sprouted up in other countries, including the United Kingdom's Institute for Economic Affairs, Canada's Fraser Institute, and Australia's Institute for Public Affairs (Dunlap and McCright 2010). Such organizations have longstanding international collaborative ties. Moreover, climate change denial was adopted by many populist movements, which painted attempts to limit carbon emissions as part of a secretive global cabal of liberals, experts, and "elites" (Lewandowsky 2021). Such groups often painted scientists as having ulterior motives, such as making money and preserving their privileged social position.

Climate change denial is a form of pseudoscience (Hansson 2018). Because denialists learn and borrow from other, earlier anti-science struggles, "The tactics invented in one battle of science denial are often appropriated for the next" (McIntyre 2018, p. 138). Like the war to defend tobacco, climate change denial involves fabricated controversies, such as the claim that it is not well-established science. Climate change denial takes a variety of forms, including refusal to admit that CO_2 levels are rising; claims that if they are rising it is due to natural causes; the claim that rising CO_2 levels have no substantive impacts; and the notion that such increases are inherently beneficial. Deniers may use fake experts, pseudo-science, and selectively cherry-pick occasional papers that challenge the established consensus. They exaggerate scientific uncertainty. They often rely on "contrarian" scientists, often physicists such as Fred Singer and Frederick Seitz, to back their claims. Such actors often attacked the entire scientific community, including scholarly journals and peer review. Denial often includes notions that "not all the facts are in" and more research is needed. Deniers often rely on anecdotes rather than large quantities of data, such as when Senator James Inhofe (R-OK) famously brought a snowball onto the Senate floor. The goal of such actors is to generate doubt about the scientific validity of climate change, leading the public to believe there is a controversy when in fact there is none. Because it is rooted in post-truth politics, no amount of facts will change the minds of climate change deniers (Fischer 2019). What started as a tool of oil companies quickly metastasized into a political ideology. In due course, climate denialism was picked up and amplified by Fox News, the *Wall Street Journal* and the *New York Post* (all owned by Rupert Murdoch), and the Unification Church, which owns the *Washington Times*.

Climate change deniers argue that moving to a post-carbon-based economy would generate incalculable harm. Moving toward a green economy, it was often alleged, would undermine American competitiveness. Undoubtedly there are costs to such a massive shift, and even the most effective actions, such as a carbon tax, would be difficult to implement and enforce. But companies with a long hostility to environmentalism, as Oreskes and Conway (2011) point out, soon began labeling climate change scientists as environmental "alarmists." Climate skeptics questioned the unanimity of scientific opinion, upholding that the matter was a subject of "debate" even when it was not. They reposition it as a theory rather than a fact. Climate change skeptics are quick to point to any error on the part of climate scientists and amplify it accordingly. As climate change skeptics gradually lost the scientific war, they turned increasingly to personal attacks on scientists or promoted the idea that it was a global conspiracy.

Climate change denial was greatly accelerated by the media's practice of reporting "both sides" of a story, even if one side is bogus: because the media loves controversy more than the truth, climate denialists receive undue and unwarranted attention. In contrast to the measured tones of climate scientists, deniers often use inflammatory hyperbole designed to appeal to emotions. As a result, the media often treat climate change as a scientific dispute rather than scientific reality (Lopez and Share 2020), a false equivalence that gives equal credence to both sides of a debate when in fact one side has no scientific credibility whatsoever. As Oreskes and Conway (2011, p. 214) note, "Journalists were constantly pressured to grant the professional deniers equal status – and equal time and newsprint space – and they did." Boycoff and Boycoff (2004, p. 127) hold that "Balanced reporting has allowed a small group of global warming skeptics to have their views amplified." Similarly, Lewandowsky (2021) states that "False-balance coverage constitutes one of the most insidious, albeit sometimes inadvertent, forms of climate misinformation." Thus, in claiming to be objective, media outlets give voice to fringe opinions that lack scientific credibility. This notion of "balance" led the media to give a right-wing fringe view much credence than it deserved. This strategy greatly enhanced climate change denialists' standing among the public. As Strong (1017, p. 139) notes, "Resistance to change is particularly pronounced when people are presented with both sides of a controversy, as is routinely the case in legal and political debates."

Social media is rife with climate change denialism (Bensinger 2021). Because giant corporations such as YouTube (owned by Google) and Facebook do not treat the issue with urgency, they allow misinformation and disinformation about the topic to proliferate with abandon. They rarely append warnings directing readers to more accurate sources. As a result, blatant lies and conspiracy theories abound. Facebook posts denying climate change are viewed as much as 1.36 million times per day. Websites such as Climate Change is Crap, Watts Up With That, and Britain's Global Warming Policy Forum operate with impunity. They frequently attack mainstream climate science, ignore the evidence in favor of it, and take anecdotes out of context. They focus on showy topics to gain public interest. They are often coupled with suspicions of renewable energy and view attempts to combat climate change as government overreach. Such sites often give the appearance of credibility by reposting and hyperlinking (Bloomfield and Tillery 2019). Similarly, Dunlap and McCright (2010) describe how climate denial information "zooms" through online spaces via the "climate denial blogosphere." Many denialist blogs are cross-linked, making them into a giant, right-wing echo chamber.

In American politics, denial of climate change has become an article of faith in the Republican Party. The GOP has long waged war on science (Mooney 2006), in part to curry favor with religious fundamentalists. But climate change denial has become widespread. In 2019, the League of Conservation Voters identified 130 members of Congress – of whom 129 were Republicans – who denied the scientific consensus on climate change. A selection of quotes from Republican politicians reflects the GOP's opposition to the science of climate change:

> I believe that climate change in this country is largely leftist propaganda to change the way we live. – Rep. Jim Banks (R-IN)

> The idea that CO2 is somehow causing global warming is on its face fraudulent. – Sen. Keven Cramer (R-ND)

> Global warming is the greatest hoax ever perpetuated on the American people. – Sen. James Inhofe (R-OK)

> The idea that climate change is the biggest scam since Teapot Dome – Rep. Don Young (R-AK)

> There isn't any real science to say we are altering the climate path on the earth. – Sen. Roy Blunt (R-MO)

> The concept of global warming was created by the Chinese in order to make U.S. manufacturing non-competitive. – Donald Trump

Like climate change itself, climate change denial has a geography. It tends to be most pronounced in Anglophone countries (Björnberg et al. 2017), where the right-wing disinformation infrastructure is most developed. Not surprisingly, denialism is most pronounced in countries with the most to lose from mitigating CO_2 emissions. Because knowledge always serves an interest and is embedded in historically and geographically specific contexts, climate change denial exhibits a spatiality that reflects vested interests, notably conservatives and energy companies.

Climate change denial is only one of a series of fabrications promoted by conservatives in the cause of protecting corporate interests. Others include fallacious attacks on public health care programs, such as Obamacare in the U.S., such as Sarah Palin's famous, malicious, and utterly unfounded allegation that it would erect "death panels" that decide who would live and who would die. Opponents of immigration reform, such as the Heritage Foundation, alleged that Democrats would give amnesty to all undocumented immigrants and give them permanent residency, part of a "Reconquista" of the American Southwest by Mexico. Ardent defenders of gun ownership, such as the National Rifle Association, spread the lie that possessing more guns saves lives from the threat of criminals, when in fact gun ownership is closely tied to the probability of being murdered by a family member. The Republican Party has insisted on strict voter ID laws to combat the non-existent threat of voter fraud, using the restriction to limit voting access for people of color. Abortion opponents spread lies that women who have had abortions will become sterile, develop breast cancer, or suffer mental health problems. Reactionaries against gay marriage held that it was slippery slope to legalized bestiality, pedophilia, and incest, and that children of same-sex couples were prone to social and psychological problems, none of which is true. In all of these cases, the utility of lies is in "their power to halt progress and justify political positions that would otherwise seem cruel, irrational, or extreme" (Rabin-Havt 2016, p. 189).

The Right-Wing American Mediasphere

Starting in the 1990s, a vast web of conservative media outlets and websites has emerged in the U.S. and, increasingly, across the Western world (Meagher 2012). In the U.S. it is anchored by Fox News, but also includes *The Washington Times*, Breibart, the Drudge Report, Sinclair Broadcasting, Infowars, Newsmax, One America News Network, World Net Daily, the Blaze, Red State, and the Daily Caller. The outrage industry, as these outlets comprise collectively, serves up a daily diet of apocalyptic predictions, vilification of liberals, and wild exaggerations designed to keep their audiences in a constant state of fear and indignation. Frequently these are coupled with implicitly racist notions that exaggerate white grievances, targeting minorities, immigrants, Muslims, and other disadvantaged groups. In so doing, the right-wing media serves to normalize extremist political views and inject them into the mainstream.

The rise of the right-wing mediasphere on the heels of neoliberalism is no accident. Reactionary television channels and websites serve a variety of purposes to provide ideological cover for neoliberal politics around the world, including stoking discord and amplifying social divisions, demonizing liberal opponents, promoting Islamophobia, safeguarding corporate interests, sowing doubt and uncertainty about science, and advancing conservative views in the culture wars to distract from issues of class and inequality. If there is any one, single cause of post-truth, it is conservative media that has given up accuracy for the sake of political partisanship. Manjoo (2008, p. 157) notes that the constellation of right-wing television stations, radio channels, and websites constitute "a massive conservative media structure that, more than ever, determines the shape and scope of our political agenda."

This interlocking set of channels has created a vast echo chamber in which pre-existing prejudices are reaffirmed and no dissenting ideas creep in, leading consumers of conservative news to become impervious to facts. Amplified by filter bubbles, many conservatives have fallen into an information abyss. Wehner (2019) argues that

> for a significant number of Americans – including many people on the right who long defend-ed the concept of objective truth and repeatedly rang the alarm bell about the rise of relativ-ism – truth is viewed as relative rather than objective, malleable rather than solid; as instru-mental, as a means to an end, as a weapon in our intense political war.

Thus, under George W. Bush, a senior advisor (widely believed to be Karl Rove) fa-mously told Ron Suskind (2004) of the *New York Times:*

> We're an empire now, and when we act, we create our own reality. And while you're studying that reality – judiciously, as you will – we'll act again, creating other new realities, which you can study too, and that's how things will sort out. We're history's actors ... and you, all of you, will be left to just study what we do.

For such actors, truth is simply too inconvenient, such as the truth about climate change. The explosion of right-wing media has created a vast echo chamber in which large numbers of people willfully subscribe to the falsehoods perpetuated by professional political liars, fakes, and frauds. Telling lies has been a frequent tactic among many types of politicians, but recently the denial of objectivity and the manipulation of facts and scientific data for political purposes appear to have become a monopoly of the political right (Fuller 2018).

The tribalism of truth reflects the intense political polarization of American society, in which winning has become more important than learning (Fisher et al. 2018). The effects are deeper than systemic anti-intellectualism, because as Ste-phens (2019) points out:

> it is further poisoning a society in which the idea of truth was already being Balkanized (*our* truth), personalized (*my* truth), problematized (*whose* truth), and trivialized (*your* truth) – all before Trump came along and defined truth as whatever he can get away with.

At the heart of the right-wing media universe is Fox News, the largest cable tele-vision station in the world. Founded by the reactionary Australian billionaire Ru-pert Murdoch, whose News Corporation owns it, and relying heavily on Roger Ailes in its early days (Sherman 2014), Fox debuted in 1996 and is headquartered in New York. Fox is the most commonly watched channel in the U.S., reaching 90 million people and two million daily watchers. Its audience tends to be overwhelmingly white, heavily male, often rural, and elderly.

The over-riding character that defines Fox News is its aggressive, sustained, and unapologetic reactionary conservativism, which permeates its news and especially opinion divisions (Jamieson and Cappella 2008). As media critic Michael Wolff (2002) put it early in the network's history:

> Fox is not really about politics. ... Rather, it's about having a chip on your shoulder; it's about us versus them, insiders versus outsiders, phonies versus non-phonies, and, in a clever piece of postmodernism, established media against insurgent media. ... Pull their strings. Push their buttons. Build the straw man, knock it down. Night after night. Here's the way not to get labeled a phony: Accuse the other guy of being one. Always attack, never defend. And have fun doing it.

Essentially, Fox imported Limbaugh's model of reactionary post-truth from radio to television. Conway et al. (2007, p. 199) note "Fox News, with its "Fair and Balanced" slogan [since retired], positioned itself not simply as another competitor, but as a brash, opinionated, and unashamedly patriotic channel and as a counterpoint to what some regard as a liberal bias among mainstream news outlets." Roughly 94 % of its viewers lean or identify as Republican. To cater to its audience, Fox dishes out a daily diet of attacks on liberals and Democrats, often half-truths mixed with outright lies. On the other hand, it tends to lionize Republican politicians and enthusiastically backed Donald Trump; Fox shared several personnel with the Trump White House (Stelter 2020). Never has the U.S. seen a major media outlet so highly dedicated to serving the interests of only one political party. Not surprisingly, the channel has had significant impacts of voting patterns and American politics (DellaVigna and Kaplan 2007; Cassino 2016). Fox's journalistic standards are so low and its biases so pronounced that it is widely not regarded as a "real" news station. Indeed, it is widely seen as a mouthpiece for the Republican Party, much like *Pravda* during the days of the Soviet Union. Brock and Rabin-Havt (2012) detail how Fox spreads lies, disinformation, and propaganda in the service of the GOP on issues such as guns, abortion, gay rights, ethnic equality, female political candidates, anti-Christian bias, Muslims, and other issues. Several studies found that Fox News viewers were *less* well informed than those who watched no news at all (PublicMind 2011; Licari 2020).

One of the most influential aspects of Fox News is its status as a pundit factory. A long list of reactionary commentators has made their careers there, including Bill O'Reilly, Sean Hannity, Lou Dobbs, Glenn Beck, Greta Van Susteren, Tucker Carlson, Geraldo Rivera, Bret Baier, Neil Cavuto, Jeanine Pirro, Steve Doocy, Brit Hume, Laura Ingraham, Brian Kilmeade, and Andrew Napolitano, among others. The bombastic, domineering Bill O'Reilly, long the star of Fox News political commentary, was featured in *The O'Reilly Factor,* which was shown in 30 countries. He made a number of controversial statements: He wished Hurricane Katrina had destroyed the United Nations. He hoped Al Qaeda would blow up San Francisco. He said the ACLA was second only to Al Qaeda as a danger to the U.S. He made racially charged statements about Black politicians. His rhetorical strategy mimics that of military propaganda, including the habitual use of fear, clear distinction between good guys and bad guys, and the attribution of problems to outgroups (Conway et al. 2007). In 2004, Media Matters for America awarded its annual "Misinformer of the Year" title to O'Reilly. Similarly, Sean Hannity has promoted the QAnon and "deep state" conspiracy, made numerous anti-gay comments, warned that sharia law was taking over the U.S., equated the Quran with *Mein Kampf*, supported the use of torture on political prisoners, advocated for the invasion of Iraq, called the coronavirus a hoax, and promoted conspiracy theories about the Democratic Party. Laura Ingraham issued forth homophobic slurs, denounced immigrants, and ridiculed survivors of school shootings. Tucker Carlson has repeatedly questioned climate change, minimized the threat of the corona pandemic, misrepresented the safety of vaccines, questioned the need for face masks, attacked immigrants in racialized terms, given voice to Islamophobia, called Black Lives Matter a threat, echoed Russian propaganda, and promoted white supremacy. He is an advocate of the Great Replacement theory, a white nationalist conspiracy theory that holds that the white population will decline in the face of low birth rates and immigration of non-whites. He falsely said that the South African government had changed its constitution to give white-owned farmland to blacks. He defended the attack on the capitol building on January 6, 2020, and pushed Trump's Big Lie claiming the 2020 presidential election was fraudulent. In short, Fox News pundits deliberately and insistently blurred the boundary between news and opinion by asserting questionable "truth claims" (Peters 2010).

One example of Fox News's deceit is Lou Dobbs, a fountain of geographic lies. Dobbs argued that NAFTA would lead to a "North American Union" modeled after the EU. He argued a non-existent NAFTA superhighway formed the backbone of this new union. He claimed in 2003 that one-third of all inmates in the federal prison system are Mexican immigrants, a number proven wrong by the US Justice Department, and gave airtime to a White nationalist conspiracy theorist who claimed that Mexican immigrants molested their children (Leonhardt 2007). These narratives reinforce the ideas of racial association with disease and reinforce the "unclean subjects" idea (Briggs and Mantini-Briggs 2003). These arguments continued in Dobbs's other "reporting" in his position at Fox Business, where he helped to advance many conspiracy theories such as the Obama birther theory, and maintain that immigrants bring leprosy to the U.S. (Folkenflik 2009). After Dobbs spouted lies about voting machines switching votes from Trump to Biden in 2020, Fox canceled his show.

Fox News has given birth to numerous post-truth geographies. For example, on January 11, 2015, Fox News commentator Steve Emerson claimed "In Britain ... there are actual cities like Birmingham that are totally Muslim where non-Muslims simply don't go in," echoing the falsehoods of Heart's yellow journalism but substituting Islamophobia for Sinophobia. Fox spread disinformation about a proposed mosque in Manhattan. Other whoppers propagated by Fox: that secondhand smoke does not harm people; that President Obama released ISIS leader Abu Bakr al Baghdadi; that most homicides in the U.S. are committed by undocumented immigrants; that everyone banned from Facebook is a conservative; that ISIS was spreading the Ebola virus; and that food stamp recipients can use their funds to buy marijuana. Fox News also has questionable cartography: it has confused New Hampshire with Vermont, Bulgaria with Serbia, Serbia with Hungary, Egypt with Iraq, and Arkansas with Missouri (Ward 2014). In 2019 it announced "Trump Cuts Aid to 3 Mexican Countries" (Atkinson 2019). In this way anti-intellectualism achieves a wide audience.

Today, Fox News operates in 40 countries, including all of the Western hemisphere, parts of Europe, and Africa, India, China, Japan, Indonesia, and Australia. It has also spawned imitators, such as Britain's News UK TV, France's CNews, and Brazil's Globo Media.

If Fox News is the core of the right-wing mediaverse, other, smaller, more extreme species hover around the periphery, appealing to a fringe audience of extremely conservative readers. They are central to the organization and publicity of the alt-right movement. InfoWars is an extreme right-wing website founded by "shock jock" Alex Jones, who became famous for his aggressive promotion of false conspiracy theories. InfoWars has dismissed school shootings, attacked the HPV vaccine, republished Russian state-sponsored news stories, and claimed that undocumented immigrants widely voted in presidential elections. Jones also ranted about "interdimensional travel," human-fish hybrids, and a vampiric elite of baby eaters. Jones claims 5 million daily radio listeners, and his website receives 10 million monthly visits. It has also been promoted by bots connected to the Russian government. However, InfoWars is so extreme that it and its founders have been barred from Facebook, YouTube, Pinterest, and LinkedIn. Alex Jones faced his comeuppance in 2022, when his lies that the Sandy Hook murders of 20 children in Newtown, CT were staged were finally exposed in court, leading to punitive penalties amounting to almost one billion dollars.

Founded in 2004, The Gateway Pundit is a right-wing fake news website; at its peak, in 2020, it received one million visitors per day. Twitter halted its founder's account for publishing false and misleading information. Breitbart News is an extreme right-wing website founded in 2006 by conservative activist Andrew Breitbart, who died shortly thereafter. It has since become a font of conspiracy theories and racist, misogynistic false news, advancing the causes of neo-Nazis and white supremacists. Funded by conservative billionaire Robert Mercer, it hired as editor Trump confidant Steve Bannon before he became Trump's campaign manager in

2016. Breitbart has published a series of false stories about covid, wildfires, immigrants, voter fraud, and climate change. The One America News Network (OANN), a cable channel launched in 2013, likewise has published a slew of unsubstantiated conspiracy theories and fake news stories, including ones about Black Lives Matter protestors, George Soros, voter fraud, Hillary Clinton, and Planned Parenthood. It has falsely claimed that California's government wanted to ban bibles and attacked survivors of school shootings such as David Hogg. Newsmax, which began in 1998, has published a series of false stories, including ones about covid vaccines and voting machines, among other things. After Fox News declared that Biden won Arizona in the 2020 election, OANN and Newsmax mounted a challenge to the station from the right. The Daily Caller, a website founded by Fox News anchor Tucker Carlson in 2010, is well known for its non-existent journalistic standards, which led it to publish numerous false stories about Democratic politicians, George Soros, climate change denial, and the Environmental Protection Agency. The Daily Wire, founded in 2015 by Ben Shapiro, has also published numerous false stories about liberals, climate change denial, and ridiculing mask mandates during the covid pandemic. WorldNetDaily is yet another fringe website on the far right; starting in 1997, it has peddled white nationalism, attacked Barack Obama and Joe Biden, and promulgated conspiracy theories about American Muslims. Its own editors acknowledge "some misinformation by columnists." Finally, *The Washington Times*, started in 1982 by the Unification movement led by the Rev. Sun Myung Moon, has published a steady stream of racist stories, attacks on Obama, support for neo-Confederates, Islamophobia, and climate change denial. Without exception, and not surprisingly, all of these sites enthusiastically supported Donald Trump.

Blogs are another star in this galaxy. Some right-wing bloggers have been spectacularly successful. Mike Cernovich, for example, a conspiracy-theory advocate, played a major role in promoting fake news about pizzagate, that the Clintons participated in a satanic sex cult, and that date rape does not exist. Other examples include blogs by Michele Malkin, Mark Levin, Matt Drudge, and Hugh Hewitt. All trolled on behalf of Trump, and many offer podcasts as well.

The right-wing mediaverse also extends into talk radio, where it enjoys virtually a monopoly over the airwaves (Mayer 2004). Famed reactionary commentator Rush Limbaugh (who died in 2021), for example, became one of the most well-known and influential representatives of the right, with the most-listened-to radio show in the U.S. As Nichols (2017, p. 146) points out, Limbaugh set "himself up as the source of truth in opposition to the rest of American media." A controversial and polarizing figure, Limbaugh was also a fountain of fake news, spewing racist, sexist, homophobic, and Islamophobic diatribes designed to appeal to his deeply conservative listeners (Jamieson and Cappella 2008). Politifact rated 84%

of his comments "Mostly False" or "Pants on Fire" lies. For example, he asserted the coronavirus was just like the common cold and pushed false cures such as hydroxychloroquine. He stated "[I]f you're Al Qaeda, come on in over the southern border! The Democrats will take your votes as well!" (quoted in Fishel 2006). He also said nicotine was not addictive, that Obama was not born in the U.S., that eco-terrorists caused the Deepwater Horizon oil spill in the Gulf of Mexico, and that climate change was not real. Limbaugh helped to lead the conservative charge against climate science. He repeatedly stated "The Four Corners of Deceit are government, academia, science, and the media" (Waldman 2020). Limbaugh's critics had a field day announcing his lies and falsehoods (e. g., FAIR 1995; Franken 1996). Another facet of reactionary radio is Clear Channel (Foege 2009), now iHeartCommunications, which, with 1,200 stations, is the largest such owner in the U.S. Clear Channel has been unrelenting and unprecedented in pushing a conservative political agenda and syndicating right-wing voices such as Limbaugh, Glenn Beck, and Laura Schlessinger. It aggressively promoted the lie that Saddam Hussein had weapons of mass destruction in Iraq during the lead-up to the American invasion in 2003.

Howling at the Moon: Right-Wing Conspiracy Theories

> Blind belief in authority is the greatest enemy of truth.
> Albert Einstein

Conspiracy theories are not new in right-wing political culture (Fenster 2008). In the U.S., they are as old as the country itself, or older (Knight 2003). Such views of the world are especially appealing to those who adhere to authoritarian politics (Grzesiak-Feldman 2015). As Forgas and Baumeister (2019, p. 3) note, "Believers in conspiracy theories also often see themselves as careful, motivated skeptics who are motivated by a quest to avoid gullibility, while those who doubt their beliefs are the gullible ones." Concerns about the Illuminati, Freemasons, Irish immigrants, the Pope, slave rebellions, labor unions, Jews, bankers, Japanese-Americans, the Antichrist, communists, UFOs, the United Nations, the New World Order, and the Trilateral Commission have popped up among reactionaries with great regularity. In the 1950s, the John Birch Society presented anti-communist conspiracies as facts. Essentially, these offer followers a narrative that allows them to interpret political events in comforting and convenient terms. They united people around a common enemy, even if that enemy is not real.

More recently, one of the more famous, if bizarre, instances of fake news in U.S. politics was Pizzagate. In 2016, Russia's Internet Research Agency spread lies, amplified by Alex Jones on InfoWars, that Hillary Clinton was running a Satanic child sex ring out of the basement of a Comet Ping Pong pizza parlour in Washington, DC. Fired up by fake news, 28-year-old Edgar Maddison Welch drove across the country to "self-investigate" the conspiracy; armed with an AK-15 assault rifle, he began shooting (Fisher et al. 2016). Although no one was hurt, the incident became emblematic of the power of fake news to provoke real world violence. Tuters et al. (2018) called it an instance of "post-truth protest."

Right-wing conspiracy theories are widespread, and most are ineffectual, dying out within a short time. One exception, however, is the QAnon movement, which has millions of followers. The cult claims, without evidence, that Democratic politicians, officials, and some Hollywood actors formed a cabal of cannibalistic pedophiles operating a child sex-trafficking ring out of Washington, DC (Rothschild 2021). In this fantasy, "Q" is an anonymous, high-ranking official trying to save the government from liberals (the "deep state") by posting on right-wing media sites such as 4chan starting in 2017. Q warned about the "deep state" of government officials trying to undermine the heroic President Trump and his agenda. Stories about Q received enthusiastic support on Russian-backed Twitter accounts, and most Q followers post anonymously on social media (Hannah 2021). In 2018, *Time* magazine declared Q one of the 25 most influential people on the internet. QAnon rhetoric is often steeped in racism and anti-Semitism, and many supporters viewed covid vaccines as part of a conspiracy. It promises an event called "The Storm" in which liberal, child-eating politicians will be arrested *en masse* and executed; precise dates for when The Storm will occur have come and gone, only to be postponed again and again.

QAnon was espoused by former National Security Advisor Michael Flynn in the Trump administration. Some members of Congress, such as Marjorie Taylor Greene (R-GA) and Lauren Boebert (R-CO), have openly expressed support for the conspiracy. Greene also claimed that forest fires in California were started by "Jewish space lasers," apparently a reference to the Rothschild family, an old anti-Semitic trope. Hundreds of Republican candidates have run for office on the QAnon agenda. The Q movement has also found favor with some evangelical Christians and is sometimes viewed as an extremist Christian movement. President Trump retweeted QAnon messages more than 200 times. After some Q followers committed acts of violence, the FBI labeled QAnon a domestic terrorist threat. Not surprisingly, QAnon members actively supported Donald Trump's attempts to overthrow the results of the 2020 election, and some were involved in the January 6, 2021 storming of the Capitol building, including Ashli Babbitt, who died there. The movement has also found followers in Britain, Germany, France, and Japan, has become globalized through the app Telegram after it was banned on other social media networks.

Another widespread conspiracy theory born of fake news concerns 5G ("fifth generation") telecommunications technology, which is widely used in internet connections and mobile phones (Bruns et al. 2021). 5G began to spread widely in 2019, the year the covid pandemic started. Conspiracists have alleged that 5G weakens the immune system; causes brain tumors, various cancers, and the covid pandemic; that it causes vaccinated people to explode; and that it burns the skin. Ironically, many of these rumors circulated through cyberspace on 5G. Some rumors are linked to wider fears about a mysterious global order led by Bill Gates bent on worldwide depopulation. The 5G conspiracy is also promoted by followers of QAnon. Some celebrities such as actor John Cussack and R & B singer Keri Hilson spoke out in its defense. Donald Trump weighed in, claiming that 5G was part of a Chinese government plot to destroy the U.S. The conspiracy went global, sprouting up in dozens of countries. In Britain, rumors abounded that the new £20 banknotes had secret symbols that revealed that 5G spread covid. This disinformation led many people to become afraid of fiber optic cables, cell phone towers, and mobile phones. In Britain, the conspiracy led several people to attack mobile phone towers. Followers of the 5G conspiracy were impervious to evidence that viruses do not spread through radio waves and cell phones.

The popularity of conspiracy theories speaks to the degraded nature of public discourse and the naivete of large swaths of the public. As Zuckerman (2019) argues, "A movement like QAnon is an inevitable outgrowth of the Unreal, an approach to politics that forsakes interpretation of a common set of facts in favor of creating closed universes of mutually reinforcing interpretations." Despite the ubiquity of information that digital media offer, many people inhabit a dark information age (Hannah 2021).

Fake News and the 2016 and 2020 U.S. Presidential Elections

> Truth isn't truth.
> Rudy Giuliani

The 2016 U.S. presidential election was a milestone in the history of fake news. It saw an unprecedented role for social media, through which disinformation circulated at the speed of light. Fake news played a central role in the surprising victory of Donald Trump, who lost the popular vote but succeeded in the Electoral College. The story of fake news involves a host of curious characters, including Macedonians, Russians, and others.

Oddly, during the 2016 presidential election, a group of teenagers in Macedonia played an important role in promoting fake news with more than 100 pro-

Trump websites, often duping Trump supporters in the process (Silverman and Alexander 2016). Most were concentrated in the town of Veles (pop. 55,000). They set up domain names with American-sounding names, such as WorldPoliticus.com, TrumpVision365.com, USConservativeToday.com, DonaldTrumpNews.co, and USADailyPolitics.com. Some have Facebook pages with hundreds of thousands of followers. Their stories included fables that Hillary Clinton would soon be indicted for crimes pertaining to her email account, that the Pope forbid Catholics to vote for Hillary, that proof had emerged that Obama was born in Kenya, and that Oprah Winfrey said some white people must die. Some simply plagiarized stories from right-wing American media. The teenagers themselves tended to be apolitical, but earned fractions of a penny per click on their stories from automated advertising machines such as Google's Adsense (Subramanian 2017). Some teens earned up to $16,000 in a country where the average monthly salary is roughly $400. Similarly, the New York Times reports in a story titled "Inside a few news sausage factory" that in Tbilisi, Georgia, a university student named Beqa Latsabidze earned substantial funds when he made up stories about Hilary Clinton and claimed that if Trump won the election, Mexico would close its borders with the U.S., a story that received widespread attention (Higgins et al. 2016).

In the 2016 presidential election, fake news articles shared on Facebook tilted heavily in favor of Donald Trump. For example, Allcott and Gentzkow (2017) report 115 fake stories deemed to be pro-Trump were shared on Facebook 30 million times while there were only 41 pro-Clinton ones that were shared 7.6 million times. Fake news convinced numerous voters who supported Obama in 2012 to switch to Trump in 2016 (Gunther et al. 2019).

The pattern established in 2016 was successfully maintained in 2020 (DiResta 2021). For example, the Gateway Pundit published numerous false narratives about stuffed ballot boxes, malfunctioning voting machines, and fake ballots marked for Biden. Over and over again, pro-Trump influencers picked up misleading stories and inserted them into the mainstream media and even the White House Press Secretary. Many stories hinted at a conspiracy at work but none offered evidence. As Rutenberg et al. (2021) note, "Allegations of Democratic malfeasance had disintegrated in embarrassing fashion. A supposed suitcase of illegal ballots in Detroit proved to be a box of camera equipment. "Dead voters" were turning up alive in television and newspaper interviews." A postal worker in Erie, Pennsylvania, claimed to have overheard supervisors discussing backdating postmarks on ballots that had arrived too late to be counted; his affidavit turned out to be written by the conservative activist group Project Veritas, well known for its tactics of deception. Trump tweeted a story about a truck driver in Long Island who claimed he had delivered thousands of illegal ballots; later it emerged the driver had been committed to mental health institutions several times.

Rudy Giuliani, former mayor of New York and Trump's personal attorney, emerged as one of his foremost advocates of conspiracy theories. Giuliani claimed, among other things:

> Pennsylvania received more absentee ballots than it had sent out before the election. That Trump was pursuing a claim of voter fraud in the Pennsylvania courts when in fact he was not. That dead people – sometimes 8,021, at another point as many as 30,000 – voted in Philadelphia, including heavyweight boxer Joe Frazier. And: That Dominion Voting Systems machines manipulated the final tallies in Georgia. That thousands of underage voters, variously 65,000 or 66,000 or 165,000, cast ballots in Georgia, along with numerous felons and dead people. That security cameras showed Georgia election officials illegally counting mail-in ballots. That "illegal aliens" voted in Arizona (Marcus 2021).

At one press conference, as he made wild accusations, hair dye ran down Giuliani's face, earning him wide ridicule. In June 2021, the New York State Bar authorities temporarily suspended his license to practice law due to the falsehoods he spread, noting that he "communicated demonstrably false and misleading statements" (quoted in Weiner 2021), and he faced the prospect of being permanently disbarred.

Extremely right-wing defamation lawyer L. Lin Wood of Georgia echoed some of Trump supporters' wildest accusations. Wood filed multiple lawsuits challenging the election results and spread baseless conspiracy theories (Peters and Feuer 2020). He accused Georgia governor Brian Kemp of corruption and led chants of "lock him up!" He called Vice-President Mike Pence a traitor. Arguing that the Georgia electoral system was corrupt, he urged Trump supporters to sit out the run-off elections for two open Senate seats on January 5, 2021, thus contributing to Democratic victories there. Wood later lost a bid to stop the Georgia bar from requiring him to undergo a mental health evaluation as part of a probe into whether he should lose his license to practice law. He was also investigated for the crime of living in South Carolina but voting in Georgia.

Maverick attorney Sydney Powell took the conspiracy theory of a rigged election to new heights. Attacking the accuracy of the vote counting machines, she alleged that a Venezuelan plot to rig the machines was underway, somehow involving dead Venezuelan president Hugo Chavez. The notion of rigged vote counting machines became widely popular in Republican circles, as Republicans insisted that the devices miraculously transformed thousands of Trump votes into Biden votes. In fact, Chavez had nothing to do with the machines (Swensen 2020). Powell also threatened to "release the kraken," which would provide definitive proof of a stolen election, but never actually came up with evidence (Alba 2020). In response to the allegations, the two companies that made the machines, Dominion Voting and Smartmatic, both sued Sydney Powell and Rudy Giuliani each for $1.3 billion for libel, and forced conservative media outlets to retract their false statements, including Fox News, leading it to cancel its Lou Dobbs show. Dominion also sued Fox News for $1.6 billion, alleging that the network gave prominence to the election-fraud theory to raise its ratings. Subsequent evidence revealed that Fox News hosts did not believe the election denial claims but promoted them anyway.

Many of the trends found in the 2016 election continued in 2020, including widespread Russian disinformation and Trump's claims of election fraud. The volume of fake news surged, with the number of websites spewing disinformation doubling between 2019 and 2020 (McDonald 2021). The phenomenon was mostly confined to the political right: as Calvillo et al. (2021, p. 175) note, "consuming more politically conservative election news was associated with greater belief in false headlines. ... The more right-leaning news that participants consume (in particular, Fox News), the poorer their political news discernment."

Trump lost the 2020 election but refused to concede. Instead, he insisted repeatedly that the election had been stolen from him ("the Big Lie") and that Biden was not legitimately elected, a falsehood that became a sacred truth to his followers. In fact, there was no widespread fraud in the 2020 election (Corasaniti et al. 2020). Trump's own cybersecurity official, Christopher Krebs, called the election "the most secure in American history," only to be fired by the president for contradicting him. Trump's own Attorney General, William Barr, as well as Acting Attorney General Jeffrey Rosen, also said they saw no significant evidence of fraud.

Trump's rhetoric encouraged the mob that overran the Capitol on January 6, 2021, a violent example of post-truth geographies. Trump called on his followers to join him at a "Save America" rally at the Ellipse in Washington, DC, on January 6 to "stop the steal." Shortly thereafter a mob of roughly several thousand mostly White Trump supporters, waving Trump flags and wearing Trump regalia, marched to the Capitol building. Many believed they were patriots saving the country. Upon arrival, about 800 of them forced their way in and occupied it in an attempt to stop the formal certification of Biden's victory (Figure 4.2). What started as energetic protest quickly devolved into the most serious attack on the Capitol since the War of 1812. As the mob moved into the building, lawmakers hid under their desks, barred entrance to their rooms, or fled to secure locations. The Senate stopped its proceedings and the Electoral College vote certification was postponed until early the next morning. Police fired tear gas at the protestors. Some 151 police officers were struck with flagpoles, had fire extinguishers thrown at them, were beaten and kicked, suffered broken bones, were Tasered, and had their badges stolen. Altogether, seven people died during or immediately after the attack. In the months after the riot, federal prosecutors arrested and indicted more than 1,000 people on federal crimes in the largest criminal investigation in the history of the Department of Justice. The January 6 riot is a stunning example of fake news gone wild, of how right-wing disinformation plays out socially and spatially with devastating consequences. Trump's Big Lie became a litmus test for aspiring GOP politicians and the basis of a sustained nationwide Republican campaign to suppress voting rights under the guise of "securing elections" and "protecting election integrity." More than half of Republicans believe that Trump was re-elected and that the presidency was stolen from him (Reuters 2021). Although even some GOP leaders did not believe Trump won the election, they clung to the lie to curry favor with his base.

Figure 4.2: Trump Supporters Storm the Capitol Building, January 6, 2021.

Donald Trump's Lies and their Fake Geographies

> When I can, I tell the truth.
> Donald Trump

Among the greatest of Donald Trump's numerous flaws is his persistent, chronic, and habitual mendacity. He was the first post-truth president in American history. Donald Trump is the most mendacious person ever to occupy the White House, and one of the greatest liars in human history. The volume of his lies has no precedent. Trump lies so frequently that if he tells the truth, it is by accident. Trump has even admitted to lying: in *The Art of the Deal*, he referred to the practice as "truthful hyperbole." As Waldman (2019a) puts it:

> Trump is blessed with a preternatural shamelessness; while ordinary people would ask themselves, "What will happen if I get caught in this lie?" Trump never seems to. He simply updates the old lie with a new one, and when that one is exposed, he offers up yet another.

Other observers have made the point similarly: As Gerson (2020) writes,

> The president is a bold, intentional liar, by any moral definition. A habitual liar. A blatant liar. An instinctual liar. A reckless liar. An ignorant liar. A pathological liar. A hopeless liar. A gratuitous liar. A malevolent liar.

Similarly, Bruni (2020) notes

> He lies because he grew up among liars. He lies because hyperbole and hooey buoy his fragile ego. He lies because he is practiced at it, is habituated to it and never seems to pay much of a price for it.

Trump's constant, incessant lying has given him a reputation as a habitual abuser of the truth, reinforcing stereotypes about his intelligence, and deeply undermining his credibility. Indeed, in late 2018 the U.N. Special Rapporteur on Freedom of Expression and Opinion, Daniel Kaye, called Trump "the worst perpetrator of false information in the United States" (*Policy Times* 2018). Oddly, his mendacity became a source of political strength. Holman (2020, p. 378) writes that "What shocked the political left was not just the detachment of Trump's rhetoric from reality, but that his complete disregard for being caught in outright lies did not disqualify his candidacy. Indeed, in Orwellian fashion, it won him a reputation for 'telling it like it is.'"

Donald Trump's proclivity to exaggerate, misstate the truth, make unfounded claims, and assert flat-out falsehoods has been widely documented. Trump pulls figures out of thin air, rewrites history, and contradicts his own past statements. According to the *Washington Post* database, he lied more 30,573 times in his four years as in office, an average of roughly 12 per day and sometimes up to 40 per day. The *Post*'s fact checker crew even published a book about Trump's assault on the truth (Kessler et al. 2020). What was once considered to be shocking presidential behavior has become normalized, or mere background noise.

Trump has a long history of lying. His carefully groomed public image of the self-made billionaire businessman was built on a foundation of lies. His "birtherist" stance on President Obama's birthplace was filled with racist innuendo, an attempt to delegitimize his predecessor. He claimed that five young men imprisoned for a rape in Central Part were guilty even after they were exonerated by DNA evidence, asserting "They admitted they were guilty" (Waxman 2016). In 2014 he tweeted that "I am being proven right about massive vaccinations – the doctors lied" (Blake 2017). Trump has lied about his wealth; the cost of membership in his golf clubs; how many condos he has sold; how much debt he owes; whether he associated with members of organized crime; that he had opposed the Iraq war when he had not; and who had endorsed his presidential bid (O'Brien 2017). Trump has lied about the ratings of news outlets he does not like, like CNN; the rate of taxation in the U.S. relative to other countries; that Immigration and Customs Enforcement and the Border Patrol endorsed him; and that Obama's policies created ISIS. He has lied about U.S. contributions to NATO and falsely claimed dozens of times that Democrats colluded with Russia in the 2016 presidential election. He told evangelicals that he had ended the Johnson Amendment, which prohibits religious groups from endorsing or financially supporting political candidates, when in fact he had not.

Perhaps the most frequent lie Trump tells is the claim that the proposed wall on the U.S.-Mexican border is under construction. He also claimed that Middle Eastern terrorists have sought to enter the U.S. through the border with Mexico, and at times claimed they carried Ebola. He falsely claimed that the GOP tax cut bill signed in December 2017 was the largest in history, which it was not. Some of Trump's lies are infamous whoppers. He made his first press secretary, Sean Spicer, lied about the size of his inauguration crowd when he claimed "This was the largest audience to ever witness an inauguration – period – both in person and around the globe" (Kessler 2017). The claim was easily disproven by data on ridership on mass transit, eyewitness testimony, independent crowd counts, and Nielsen television ratings. Given the evidence against Spicer's lie, it fell to Trump advisor Kellyanne Conway to famously claim that he was relying on "alternative facts." Conservative commentator Scottie Nell Hughes went even farther when she said "There's no such thing, unfortunately, anymore as the facts" (Wemple 2016). Her line echoes the famous dictum widely attributed to Nietzsche, "There are no facts, only interpretations."

Trump also falsely claimed to have written his own inauguration speech. Incensed that he lost the popular vote in 2016 to Hillary Clinton, Trump claimed that "Between 3 million and 5 million illegal votes caused me to lose the popular vote" (Phillip and DeBonis 2017). Later, he argued "Terrible! Just found out that Obama had my 'wires tapped' in Trump Tower just before the victory. Nothing found. This is McCarthyism!" (Nussbaum 2017). He lied about attending the famous June 9, 2016 meeting in Trump Tower to discuss cooperation with the Russians, then lied about writing the reason it was held (allegedly to discuss adoptions), then lied about personally dictating the public response to media scrutiny about it.

Trump also lies about matters of less significance. Leonhardt and Thompson (2017) compiled a long, helpful list, although it grows daily. He claimed that Trump Tower is 68 stories high when it is only 58. He bragged that the Trump winery is the "largest winery on the East Coast" (Gorman 2016) when it is not even among the 10 largest in Virginia. Before the 2018 midterm elections he claimed that work on a middle-class tax cut was underway. In a visit to troops in Iraq in December 2018, he invented a magical 10 % pay raise for service members, "the first in ten years." He claimed windmills cause cancer (Bump 2019b), which they most assuredly do not. These are not simply careless errors; Trump tells these lies knowing fully that they are false.

Trump lies so much that the *Washington Post* invented a new category, the Bottomless Pinocchio, for false claims that he repeated more than 20 times. Kessler (2018a) notes "That dubious distinction will be awarded to politicians who repeat a false claim so many times that they are, in effect, engaging in campaigns of disinformation." Some lies Trump has told more than 100 times. Most politicians dread the *Post*'s rating, and stop telling lies when caught. Not Trump. Kessler (2018a) notes:

> The president's most-repeated falsehoods fall into a handful of broad categories – claiming credit for promises he has not fulfilled; false assertions that provide a rationale for his agenda; and political weaponry against perceived enemies such as Democrats or special counsel Robert S. Mueller III.

Trump is such an incorrigible liar that his own lawyers refused to let him be deposed by the Robert Mueller investigation on the grounds that their client was incapable of telling the truth. As Schmidt and Haberman (2018) note, "His lawyers are concerned that the president, who has a history of making false statements and contradicting himself, could be charged with lying to investigators." Trump even lies about lying. After he accused President George W. Bush of lying about weapons of mass destruction in Iraq, he said "I didn't say lie. I said he may have lied" (Lavender 2016). In reality, he did say that Bush lied, with no qualifiers (Kiely 2016).

Trump lies as if everyone simply believes him, or takes him at face value. This is a sign of pathological narcissism. He is so important that we must accept whatever he says is true. His lies are thus a function of his narcissism, which produces a self-imagined reality, a delusional fantasy in which he is at the center of everything. This worldview reflects a sense of entitlement in which he can say anything he wants to anyone, and never pay for consequences. Indeed, Trump has never paid a penalty for the whoppers he repeats year after year. Without a cost to his lies, Trump has no incentive to stop issuing them.

Whether Trump believes his own lies has been the subject of much debate. "When he lies, does he know he is lying, or does he believe his own lies?" (Kessler and Lee 2017, p. 7). If Trump does realize he is lying, then his behavior constitutes a classic case of "gaslighting," a deliberate attempt to convince others that the proposed reality is more real than what they experience in daily life. The term originated with the 1928 play *Gaslight* and subsequent film, in which the protagonist attempts to convince his wife that she is going insane and cannot trust her own eyes. The tactic is commonly used by pathological narcissists. As Schwartz (2017, p. 71) puts it about Trump, "His aim is never accuracy, it's domination."

Even worse, much of the public tolerates or even adores Trump's lies, as Carpenter (2018) notes in *Gaslighting America*. She argues that his lying is methodical, following a consistent, strategic pattern: first he makes an outrageous claim; next he denies it, while simultaneously advancing it; third, he claims more information is coming; fourth, he attacks those who accuse him of lying; and fifth, he declares victory under any and all circumstances regardless of the evidence. She makes a prescient point (pp. 7–8):

> He learned that people actually love it when he lies. ... We want to think his crazy lies are his greatest weakness when they are, in fact, the source of his strength. ... The conventional wisdom currently says that when Trump tweets something laughably incorrect, the fact-checkers will reveal the truth, the public will turn against him, and his political allies will desert him. This is has not borne out.

Trump's lies are necessary for his political success, to ward off opponents, and keep his base in line. Blow (2019) points out, "He lies to brag. He lies to deflect. He lies to inflate. He lies to defame. He lies to praise. He sometimes seems to lie just for the sport of it." Trump uses mendacity to attack his critics, demean the press, and advance his political agenda. For example, in 2019 he claimed that "The Democrat [sic] position on abortion is now so extreme that they don't mind executing babies AFTER birth" (Grady 2019). In April 2019 he stated that Democrats approve of situations in which "The baby is born. The mother meets the doctor, they take care of the baby, they wrap the baby beautifully, and then the doctor and the mother determine whether or not they will execute the baby" (Cameron 2019). He claimed "The Democrats want to invite caravan after caravan of illegal aliens into our country. And they want to sign them up for free health care, free welfare, free education, and for the right to vote" (Valverde 2018). He added that Democrats wanted to purchase a new car for all undocumented immigrants (Jacobson 2018).

The news media have been complicit, spreading Trump's falsehoods repeatedly. Trump knows that his lies will be broadcast by the very channels he denounces as "fake news." "Fake news," in this reading, does not mean false reporting, but anything that criticizes Trump. Of course, any other politician would have long ceased to have a career after being exposed as a liar at any level approaching Trump's, but given the depth of the personality cult that surrounds him, Trump has political Teflon like no other, and seems impervious to the repeated demonstrations of his falsehoods. His fans believe him more than the truth.

Trump both publicizes the conspiratorial views of the extreme right, such as Alex Jones and Fox News. He has retweeted theories of far-right activists, such as the claim that Obama and Clinton founded ISIS, that the media covered up terrorist attacks, and that Mexican cartels carry bags of drugs across the Rio Grande. He thus makes those views part of the "mainstream," first by circulating them among alt-right political circles, and then the gullible viewers of Fox News, where Sean Hannity and Tucker Carlson bring them into the mainstream as truth. Trump's lies have also been spread far and wide by an army of online trolls.

An unfortunate byproduct of Trump's habitual lying is that it is contagious, and other members of his administration have followed suit (*New York Times* 2018). Some lie to impress or support their boss, others to justify administration policies, yet others regard honesty as a handicap. Examples include Brock Long, former head of the Federal Emergency Management Agency, who lied about the deaths from Hurricane Maria; Wilbur Ross, Trump's Secretary of Commerce, who lied about attempts to insert a citizenship question in the national census; Kirstjen Nielsen, Trump's Secretary of Homeland Security, who lied about Russian interference in the 2016 presidential election; and Sarah Huckabee Sanders, the former White House press secretary, who lied about African American unemployment rates. A vast cadre of Trump fans, sycophants, aides, and surrogates back up his lies on television talk shows and op-ed pieces, deliberately overlooking the most extravagant falsehoods and attempting to shore them up when possible.

Trump succeeds in lying in part because his base and most Republican Party leaders accepted anything he says or does without question. This issue is aptly summed up by Waldman (2019b), who notes:

> There is no volume of lies he could tell, no extent of his corruption that could be revealed, no amount of bigotry he could spread, no number of family members he could appoint to high positions in government, no degree of profiteering off the presidency, no amount of admiration he could express for authoritarian dictators, no obstruction of justice he could engage in, no assault on the integrity of his office too appalling for them not to enthusiastically defend him.

Critically, Trump's discourse is used to cement political loyalty regardless of the facts. Douglas (2017) offers an insightful summary of this phenomenon:

> In Trumpspeak, truth is not factual, it's imagistic. ... Truthful statements do not necessarily offer an accurate account of events in the world. They provide an approximation or exaggeration of something that might, in theory, have occurred. ... In Trumpspeak, belief is a signal of truth. If his supporters believe him, then what Trump is saying must be true. Conversely, if his detractors disbelieve him, this too is evidence that what he is saying must be true. ... Finally, Trumpspeak is transactional. It places no independent value on truth. The value of speak is to be measured exclusively in terms of its effects. If a statement gets me closer to my goal, then it is valuable; if it does not, it is worthless. Valuable statements, then, are true by virtuated of the fact that they advance my interests. Statements that fail to do so are worthless and thus false.

No clearer rejection of the correspondence theory of truth and definition of the pragmatist definition could be found.

Trump's lies have very real material effects on people, landscapes, and social relations. Many of Trump's lies have a profoundly geographic dimension. For example, he frequently claimed, with no evidence, that U.S. Steel is "opening six new plants" (Tobias 2018) (sometimes seven, eight, or nine). He also claimed Californians were rioting "to get out of their sanctuary cities" (Bump 2018).

Trump has lied repeatedly about immigrants, arguing that more undocumented people are crossing the border than ever, even though apprehensions at the border dropped. He argued that "Over the years, thousands of Americans have been brutally killed by those who illegally entered our country and thousands more lives will be lost if we don't act right now" (Nakamura 2019). However, statistically, undocumented immigrants commit far fewer crimes than do American citizens. During the 2016 campaign, he argued that undocumented immigrants were bringing "tremendous" amounts of disease into the U.S. The World Health Organization notes that "Nicaragua, Costa Rica and Mexico all have higher average vaccination rates than the United States, making people from those countries on average less likely to transmit diseases like tuberculosis, diphtheria and hepatitis B" (Rizzo, Kessler, and Kelly 2019). Trump also claimed "The drugs are pouring into this country. They don't go through the ports of entry" (Lewis 2017), which is simply not true, according to the Drug Enforcement Administration, which reports that the most common trafficking technique by transnational criminal organizations is to hide drugs in passenger vehicles or tractor-trailers as they drive into the U.S. though entry ports. The wall will do nothing to stop the influx of drugs. Trump also claimed that terrorists often cross the U.S.-Mexico border, which has no basis in reality (Bergen 2018). In 2017, the Department of Homeland Security apprehended 3,755 suspected terrorists trying to enter the U.S. through all points of entry; 2,170 of these attempted entry through airports. Trump's own State Department noted in 2017 that "there was no credible evidence indicating that international terrorist groups have established bases in Mexico, worked with Mexican drug cartels, or sent operatives via Mexico into the United States" (Bump 2019a).

If anything demonstrates the fictitious geographies that Trump calls into being, it is the famed border wall with Mexico, a central feature of his 2016 election campaign. He has claimed more than 134 times that the wall on the U.S.-Mexico border is under construction, which is simply not true. In 2018 Trump claimed "We started building our Wall. I'm so proud of it. We started. We started. We have $1.6 billion, and we've already started" (Kessler 2018b). In fact, the $1.6 billion was explicitly not for a wall. The 2006 Secure Fence Act resulted in about 1,050 kilometers of border barrier, but under Trump no part of the wall has been started, and perhaps never will be. Trump's lies create geographies where none existed beforehand. The wall with Mexico, for example, is simply dreamed into existence by sheer force of rhetoric. Trump repeatedly claimed Mexico would pay for it, then forced the longest government shutdown in American history over Congress's refusal to appropriate funds. When that tactic failed, he declared a national "emergency" where none existed, with the backing of an obsequious Republican Party (which showed some resistance when the Senate condemned the measure as executive overreach). He also claimed that a reworking of the North American Free Trade Agreement (NAFTA) will earn enough money for pay for the wall (Kessler 2019), which reveals a lack of understanding of basic economics. Similarly, Trump told the Spanish Foreign Minister to build a wall across the Sahara Desert to stop immigrants (Meixler 2018).

Nor do refugees get any better treatment from Trump, who has called them "the ultimate Trojan horse" (Kopan 2015). Indeed, his lies about them have served to restrict the movement of desperate people fleeing poverty, crime, and violence. He argued that "Refugees are pouring into our great country from Syria. We don't even know who they are. They could be ISIS. They could be anybody," adding that there are many "who are definitely, in many cases, ISIS-aligned" (Byrnes 2015). Trump threatened to deport the roughly 12,000 Syrian refugees currently living in the U.S. These lies and actions are part of the broader Islamophobia that pervaded his administration. Following the collapse of the World Trade Center in 2001, Trump claimed that "I watched when the World Trade Center came tumbling down. And I watched in Jersey City, New Jersey, where thousands and thousands of people were cheering as that building was coming down. Thousands of people were cheering" (Kessler 2015). These lies are simply not true (Kessler 2015). His hatred of Muslims, and use of Islamophobia for political ends, culminated in the so-called "Muslim ban" that sought to restrict immigration from several Muslim-majority countries (it was rejected by the courts until finally approved in a limited manner by the Supreme Court).

Trump also invents fictitious geographies about sanctuary cities. Angry that many have refused to turn undocumented immigrants over to the federal government, he boasted to his supporters that he was "dumping" refugees on these places. The claim, however, is simply untrue, and lacks any legal basis for doing so.

Trump also lies about the environment. On climate change, he argued that climate scientists "have a very big political agenda" (Samenow 2018). He tweeted in 2012 that "The concept of global warming was created by and for the Chinese in order to make U.S. manufacturing non-competitive" (Wong 2016). Whenever the U.S. is faced with a cold front during the winter, he uses it as evidence that climate change is not real. Regarding the vast majority of climate scientists who insist that anthropogenic climate change is real, he said "It's a hoax. I mean, it's a money-making industry, okay? It's a hoax, a lot of it" (Jacobson 2016). Later he added "Look, scientists also have a political agenda" (Rubin 2018). When he withdrew the U.S. from the Paris Climate Accord, he claimed that it would cost the country 2.5 million jobs, even though most experts hold that it would save far more money than it cost (Kessler and Lee 2017). Trump's stance has left the U.S. essentially alone in denying the greatest existential threat to the planet. Trump's own National Climate Assessment contradicted his false claims (Jay et al. 2018). Even the victims of climate change are denied empathy by his lies: when Hurricane Maria devastated Puerto Rico in 2017, Trump claimed "3,000 people did not die" (Klein and Vazquez 2018), and that the statistic was manufactured by Democrats desperate to make him "look as bad as possible" (Qiu 2018). When California was devastated by forest fires in 2018, he argued "There is no reason for these massive, deadly and costly forest fires in California except that forest management is so poor" (Pierre-Louis 2018).

International trade is another domain in which Trump lies frequently. Trump lied to Canadian Prime Minister Justin Trudeau about the U.S.-Canada balance of trade, and later bragged at a fundraising speech that he had made up facts during the meeting (Dawsey et al. 2018). Although the U.S. has a trade surplus with Canada, Trump claimed it was a deficit. He claimed "There's a tremendous tax that we pay when we [American businesses] go into China, whereas when China sells to us there's no tax" (Greenberg 2016). China's tariffs are higher than those imposed by the United States.

Trump's lies reflect the culmination of a long-standing, and increasingly virulent, form of American anti-intellectualism (Gore 2007; Jacoby 2008). This phenomenon has been taken to new heights by the Republican Party. For example, two-thirds of Trump supporters believe that President Obama is a Muslim not born in the U.S. (Gangitano 2016) and most Republicans believe that Trump won the popular vote in 2016 (Oliver and Wood 2016). Others assert that millions of immigrants voted illegally in the election. Conservative commentator and never-Trumper Charlie Sykes (2017) lamented how this mediasphere created an alternative reality that empowers the most reckless elements of the far right.

Trump's view is that truth – and that of the right-wing mediasphere more generally – is whatever benefits Trump and friends, not facts (or as Kellyanne Conway called them, "alternative facts"). More radically, one might say that Trump's view of truth is decisively nihilist: there is no truth. This line of thought is perhaps the ultimate apotheosis of postmodernism, of the "anything goes" view. Trump's epistemology is not grounded in philosophical debate or historical reality: in this view, truth is simply a means to an end, a self-serving tool. Call it the "opportunistic theory of truth." Trump often repeats falsehoods over and over, until they become "alternative facts" for his base and Fox News. Fact checker Kessler (2018a) argues that

> The president keeps going long after the facts are clear, in what appears to be a deliberate effort to replace the truth with his own, far more favorable, version of it. He is not merely making gaffes or misstating things, he is purposely injecting false information into the national conversation.

Trump has openly disdained the "mainstream" media, calling it the "enemy of the people." Such a move is designed to discredit news sources and enhance his own credibility. As he told CBS journalist Lesley Stahl, "You know why I do it? I do it to discredit you all and demean you all so when you write negative stories about me, no one will believe you" (Rosenberg 2018). Trump told his followers "What you're seeing and what you're reading is not what's happening" (Kwong 2018). In this sense, Trump eerily resembles the Newspeak of George Orwell's famous dystopian novel *1984*. Orwell (1948, p. 88) noted that "The Party told you to reject the evidence of your eyes and ears. It was their final, most essential command." It tells the protagonist, Winston Smith, that "Whatever the Party holds to be truth, *is* truth. It is impossible to see reality except by looking through the eyes of the Party." Similarly, Trump appropriated the term "fake news," which was originally used by his critics, and weaponized it, using the term in attempts to discredit the media and his opponents. Such a line of thought essentially blurs the boundaries between truth and falsehood altogether.

Bruni (2019) offers a biting summary of Trump's cavalier attitude toward the truth: "a man who wouldn't know the truth if it raced toward him with sirens blaring, ran over him, then backed up and did it again." This view of truth appears at the historical moment when political tribalism in the U.S. reigns supreme, when truth is seen as a political weapon and little more. Smith (2016), in an essay entitled

"Truth after Trump," argues that "He is a mere bullshitter, and what comes out of his mouth has more to do with pathologies of personality than with any real vision of how the world, or America, ought to be brought into line with some super-empirical truth to which he alone has access." Following this line of thought, Kakutani (2018) notes that the Trump Administration ordered the Centers for Disease Control and Prevention to avoid using the terms "science-based" and "evidence-based."

Right-Wing Covid Denialism

> If the truth shall kill them, then let them die.
> Immanuel Kant

One particularly startling example of how fake news and anti-intellectualism shape behavior occurred in 2021 as the covid pandemic began to recede in the U.S. The virus killed more than 610,000 Americans in that year (and more than 1.1 million in total), including 400,000 during the Trump administration. Trump's rampant incompetence in dealing with the virus has been well documented. But the problem of insufficient covid vaccinations extends well beyond Trump: it reflects a disastrous example of post-truth conservative politics. Right-wing media played a key role in promoting fake news and conspiracy theories about covid and the vaccines that offered protection (Stecula and Pickup 2021).

Fearing that the pandemic would damage his re-election chances, Trump repeatedly downplayed the virus: On January 22, 2020, he said, "We have it totally under control. It's one person coming in from China. It's going to be just fine" (Bump 2020). As Truscott (2020) puts it rather earthily, "On Feb. 10, he puked one of his 'a lot of people' lies out of his cakehole: 'A lot of people think that goes away in April with the heat – as the heat comes in.'" On February 25 he told the American public that "I think that's a problem that's going to go away." On February 27 he called the virus the Democrats' "new hoax" (Egan 2020). Throughout the pandemic, Trump remained in a state of denial and consistently downplayed the risk. "It's fading away. It's going to fade away," Trump told Sean Hannity on Fox News (Todisco 2020). In February, he announced that the pandemic would be over by Easter, then called for premature openings of stores and schools.

Trump's response was colored by his distrust of the "deep state," the very people in his administration whose expertise and experience he badly needed. When the administration's public health team argued at the end of February that schools and business in covid hot spots would have to close, it took three more weeks to convince Trump that failure to act would have dire consequences, during which time the virus spread rapidly. As epidemiologists sounded the alarm, Trump ignored them, unwilling or unable to absorb warnings that came at him. Trump repeatedly blamed anyone and everyone for the crisis, including former President Obama, the World Health Organization (WHO), the media, China, health care workers, Democrats, and state governors. He accused hospital officials of complaining too much and hoarding ventilators (Blake 2020).

Trump's post-truth approach to the pandemic was echoed by his family and followers, who joined the ridicule of public health authorities. In October 2020, when 800 people died of the virus each day, Donald Trump Jr. dismissed the deaths as "almost nothing" (Feuer 2020). Eric Trump told Fox News in May that "They think they are taking away Donald Trump's greatest tool, which is being able to go into an arena and fill it with 50,000 people every single time," he said. "You watch, they'll milk it every single day between now and November 3. And guess what, after November 3, coronavirus will magically all of a sudden go away and disappear and everybody will be able to reopen" (Wade 2020). Famed conservative radio commentator Rush Limbaugh asserted covid was "just like the common cold" (Chiu 2020). Fox News commentators Sean Hannity, Trish Regan, and Jeanine Pirro repeatedly called the pandemic a liberal "scam" to hurt Trump (Levin 2020).

A suspicion and distrust of science pervaded the administration's response. Trump distrusted career experts because he did not consider them sufficiently loyal to him personally. In the hostile climate that enveloped the scientific wing of the federal government, hundreds of state and federal health officials were fired or resigned in protest of the indifference to facts and evidence. When experts were not purged from office, they often had to engage in degrading acts of obeisance to keep their jobs. For example, Dr. Rick Bright, who led the agency working toward a vaccine, claims he was reassigned because he "resisted efforts to fund potentially dangerous drugs promoted by those with political connections" (Goldberg 2020). Trump and aides repeatedly ignored advice from health care professionals and epidemiologists, including his own leading health care advisor Dr. Anthony Fauci, a respected and experienced epidemiologist, at one point even leading a campaign to discredit him (Mindich 2020). The White House barred Fauci from making several television appearances, lest he go off message and signal continued concern about the virus. Trump retweeted a messaged that said "Time to #FireFacuci." Death threats against Fauci from Trump supporters became so severe that he required federal bodyguards.

Worse, Trump promoted false cures. He repeatedly touted the drug hydroxychloroquine "based on a feeling" (Rucker and Parker 2020), even though medical studies showed it did not prevent or cure the virus and could cause serious side effects (Qiu 2020). Trump and his son, Donald Jr., retweeted bizarre claims by a Houston physician who promoted hydroxychloroquine but added that gynecological problems were caused by dreams of sex with demons and that alien DNA was being used in medical experiments to create a vaccine that would make everyone an atheist (Pitofsky 2020). Trump himself began to spout odd, medically unfounded claims: "Supposing we hit the body with a tremendous – whether it's ultra-violet or just very powerful light?" (quoted in Broad and Levin 2020). He also suggested that drinking or injecting bleach might help (Rogers, Hauser et al. 2020), earning him widespread ridicule.

The surge of hostility to the lockdown, masks, and social distancing exhibited by conservatives undoubtedly raised the pandemic's death toll. Trump fans are more likely than most of the population to attend religious services without masks (Nortey 2020). Many Trump supporters thought that the pandemic was "over" or part of a nefarious anti-Trump plot. Avid viewers of right-wing media such as Fox News were more likely than most people to deny the pandemic's importance, contract the virus, and die from it (Ingraham 2020; Moore 2020; Sullivan 2020).

Unsurprisingly, Trump's popularity declined in proportion to the rise in cases, with the majority of people disapproving how he handled it; his failure to manage it contributed significantly to his electoral defeat in November, 2020, when the bill for his contempt for the truth, facts, science, and evidence finally came due. Even in the days before the election Trump professed his contempt for facts and denial of reality: At a rally in North Carolina, he said "That's all I hear about now. That's all I hear. Turn on television—'Covid, Covid, Covid, Covid, Covid, Covid.' A plane goes down. 500 people dead, they don't talk about it. ... By the way, on November 4, you won't hear about it anymore" (Beer 2020). Trump may well have won re-election if he had handled the pandemic better; he lost many battleground states by narrow margins.

Right-wing truth-denial continued throughout the covid vaccination program, which began in December 2020, and significantly reduced the number of new infections and deaths. However, the politicization of the pandemic became a politicized response to vaccines, with many conservatives denying the need for them or their efficacy (Lerer 2021). Covid disinformation comes in various forms and from different sources (Brennen et al. 2020). Some of the most egregiously stupid rumors were that the vaccines modified recipients' DNA, that covid-infected people would be locked in camps, or that the vaccines contained a microchip implanted by Microsoft CEO Bill Gates (Bodner et al. 2020). The problem was exacerbated by Russian bots that spread rumors (Broniatowski et al. 2018). Disinformation about covid became so widespread that the World Health Organization expressed concern about an "infodemic" that paralleled the viral pandemic.

Conspiracy theories became a major roadblock to the acceptance of vaccinations (Romer and Jamieson 2020). Reactionary commentators such as Fox News's

Tucker Carlson spread lies that the vaccines were killing people, saying the vaccination program was the "greatest scandal of my lifetime, by far" (Hsu 2021). Unsurprisingly, those who watched Fox News regularly were more likely to be unvaccinated and to die from the virus (Pinna et al. 2022). When one Ohio woman claimed that covid vaccines left people "magnetized," Republican lawmakers thanked her for her "enlightening" comments. As a result of this science denial, most people skeptical, hesitant, or hostile to vaccines are conservatives (Diamond et al. 2021). Vaccinations are critical because they save lives: 97 percent of people hospitalized for the virus are unvaccinated. One poll indicated that 47 percent of Republicans would not get vaccinated; among viewers of extreme right-wing outlets such as Newsmax and One America Network, 68 percent refused to get a vaccine (Hsu 2021). Thus, although more than half of Americans had received at least one vaccine shot, there were significant differences between conservatives and liberals: in June, 2021, among Democrats, 67 percent reported living in households where everyone had been vaccinated, whereas among Republicans only 37 percent did so (Levenson 2021). Many Republican politicians well knew the benefits of vaccination but tolerated and disseminated lies about vaccines for political expediency (Weisman and Stolberg 2021).

These political differences were accompanied by geographic ones. In counties that Biden won in the election in 2020, 47 percent of residents had been vaccinated; in contrast, in counties won by Trump, only 35 percent had done so. The result of right-wing science denial was a surge in coronavirus cases in the summer of 2021, a reflection of the spread of the Delta variant, which was primarily evident in rural, conservative areas such as southern Missouri and Arkansas. Republican states such as Alabama, Mississippi, and Louisiana have the lowest rates of vaccinations in the country. Republican governors in Texas, Florida, Iowa, and elsewhere refused to implement mandatory face masks. As a result, as Boot (2021) puts it, "people are dying because of Republican hostility to science." These unnecessary deaths due to covid reflect the costs of living in a post-truth world and the accompanying distrust of science and expertise that it includes.

Fake News and Brexit

> There are two ways to be fooled. One is to believe what isn't true;
> the other is to refuse to believe what is true.
> Søren Kierkegaard

Britain's decision to leave the European Union in 2016 offers a textbook example of post-truth geopolitics. By a narrow margin (51.9 to 48.1%), British voters chose to leave the EU. As with similar political events around the world, Britain's cities heavily voted Remain while small towns and rural areas voted to leave. Turnout was quite high. Brexit marked the culmination of decades of effort by right-wing Britons who were skeptical of the EU and of supranational organizations more generally. Like Trump's MAGA movement, Brexit was fueled by a deep desire for change.

The Leave campaign was inspired by post-truth politics that inflamed passions and misled wide swaths of the public (Marshall and Drieschova 2018). In contrast to the Remain campaign, Leave aimed at the level of affect and emotion. Arron Banks, who bankrolled LeaveEU, wrote "The Remain campaign featured fact, fact, fact, fact. It just doesn't work. You've got to connect with people emotionally. It's the Trump success" (D'Ancona 2017, p. 17). The notion reflects the right's widespread desire for simplicity and emotional resonance rather than the subtleties and complexities of data.

As the event became an opportunity for politicians to peddle lies and fantasies, the debate about Brexit was widely plagued by falsehoods, lies, and fake news (Henkel 2021; Fig. 4.3). Rather than target the entire UK population, Leave focused on "persuadables," a marketing term that entered politics. Leave supporters united around the slogan "Take Back Control," although it was deliberately vague and misleading about EU decision-making. One lie was that without Brexit, the EU would allow unlimited immigration into Britain, especially from poorer countries such as Turkey, Albania, Serbia, and Macedonia. Armed forces Minister and Leave campaigner Penny Mordaunt fraudulent popularized the notion that Turkey would enter the EU, opening the door for countless dark-skinned immigrants to flood into Britain. As Wren-Lewis (2018, p. 4) notes, "Scare stories like Turkey joining the EU within 10 years were allowed to gain traction rather than being knocked down as ridiculous." Similarly, Nigel Farage, then leader of the UK Independence Party, unveiled a poster of a long queue of Syrian refugees under the slogan "Breaking Point," indicating that without Brexit they would be allowed asylum in the UK. As D'Ancona (2017, p. 20) notes, "This was Post-Truth politics at its purest – the triumph of the visceral over the rational, the deceptively simple over the honestly complex." He adds (p. 125) "in the Brexit referendum, the Remain camp's greatest mistake was to assume that torrents of statistics would win the day." Other observers such as Collins (2019) confirm that post-truth was overwhelmingly used by the Leave rather than Remain campaign.

The most frequent and insidious lie told by Brexit supporters – the defining one of the campaign – was that the UK was sending £350 million ($480 million) per week to the EU, funds that could be better used to fund the strapped National Health Service. This bit of fake news was repeated on hundreds of busses throughout the country. The claim ignored the funds that the EU would spend on the UK if

Figure 4.3: Sign Opposing Brexit Lies, photo by Matt Brown.

it remained in the union, notably subsidies to British farmers. The UK Statistics Authority called the claim a "clear misuse of official statistics." The claim ignored the rebate that Britain received from the EU, which lowered the UK's weekly contribution to £250 million. Another lie, told by Boris Johnson, was that the EU wanted a European superstate, a fantasy he compared to Hitler's. Yet another, by Liam Fox, was that a post-Brexit deal with the EU would be "the easiest thing in human history." Even more claims, such as the one that the UK economy would surge once it left the EU, were difficult to counter with facts. The mainstream media did little to counter these bits of fake news or offer counter-narratives.

With a long history of Euroskepticism, often by peddling "Euromyths," conservative British tabloids zealously supported Brexit. As Klikauer and Simms (2021) point out, "In 2019, just three companies – the Daily Mail and General Trust, Reach and Murdoch's News UK – controlled 83 % of the British newspaper market. Only the secretive state of North Korea comes close to such numbers!" Outlets such as *The Sun, Daily Mail, Daily Telegraph, Sunday Telegraph,* and *Daily Star* all published a series of pro-Brexit stories with varying degrees of accuracy. *The Sun* falsely reported that Queen Elizabeth supported Brexit. Their readership, typically older and less educated, is similar to Trump's base in the U.S. British tabloids often published lies about Brexit, including, for example, "the 350 million pounds (about $450 million at current rates) that Britain paid to the European Union every week (false) and the prospect of millions of Turks making their way to Britain if it stayed in the union (Turkey is not joining the bloc)" (Bennhold 2017). Similarly, Zappettini (2019) summarizes some of their more ludicrous claims: "For years, titles such as *The Daily Mail, The Sun* and *The Daily Express* have been particularly active in portraying the UK as a victim of a Brussels 'cosmopolitical' conspiracy plot that, according to some headlines, would result for example in the British Parliament being forced to adopt bans on traditional British kettles and light bulbs or British women being required to return old sex toys to comply with EU rules." Some published headlines such as "The Deadly Cost of our Open Borders" (Serhan 2017).

Like many right-wing movements, Brexit was permeated with anti-intellectualism. As Hardy and McCann (2017) put it, "The unexpected 'Leave' vote gave new voice to certain forms of anti-globalism, anti-cosmopolitanism, and anti-intellectualism that comprised separate or overlapping positions." This view included the notion that "experts" are part of the "elite" intent on disparaging working people. For example, former Secretary of State for Education Michael Grove said that "people in this country have had enough of experts" (quoted in Sayer 2017, p. 92). His view speaks to the collapse of traditional gatekeepers in the media and the right's argument that the "mainstream media" is biased and untrustworthy. Even discussing the costs of Brexit was dismissed as unpatriotic blather.

Brexit promoters also engaged in a sophisticated digital strategy on social media. For the first time in British history, more money was spent on digital advertising than conventional channels. This included an army of sock puppet accounts (false online identities) and Twitterbots to promote falsehoods (Bastos and Mercea 2019). Some of this fake news was promoted by Russians (Narayanan et al. 2017). On Facebook, intense debate about Brexit reflected two distinct epistemological communities (Del Vicario et al. 2017), each with its own truths. This was the context in which "information systems" became vulnerable to "a mix of strategic disinformation from both national and foreign actors" (Bennett and Livingstone 2018, p. 127).

Britain's price for leaving the EU has been steep. Brexit ushered in a new age of economic uncertainty. London banking firms have begun to look into relocating to the continent. The 3.5 million workers from the EU in Britain have either had to leave or apply for legal residence, causing labor shortages. Supply chains have been disrupted. Some ships avoid British ports for lack of truck drivers. A fuel shortage drove up the costs of gasoline and electricity. Fruits and vegetables from Europe are in short supply. Pro-Brexit regions, which lagged behind those that opposed Leave, have declined even further (Milligan and Tartar 2023). The promises of a Singapore-on-the-Thames never materialized. As Scotland strongly opposed Leave, the movement for independence there gained strength. Northern Ireland remains in dire uncertainty, with a regulatory trade wall separating it from the rest of the UK. The majority of Britons now think that leaving the EU was a poor decision, a sort of "Regrexit." In short, in a post-truth world, the UK has learned the hard way the costs of not basing its policies and politics on the truth, in whatever form it takes.

Chapter Conclusion

> During times of universal deceit, telling the truth becomes a revolutionary act.
> George Orwell, *1984*

Post-truth and fake news are not the exclusive preserve of the right, but reactionaries the world over have employed it to the greatest effect. Those who deny democracy and favor outcomes unpalatable to large swathes of the public often use fake news to achieve their goals. It is no accident, then, that fake news is a weapon of class war, and used routinely by autocrats and oligarchs. Given the avalanche of fake news, outright lies, and conspiracy theories launched at conservatives every day, it is little wonder that many inhabit a post-truth world.

Right-wing post-truth is found in widespread anti-intellectualism, which cultivates a distrust of "experts" and academics as part of the elite, sealing people in echo chambers that reinforce their confirmation biases. This phenomenon would not be so alarming if it did not have such deleterious political effects. Ignorance and science denial lie behind the movement against vaccinations, which has endangered the lives of millions, notably during the covid pandemic. Most insidiously, it allows petroleum and coal companies to deny the reality of climate change and inhibit progress toward a post-carbon future.

The U.S. has spawned an enormous – and enormously powerful – right-wing mediaverse, a constellation of television outlets (notably Fox News), pundits, radio shows, and websites that ceaselessly demonizes liberals and spews forth a maelstrom of fake news. This apparatus is in no small part responsible for accelerating the political divisions that have emerged in the wake of neoliberalism. Such outlets become vehicles for importing extremist ideas into the mainstream. In its most extreme forms, the conservative mediaverse facilitates conspiracy theories, such as the ludicrous QAnon movement. This network of outlets, often funded by right-wing billionaires (Peter Thiel, the Koch Brothers) gave cover to Donald Trump and his followers, allowing falsehoods to be spread without consequence. When politicians can boldly lie or make claims with no evidence, and face no consequence whatsoever, post-truth has become a reality.

The dangers of the global right-wing mediaverse are sobering. Reactionary outlets may shape the creation of news in more mainstream channels, setting agendas and coloring their coverage of controversial topics and liberals (Benkler et al. 2017). Moreover, selective exposure to hyper-partisan right-wing views creates an internally coherent, insulated echo chamber that has no equivalent on the political left. Thus, Manjoo (2008, p. 46) holds that "conservatives exhibit greater partisan selectivity in their news choices." As a result, Ingraham (2016) notes, they are less reflective in information processing, more likely to be duped by nonsense, and more susceptible to fake news.

Both Brexit and Trump's victory were predicated on post-truth politics (Rose 2017; Sayer 2017). In both cases, the lies that sustained them were part of a populist broadside against "elites," usually taken to mean liberal experts out of touch with working class families (Norris and Inglehart 2019). Both relied on a cocktail of racism, xenophobia, "traditional values," and fears of globalization. Trump's election in 2016, the border wall that was never built, and Brexit all reflect a broader dynamic of post-truth geopolitics.

Neoliberal populism has flourished in the post-truth age, and the links between post-truth and authoritarianism are clear. Like neoliberalism, it is deeply anti-democratic. As historian Timothy Snyder (2017, p. 70) puts it, "post-truth is pre-fascism."

Chapter 5
The Urban and Rural Landscapes of Post-truth

Post-truth does not float in some aspatial world; it is produced on the ground, somewhere. Because it is constructed socially, post-truth is the product of actors embedded in networks. In this sense, post-truth consists of a series of sociospatial activities and situated practices. To understand where post-truth comes from, and who believes in it, one must approach it geographically. This observation is critical to understanding the origins and impacts of fake news: *where* it is produced is fundamental to *how* it is produced; *where* it is consumed is foundational to *how* it is consumed.

The global information economy has increasingly focused its rewards on well educated, white-collar professionals in large metropolitan regions. This process plays out unevenly, of course, in different countries and has markedly different impacts on urban and rural areas. As a result, large numbers of poorly educated people have been left in the lurch; many, resentful of vilified urban "elites," support populist movements in which fake news plays a major role.

The chapter begins by summarizing the urban economy of cognitive-cultural capitalism, the information-intensive form of capitalism today that demands large volumes of skilled intellectual labor. This phenomenon has led to the explosive growth of globalized metropolitan areas around the world with an economic niche in financial and producer services. In the process, contemporary capitalism has created large pools of college-educated workers, sometimes called the creative class. Next, the chapter explores the relations between urbanity, diversity, and tolerance, arguing that people who live in cities are more likely to be exposed to cultural and ethnic differences and thus resist the simple stereotypes that feed reactionary politics. The third part turns to news deserts, a geographical outcome of the restructuring of the media that has led many people in small towns and rural areas to be deprived of a wealth of news sources. Fourth, it argues that post-truth unfolds over a landscape of gullibility, in which the college educated, concentrated in cities, enjoy an economic and intellectual premium; in contrast, the poorly educated, many of whom live in news deserts, are more likely to fall prey to fake news and conspiracy theories. Fifth, it touches on European urban-rural dichotomies. The conclusion highlights the chapter's major points.

https://doi.org/10.1515/9783110749847-006

Cities and Cognitive-Cultural Capitalism

Capitalism has been associated with the growth of cities throughout its history. Cities are reflective of the division of labor, particularly the insistent tendencies of firms to cluster to take advantages of the agglomeration economies and network externalities found there. By grouping together, firms minimize transport costs of inputs and outputs, and maximize their access to specialized labor and information. Cities are thus much more than simply conglomerations of people, but consist of networks of interdependencies.

Since the late 20th century, the hallmark of the global economy is what Scott (2007, 2008, 2011, 2012, 2019) has called "cognitive-cultural capitalism," a particular form of information-intensive capitalism that relies heavily on the commodification of culture. In such a labor market, employers place a premium on laborers with the intellectual capacities to process, analyze, and communicate large volumes of information. Scott (2014, p. 570) holds that they are "called upon increasingly to deploy high-level cognitive and cultural skills such as deductive reasoning capacities, technical insight, leadership, communication abilities, cultural awareness and visual imagination – in other words, more or less creative capacities – in the workplace." Firms engaged in such activities rely heavily on the agglomeration economies of large cities. The rise of cognitive-cultural capitalism is thus manifested in the explosive growth of producer services across the globe, including finance, legal services, computer software firms, advertising, public relations, engineering and architecture, and other assorted companies that engage in the production of specialized expertise. It also includes the management functions of many large corporations, as well as research and development. Such jobs often require technical experience and involve decision making in a variety of complex tasks, which are difficult to automate. Historically, intellectual labor has been marginal to the production process; under cognitive-cultural capitalism, it has moved to center stage.

The emergence of cognitive-cultural capitalism is synonymous with the growth of global neoliberalism. From global cities that act as the command-and-control functions of the world economy to smaller urban areas, these places have increasingly developed a competitive niche as Marshallian nodes embedded within worldwide commodity chains. This notion has been observed by several authors, including Robert Reich's (2010) "symbolic analysts." Most famously, Richard Florida's (2004; 2005) celebrated notion of the creative class has drawn enormous attention. The creative class involves an array of occupations and workers involved in information-processing, notably software, finance, producer services, parts of health care, law, the media, the arts, entertainment, and education. They are clustered in metropolitan regions where urban agglomeration economies are powerful magnets that link firms in dense networks of interactions. The creative class reflects the convergence of the cultural and the economic, of symbolic and use values. Such workers tend to like their jobs and put a premium on self-expression. Their work and personal lives are deeply intertwined. The creative class is disproportionately represented in startups, and its education and creativity is essential to invention, innovation, solving problems, product development, marketing, and entrepreneurship. In this reading, the skilled professionals so central to cognitive-cultural urban economies place a high value on amenities, recreational opportunities, and local social climates that value diversity, including ethnic differences and tolerance of alternative lifestyles (notably gays). Cities that are tolerant, Florida maintains, are economically healthy; those that are restrictive and xenophobic are unlikely to attract the talent they need to remain competitive. Florida and Gates (2004) are adamant that regions hoping to cultivate high technology sectors in particular must foster political contexts marked by social and cultural tolerance (see also Florida, Mellander and Stollarick 2008). In addition, it must be noted that the creative class – essentially yuppies – is sustained by vast legions of low-paid service workers who are disproportionately women, immigrants, and ethnic minorities.

In contrast to urban areas, many of which have seen their economies boom, many rural areas have witnessed prolonged stagnation and out-migration. Towns and regions dependent on extractive industries have been undercut by wave upon wave of mechanization, greatly limiting employment opportunities for the people who live there. Many small towns have been gutted by mechanization, job loss, and out-migration. Compared to cities, many small towns and rural areas offer few opportunities, higher rates of unemployment and poverty, and a rising crisis of opioid use. Indeed, many such places suffer from an epidemic of "deaths of despair" such as suicide and drug overdoses (Case and Deaton 2022).

Cities, Rural Areas, Diversity, and Tolerance

The differential geographies of the post-truth world play out unevenly, particularly in the divisions between urban and rural areas. Here, it is argued that the daily experience of social difference often found in large cities tends to render inhabitants more open to diversity and less prone to false, racist, and xenophobic discourses. In short, residents of cities are less likely to subscribe to post-truth narratives than are their rural counterparts. This is a bold claim, and requires substantiation.

Although cities have often been vilified in the popular media as dangerous and corrupting places, they may also be seen as locales in which the daily negotiation of difference is perpetual and inescapable, fostering tolerance and acceptance of difference (Binnie et al. 2006). Large cities in particular have long been seen as sophisticated and worldly. But they are also arenas in which social and economic success, including at work and in neighborhoods, often necessitates the cultivation of understanding of, and respect for (or at least tolerance of), others who are socially and culturally different. Confronting difference on a daily basis, it may be argued, mitigates against the dehumanizing stereotypes that sustain discourses of racism, xenophobia, and nationalism. Such a view is not meant to obscure the intense poverty and inequality concentrated in urban centers, or to oversimplify the very real class and ethnic tensions that are often found in metropolitan areas, which have occasionally been sites of racist violence. There is, of course, no inevitable connection between living in culturally diverse environments and becoming more empathetic, tolerant, or liberal. Daily life in such contexts includes as much social exclusion as inclusion. Indeed, pockets of racism and xenophobia exist within many global city neighborhoods (typically working-class communities under economic duress). Competition over jobs can exacerbate inter-ethnic conflicts, such as between African-Americans and Koreans in New York or between African-Americans and Mexican-Americans in Los Angeles. Yet a mounting body of evidence suggests that most people living in large cities, particularly global ones, confront the production of social difference in empathetic terms.

Evidence from social psychology indicates that diversity leads to tolerance when it challenges stereotypical expectations across multiple domains of lived experience (Crisp and Turner 2011; Roccas and Amit 2011). When difference is repeatedly experienced in personal terms in daily life, it becomes difficult to view those of contrasting backgrounds and lifestyles in simplistic, demonized terms (Gurin et al. 2004; Boisjoly et al. 2006; Valentine 2008). For example, people who know gays personally are much less likely to be homophobic; those who work with Muslims realize that claims that many are terrorists are extremely unrealistic and racist. Cities excel at bringing diverse groups together, fostering opportunities for inter-ethnic and multicultural understanding. Partly for this reason, culturally diverse cities tend to perform better economically than less diverse ones (Niebuhr 2010). Diversity tends to foster diverse cognitive skills, i.e., to make people reconsider their own opinions, to understand the perspective of others, to look past initial dislikes, to accept dissenting ideas, to see more than one side of an issue, and to reduce the drive to force one's own views on others. As Marcus et al. (1995, p. 7) put it, "diversity provides an incentive to lessen complete reliance on established beliefs and predispositions." Mutz (2006) demonstrated that people whose personal networks include those with divergent political opinions are more likely to be politically tolerant. Intergroup contacts reduce prejudice primarily through a process of identification with out-group members (Dovidio et al. 2003; Brown and Hewstone 2006). Diverse social and cultural environments offer opportunities for inter-action in multiple arenas, to cultivate trust, to define mutually beneficial objec-tives, and to learn to think of different groups as part of a larger, more comprehen-sive social project. In short, social and cultural diversity tend to make urban residents less prone to believe fake news and subscribe to simplistic stereotypes, conspiracy theories, and false information.

Conversely, it is most certainly the case that *not* living in a diverse urban en-vironment, such as ethnically and religiously homogeneous small towns and rural areas, often leads to a dehumanization, even if subtle, of the perceived Other, usu-ally meaning ethnic, religious, and sexual minorities. A diverse literature from so-ciology, political science, psychology, and economics confirms this point. Commun-ities lacking cultural diversity often suffer a wet blanket of conformity that acts as an echo chamber in which alternative views and lifestyles are not imagined, or what psychologists call confirmation bias (Nickerson 1998), leading to exaggerated views of the normality of one's own worldview and lifestyle. Moore and Ovadia (2006) tested the extent of social heterogeneity using census-tract information about the religious, educational and racial composition of areas and concluded di-verse communities tend to be relatively tolerant ones. Indeed, small towns and rural areas frequently exhibit higher rates of racism, religiosity, and nationalistic fervor (Wimmer 1997; Branton and Jones 2005). Thus, for people enmeshed in ho-mogeneous environments, it is much easier to fall victim to stereotypes of foreign-ers, immigrants, and minorities. Lack of diversity makes one prone to believe in fake news.

Conversely, living in urban environments affords opportunities for pleasant encounters with difference, such as co-workers from different backgrounds or eth-nic foods, music, dance, art, and festivals. These statements are most certainly not to be taken as meaning that all small towns are intolerant of diversity, or that all large cities are havens of empathy, but rather that a persistent, if imperfect, pat-tern exists in which rising city size is associated with greater interaction with, and often respect for, those who are "different."

The point here is not either to romanticize large cities nor to demonize small towns and rural areas: not every denizen of small, homogenous communities is an intolerant racist, and not all residents of cities are open-minded and empathetic. Cities by no means have a monopoly on the production of empathy and tolerance. Yet the vision of urban life famously promoted by Jane Jacobs (1961) – of metropol-itan areas as diverse and bustling centers of creative engagement, of streets in which multiple lifestyles are brought into a creative collision with one another – is most explicitly manifested in those cities with a multitude of connections to the rest of the planet, with people from all corners of the globe, with various social groups living cheek by jowl (Glaeser 2000).

News Deserts

Post-truth in various forms has been exacerbated by corporate and spatial changes in the news media. The stark economic, cultural, and political differences between urban and rural areas is compounded by the phenomenon of news and media deserts, or communities not covered by local or weekly newspapers (Ferrier et al. 2016). In the U.S., there are more than 1,300 such places; they are disproportionately concentrated in the South. Media deserts tend to be in rural areas, have populations that are elderly, relatively low incomes, and are poorly educated (Abernathy 2016, 2018). Half the counties in the country have only one newspaper (Fig. 5.1).

■ No newspaper ■ One weekly paper ■ One daily ■ More than one newspaper

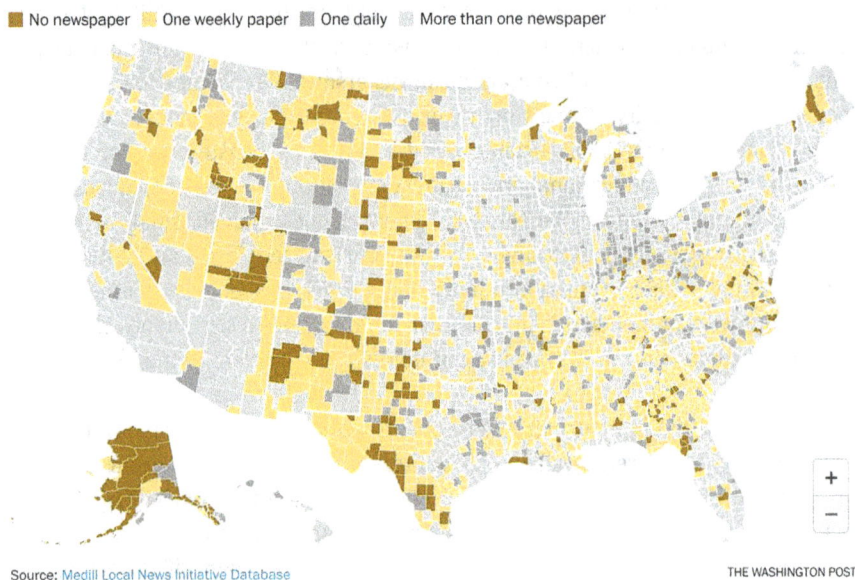

Source: Medill Local News Initiative Database   THE WASHINGTON POST

Figure 5.1: Number of Newspapers by County in the U.S., 2022. Source: Gibbs 2022.

Media deserts are the product of the restructuring of the journalism industry in the face of neoliberalism. The Telecommunications Act of 1996 led to widespread deregulation that accelerated corporate consolidation; as community service standards disappeared, corporate giants penetrated local markets with the express purpose of eliminating local outlets. Consequently, the journalism industry has been gripped by budget cuts, layoffs, corporate consolidation, financialization, and mounting challenges from television and digital media (Abernathy 2018). Many papers were complacent about the challenge posed by the internet. As a result, 2,200 local newspapers closed between 2005 and 2020, and tens of thousands of journalists lost their jobs. U.S. employment in journalism declined from 71,000 in 2008 to 39,000 in 2017. Places where papers closed tend to have higher poverty rates than the national average. The decline in readers of print media has been even greater than the collapse of the newspapers themselves. Miller (2018, p. 63) notes that "While local TV stations have tried to fill the vacuum and provide some hard-hitting local news and investigative reporting to viewers, most of the news broadcast on TV still originates in newspapers."

News deserts reflect the steady corporate consolidation of traditional media. Hedge funds, equity funds, and other investors have been buying many small newspapers (Abernathy 2016). Most of those papers acquired are located in economically struggling small towns where the newspaper is the primary source of local news. Larger chains are also responsible: the largest 25 newspaper chains own 1/3 of the country's newspapers. Corporate concentration of the media shifts editorial decisions and news coverage to people without a stake in local communities. In addition, many larger papers have scaled back coverage of their communities.

News deserts are bad news for the news. Much groundbreaking news reporting originates with humble "beat" reporters who cover mundane topics like city hall, school and zoning boards, and the local police. Fewer reporters mean less accountability, less information about local candidates, and less information about local problems and solutions. Local news may serve as watchdogs and expose local corruption. At times such news receives national coverage. The loss of local reporters thus affects the entire news ecosystem. People living in news deserts often become politically disengaged (Hayes and Lawless 2021). Finally, the loss of viewers and revenues has also accelerated the growth of fake news on social media. For good reason scholars of disinformation point to the crisis of journalism and news deserts as a major cause (Pickard 2019).

Media deserts also reflect the digital divide. In rural areas, internet and satellite connections, even cell phones, may be slow and frustrating. Many rural areas lack high-speed, broadband internet access (Ali 2020; Matthews and Ali 2022) or what Hardy (2022) calls the "rural information penalty." The broadband digital divide has been amply documented (Riddlesdon and Singleton 2014). In 2018, 86% of American urban dwellers had a broadband subscription compared to 80% of rural ones; 85.6% of urbanites owned a smart (internet-connected) mobile phone, whereas 79.5% of rural residents did so (Martin 2021). Even the ubiquity of the internet has not prevented the rise of "social media news deserts" (Thorson 2019) in which algorithms do not expose people to a diversity of news content. For people living in such communities, obtaining news is a difficult and laborious task.

Changes in the structure of the media and the rise of new deserts play out unevenly across landscapes, contributing mightily to the emerging geographies of the post-truth world. Closures of hundreds of local newspapers, particularly in low-income regions, have devastated local news outlets (Alexander et al. 2016). Lee and Butler (2019) illustrate how local information landscapes mirror the spatial inequalities of capitalism as a whole. The implications for the geography of post-truth are sobering. As Doctor (2019) puts it, "The impact is obvious. As America has moved from jokey indulgences in truthiness to a point where fact fights for its very life, it's the bankers who are deciding what will be defined as news, and who and how many people will be employed to report it." The result is news deserts. Millions of people live in a news vacuum, having to turn to television or cable to get any news at all. As Abernathy (2018) points out, "The residents of America's emerging news deserts are often its most vulnerable citizens. They are generally poorer, older and less educated than the average American." Lack of diverse media outlets has serious implications for how people in such communities receive, perceive, and process news.

In many small towns, conservative media reigns supreme (Wells et al. 2021). Unsurprisingly, Trump thrived in news deserts (Musgrave and Nussbaum 2018). Because rural states hold disproportionate power in the Electoral College, the rise of news deserts has gone hand-in-hand with the growth of reactionary populism. As Gibbs (2022) puts it, "The very places where local news is disappearing are often the *same* places that wield disproportionate political power."

The Spatiality of Gullibility: Explaining Susceptibility to Fake News

> The further a society drifts from the truth, the more it will hate those who speak it.
> George Orwell

The geography of post-truth is largely a reflection of spatial differences in education, economic opportunities, media availability, and human capital. Specifically, these dimensions vary markedly between rural and urban areas. All over the world, rural areas tend to be less educated than urban ones (Kyzyma 2018). Rural areas suffer from a variety of disadvantages, including access to education, employment, incomes, and cultural amenities. They have lower standards of living than do urbanites, less access to health care, and lower life expectancies. They are more likely to be news deserts. This phenomenon is often labeled the "rural penalty," the price paid by rural inhabitants for low population density and remoteness. About 15% of the U.S. population lives in rural areas.

A sizable literature in sociology and political science has documented the large and growing political differences between urban and rural areas (McKee 2008;

Scala and Johnson 2017; Rodden 2019). Despite a history of progressive populism a century ago, rural areas today, particularly in the U.S., tend to be deeply conservative, more traditional and religious than large cities, and supportive of the Republican Party. These political attitudes are shaped by a steady diet of right-wing news, which feeds a continual outpouring of rage, contempt for liberals, distrust of the government, and hatred of immigrants.

Compounding the gulf between urban and rural areas is the geography of access to higher education. The shift to information-intensive, post-Fordist capitalism has elevated the social and economic significance of a college or university degree, what is often called the college wage premium (Ashworth and ransom 2019; Araki 2020; Birulin et al. 2020). University degrees give, at least in theory, workers the cognitive skills and human capital necessary to compete in information-intensive careers, which lie at the heart of globalized, neoliberal cognitive-cultural capitalism (Hanushek 2012). These skills are not simply applied or technical ones but include the liberal arts (Roth 2014). Higher education imparts the ability to abstract, generalize, synthesize, contextualize, communicate, think critically, set realistic goals, and follow logical arguments. In college students have the opportunity to discover interests, be exposed to novel ideas and cultures, engage in intellectual experiences (some for the first time), understand basic science, network, meet people from different cultures, study abroad, learn to write, cultivate both social and intellectual capital, harness creativity, master a discipline, and acquire other languages. Some develop an appreciation for historical and geographic context, and even a social, and environmental consciousness. A few will acquire a lifelong love of reading and learning. Only a tiny handful will become intellectuals.

At the heart of skills acquired in college is information literacy, the ability to process and analyze large volumes of information quickly and accurately (Nicholson 2019). Exposure to such skills tends to reduce the susceptibility to conspiracy theories and fake news. Moreover, because higher education leads to greater productivity, job satisfaction, and longer life expectancies, it is both a private and a public good.

Does this mean that all college graduates are well informed and make rational decisions? Of course not. Plenty of people put in minimal effort to obtain their degrees, and some students are impervious to learning. And there are a great deal of folk who never attended college who are very smart and well informed. But, on average, a substantial body of evidence indicates that college graduates are less likely to fall for conspiracy theories and simplistic stereotypes, to be better informed, to appreciate complexity and nuance, and be more open-minded and tolerant than their non-college educated peers (Billing 2003; Hastie 2007; Hanushek 2012; Guerra-Carrillo et al. 2017).

A bachelor's degree signals to employers that the graduate has a minimal degree of maturity and responsibility. Birulin et al. (2020) note that "signaling accounts for a significant proportion of the college wage premium." Because so many well-paying, white-collar jobs rely on these abilities, a college education has become essential to gain entry into the middle class, which explains the steady growth in college enrollments in the face of decades of low birth rates. In 1990, about 24% of the U.S. population had a bachelor's degree; in 2020, 37% did so. Despite the steadily rising costs of university educations, a college degree still leads to significant financial rewards over graduates' working lives. Compared to high school graduates, college graduates earn, on average, more than 70% more over their careers, a return of several million dollars. Moreover, the college wage premium has risen over the last several decades (Ashworth and Ransom 2019), rising from roughly 40% in the 1970s to nearly twice that today. However, the premium is geographically variable (Winters 2020), tending to be higher in urbanized, service-base states than rural ones.

The rising value of a college education is closely associated with mounting income inequality in many countries (Heathcote et al. 2010; Birulin et al. 2019). Even as wages for the poorly educated have stagnated or declined, salaries for the well-educated have increased. All over the world, the college wage premium has created an income gulf between the well-educated and less well educated. Whereas technological change tends to be complementary for the highly skilled, it leads to job displacement among the poorly skilled (Doms et al. 1997; Goldin and Katz 2008; Song 2009).

Higher education is not simply a sign of who succeeds and who does not under neoliberalism, it has potent political effects (Harris 2018; Ahearn et al. 2022). It has become a major marker of how people vote, with the college-educated tending to be relatively progressive and the non-college educated more conservative (Cohn 2021). The college wage premium has thus been accompanied by the "diploma divide." Like the college premium, the diploma divide has increased over time, reflecting mounting political polarization. "I love the poorly educated," Trump proclaimed during his campaign in 2016 (quoted in Taranto 2016); while others scoffed, the poorly educated were listening (see Schaffner et al. 2017). Unsurprisingly, non-college educated voters comprise the backbone of populist movements worldwide.

Geographic differences in higher education speak to the educational gulf between urban and rural areas. In 2015, for example, 33% of urbanites had a college degree compared to 19% of people in rural areas (Marré 2017). Rural youth are less likely to attend selective schools, especially four-year ones (in part due to their ability to afford tuition), stay enrolled, and more likely to delay their entry into higher education (Byun et al. 2015). Students in rural high schools are less likely to take advanced courses. Moreover, the gap between rural and urban areas has steadily grown over time. Many college-educated residents leave rural areas for the cities (Carr and Kefalas 2009; Maxwell 2019). Rural areas with low average levels of education tend disproportionately to be poor and have high unemployment rates. Educational inequalities thus mirror the inequalities among places (Roscigno et al. 2006).

As information-intensive, white-collar jobs have boomed in metropolitan areas, the structural transformation of global and national economies under neoliberalism has left many small towns and rural areas behind, with attendant psychological and political consequences. It is not surprising that many people who live in rural areas feel oppressed and are often angry with the alleged "elites" in large cities (Cramer 2016). As Mathews and Ali (2022, p. 3) put it, "The rural penalty produces a perception among rural residents that they do not get a fair share economically, politically or socially and that they are ignored by powerful institutions of society." Many rural conservatives deeply resent and feel disrespected by allegedly condescending liberals in urban areas and feel that their regions do not receive their "fair share" of government resources, even though, on average, rural areas are more heavily subsidized than are urban ones. Rural rage, as Belert and Sunshine (2019) put it, has led many such communities to become ardently conservative, often filled with resentment at liberal, urban "elites" (Smith and Hanley 2018). As Jacobs and Munis (2022) illustrate, place-based resentment plays a major role in shaping American elections. To quote Maxwell (2019), "Rural residents feel left behind by the globalized economy and alienated from big cities' multiculturalism." Edelman (2021) goes further, arguing that capital has so hollowed out small towns and rural areas that it paved the way for authoritarian populism. Unsurprisingly, rural areas in the U.S. overwhelmingly supported the Republican Party and Donald Trump (Gimpel et al. 2020). Indeed, many White, rural Trump supporters even openly supported authoritarianism (Knuckey and Hassan 2022).

This pattern is partly, but not entirely, explained by spatial differences in economic opportunity. As Trujillo and Crowly (2022) note, "local economies of Republican-leaning districts are declining in terms of income and gross domestic product, while Democratic-leaning districts are improving." However, economic differences are often overshadowed by cultural concerns, including widespread conservative over racial and gender equality, LGBT rights, and gun rights. Because the mass media are primarily based in large cities, many rural inhabitants feel their places and lifestyles are misrepresented as retrograde, backwards, and ignorant. All of these factors, economic and cultural, define the terrain over which post-truth unfolds.

The geography of the highly educated population – those with college degrees or higher – helps to explain not only the country's economic and political geographies, but also the geography of post-truth. College-educated residents tend to read more, follow the news more closely, be better informed, and vote more frequently than non-college educated ones (Ahearn et al. 2022). Do college-educated people hold a monopoly on truth? Of course not. But higher education tends to give them cognitive and intellectual skills that make them, on the whole, less gullible and susceptible to fake news. University educations – at least good ones – lead people to be more able to contextualize, question assumptions, and be less like to believe in conspiracy theories. They are less likely to be gullible or succumb to confirmation and acceptance biases (Forgas and Baumeister 2019).

Information literacy in rural areas tends to be low. Americans living in rural areas, particularly conservatives, tend to be much more distrustful of the "mainstream media" than their urban counterparts (Hmielowski et al. 2021). Unwilling to accept news from such sources, they are more exposed to fake news, such as that presented on Fox. In the context of Trump's popularity in rural areas, Mehta (2019) documents rural areas' particular susceptibility to fake news during the 2016 election. Disinformation often confirms confirmation biases in such environments, and rural populism is prone to gullibility and conspiracy theories. As the contributors to Fogras and Baumeister (2019) demonstrate, the social psychology of gullibility is manifested in belief in conspiracy theories, fake news, and irrationality. Affect looms large in such thinking. For this reason, populist movements are often plagued by gullibility (van Prooijen et al. 2022).

To be sure, rural denizens are not some homogenous whole, and there are considerable variations among them in terms of class, gender, and ethnicity. Despite persistent myths of the idyllic rural lifestyle, rural residents have often been subject to savage stereotypes that portray them as lazy, poor, backwards, ignorant, and racist. While such tropes are unhelpful and inaccurate, the facts nonetheless indicate that many people in rural areas are less well informed than urban ones. Denied the cognitive skills offered by higher education and inhabiting news deserts, many rural people consume a steady diet of fake news, leading them to become highly susceptible to demagogues, faux populists, and political charlatans. In such an environment, post-truth flourishes and thrives. This trend is not the inherent fault of rural dwellers; it is a result of how capital has hollowed out such regions, abandoned them, and crush their dreams (Edelman 2021).

European Urban-Rural Dichotomies

Europe has large, thriving urban regions with a vibrant creative class, such as London, Frankfurt, Stockholm, and Berlin (Clifton 2008; Boschma and Fritsch 2009; Hansen et al. 2009). These have become the engines of growth for their respective national economies and the continent as a whole. As the creative class has gone global, it has fostered rounds of gentrification in cities across the world. European creative class workers, like their American counterparts, have led the continent into cognitive-cultural capitalism, and made its cities into centers of art, entertainment, tourism, and recreation.

The flip side of this, of course, is stagnant rural areas (Binelli and Loveless 2016; Giannakis and Bruggerman 2020), which exhibit the classic symptoms of low incomes, high unemployment, poor infrastructure and public services, and out-migration of the young. Although the European Union has spent lavishly on rural and agricultural subsidies, the rural-urban divide remains as strong as ever. Uneven spatial development is a stubborn thing. Europe, too, has an urban-rural digital divide (Lucendo-Monedero et al. 2019). News deserts are also found in Europe, although not to the same degree as in the U.S., largely because state regulation there is more pronounced. Examples include Britain (Gulyas 2021) and Sweden (Nygren et al. 2018).

As with the U.S., European rural areas often exhibit distrust of urban ones. Maxwell (2019) notes that "In France, for example, "yellow vest" protesters claim that President Emmanuel Macron's policies favor wealthy urbanites at the expense of poorer rural residents." The urban-rural divide, which is constantly in flux, is also evident in European voting patterns (Kenny and Luca 2021). A wealth of evidence from different countries reveals relatively liberal cities and more conservative rural areas, including Poland (Marcinkiewicz 2018), the Netherlands (DeVries 2018), and France (Ivaldi and Gombin 2015). Large European cities frequently exhibit cosmopolitan attitudes toward immigration (Maxwell 2019). Rural areas, in contrast, tend to be far more populist in their orientation. In the UK, rural areas voted for Brexit far more enthusiastically than did cities, most of which opposed it (Harris and Charlton 2016; Abreu and Öner 2020). Across the continent, opposition to the EU reflects the geography of rural discontent (Dijkstra et al. 2020). Unsurprisingly, rural areas exhibit the strongest support for right-wing populist movements; Momonova and Fraquesa (2020, p. 710) argue "the root cause of the spread of right-wing populism is the fundamental, multidimensional crisis of globalised neoliberal capitalism, particularly pronounced in Europe's countryside."

Rossi (2018), however, challenges this narrative, arguing that cities (at least in the Italian context) contributed every bit as much to the populist wave as did rural areas. Indeed, urban right-wing populism may well be an underrecognized and understudied phenomenon, borne out of housing crises and disgust with corrupt politicians; to the extent that cities are enveloped in this wave, they challenge the prevailing dichotomous geography of liberal/urban and conservative/rural areas. The geographies of post-truth are surely more complex than the simple rural-urban dichotomy would suggest.

Chapter Conclusion

> Nothing in this world is harder than speaking the truth, nothing easier than flattery.
> Fyodor Dostoevsky

Given the concentration of advanced producer services in large cities in the wake of the shift to a knowledge-based economy, metropolitan areas have done reasonably well under neoliberalism, despite the manifest poverty and inequality that are found within them. Professional white-collar workers, with college and university educations, have acquired the cognitive skills to function and prosper. As Scott (2014, p. 573) argues, "Increasing numbers of cities in both the Global North and Global South today are marked by a yawning void between their internal islands of prosperity linked to the global economy, and widely ranging tracts where social and political marginalization is the order of the day." In these urban contexts, diversity is rampant and tolerance relatively high: post-truth has enjoyed its fewest successes in cities.

Conversely, rural areas and small towns the world over have been left behind, and their populations, long marginalized, have exhibited mounting resentment at cities and urban "elites." With lower average levels of education and less access to university educations, right-wing populist movements have flourished in these places, fed by a steady diet of fake news. Many small towns and rural areas, where populations tend to be less well educated than in the cities, suffer from digital divides and lack of media outlets; they are often news deserts. Those deprived of the intellectual skills necessary to do well in a globalized, data-intensive economy are often likewise unlikely to be able to discern the difference between fake news and real news. In environments typified by pervasive gullibility, disinformation flourishes.

Chapter 6
World Regional Geographies of Post-Truth

> The chances of factual truth surviving the onslaught of power are very slim. It is always in danger of being maneuvered out of the world not only for a time, but potentially, forever.
>
> Hannah Arendt

Despite its largely American origins, post-truth has become global. Across the planet, demagogues and populist dictators deploy it to demonize opponents, rationalize unpopular policies, and stir up anxiety and hatred toward immigrants.

Following the overarching theme of this volume, this chapter traces the ways in which post-truth has emerged in different spatial contexts. It holds that neoliberalism has fomented severe income inequality and unpopular political policies, as well as populist movements susceptible to fake news. The geographies of post-truth are therefore reflective of broad trends and processes across the globe and the unique characteristics of individual social formations.

This chapter opens with comments about neoliberalism and post-truth, noting that they arose in tandem; post-truth serves to naturalize neoliberalism, to assuage those marginalized by it, and to enable its assault on democracy. Next it offers a critical world regional geography of post-truth. Post-truth plays out in different ways in different national and regional contexts. In Europe, it bears both similarities and differences from post-truth in the U.S. Russia has become a major exporter of post-truth worldwide. In Asia, post-truth includes fake news about earthquakes, the savage Myanmar regime's attempts to exterminate the Rohingya, Indian Hindutva nationalism, and far-fetched North Korean tales about its Great Leader, Kim Jong Un. In Latin America, *posverdad* largely centers on Brazil's President Bolsonaro, who imported Trump's strategy of perpetual lies and election denial. In the Middle East, autocratic regimes regularly issue forth falsehoods about political opponents, including the Saudi murder of journalist Jamal Khashoggi. Finally, in sub-Saharan Africa, post-truth has been deployed in various ways, most spectacularly in South Africa, where it was harnessed to denialism about AIDS and covid. These regional vignettes serve to illustrate how local cultural and political contexts shape post-truth, lending it a geographic specificity that makes broad but accurate generalizations problematic.

https://doi.org/10.1515/9783110749847-007

Neoliberalism and Post-Truth

Capitalism has long been typified by uneven spatial development; indeed, one might argue that geographical discrepancies in wealth and standards of living are built into the DNA of capitalist societies. This phenomenon occurs at a variety of spatial scales, ranging from the distribution of incomes among urban neighborhoods to urban-rural discrepancies to regional inequalities to the global division between North and South. Numerous authors have examined the contemporary nature of uneven spatial development. For Moretti (2012), intense competitive pressures fostered by globalization and the shift to an innovation-based service economy have accentuated inequalities among cities. Innovative places centered on software or biotechnology are relatively uncommon. Firms agglomerate in cities to minimize transactions costs and share specialized labor pools and information.

The geographies of contemporary capitalism are vital to understanding the emergence of a post-truth world. Like everything else, post-truth societies have sprouted up unevenly. Their growth reflects a multitude of factors, including geographical imbalances in education, access to the media, and job opportunities. It is no accident that post-truth has found its most fertile ground in societies most heavily plagued by neoliberalism. The slowdown in economic growth, rising income inequality, stagnating standards of living, rising prices, unaffordable health care and higher education, and a squeezed middle class have conspired to generate widespread frustration and rage at the current global situation. For the White middle class, long accustomed to comfortable lifestyles, the limits of neoliberalism are particularly galling. Post-truth offers easy, simple, and emotionally appealing explanations for this trend: immigrants, gays and lesbians, and the rising power of women and minorities. As has been widely noted, post-truth feeds upon alienation (D'Ancona 2017; Block 2018; Boler and Davis 2018).

Neoliberalism is open to interpretation, and means different things in different sociospatial contexts, but its dominant contours are clear. Many neoliberal political and economic agendas pushed by reactionary forces are deeply unpopular with the masses: privatization, budget reductions, tax cuts for the wealth, deregulation, extreme income inequality, and environmental destruction. When capitalism enters into one of its periodic crises, such as in 2008, the state bails out failing firms. At the global scale, the structural adjustment policies of the International Monetary Fund reproduce these policies in the developing world. Under neoliberalism the state has been turned into a wing of corporate capital.

It is no accident that post-truth emerged on the heels of the neoliberal social order in the late 20th century. To naturalize and justify its policies, neoliberalism relies on post-truth, the affective politics of resentment and emotion. As Mavelli (2020, p. 58) argues, "Post-truth politics, I will argue, is the instantiation of a sacralized neoliberal 'truth market' that posits ignorance and unreserved belief in the market as necessary conditions of possibility for freedom." In this reading, post-truth is the epistemology of neoliberalism.

Neoliberalism has given forth to an outburst of right-wing ethnonationalist populism around the world (Miller-Idriss 2019; Moghadam 2020). Examples include Trump's MAGA assemblage, the Brexiteers, Germany's Alternative for Germany, France's National Rally, and the political parties of Victor Orban (Hungary), Recep Tayyip Erdoğan (Turkey), Jair Bolsonaro (Brazil), and former Philippine president Rodrigo Duterte. An allegedly left-wing version is found in Venezuela under Chavez and Maduro. Such movements are heavily populated by people disenfranchised by neoliberalism, that is, they are the ones who paid the costs of globalization but enjoy few of the benefits. Such movements vary, obviously, in size, power, ideologies, and goals, but they share in common an affinity for the politics of affect, distrust of "experts," authoritarian tendencies, xenophobia, and anti-immigrant sentiments. Populist movements in conjunction with right-wing media outlets are the primary producers and consumers of post-truth. Undereducated and poorly informed, they are the most likely to believe conspiracy theories about "elites." Authoritarian populist leaders are often skilled in the use of social media: as Farias (2018) writes, "The direct connection between the speaker and mass audiences through social media lends itself to the populist logic: as the interpreter of the people's will, the leader claims to be entitled to bypass the allegedly obsolete democratic procedures that interfere with true representation." In short, there is a strong affinity between populism and post-truth. As Waisbord (2018a, p. 2) notes, "Populism opposes fundamental principles of democratic communication, namely the need for fact-based, reasoned debate, tolerance, and solidarity – essential principles for viable public life in today's globalised and multicultural societies." Populism essentially rejects the possibility of truth as a shared consensus or objective reality. In embracing polarized, dichotomous politics, it holds that truth is a weapon against "elite lies." This is the right-wing version of speaking truth to power. In this reading, facts are secondary to narratives, and are insepa-rable from power. Fact and fiction seamlessly blend into one another. Waisbord (2018, p. 10) argues "Here populism offers a watered-down cocktail of Marx and Foucault – knowledge is ideological and historical, it is embedded in social and power relations, and facts are mere cogs in epistemic systems." Such a worldview is impervious to evidence, data, or opposing views.

Neoliberalism gave rise to an extremely information-intensive form of capital-ism. The glut of information in which most people live in turn has led to an atten-tion economy, a term coined by famed Nobel Prize-winning economist and psychol-ogist Herbert Simon. This notion speaks to capitalism's relentless process of commodification, in this case, of attention. In the current historical era, which has given rise to a population of overworked, time-pressed, and exhausted people suffering from information overload, attention is scarce and competition to get it is intense (Odell 2020). In the age of the internet, the attention economy manifests itself in a perpetual and relentless avalanche of advertising, headlines, reality television, idols, celebrity worship, mobile phones, influencers, Netflix, Google, tweets, email, spam, pop-ups, alerts, updates, upgrades, Facebook "likes," social media addiction, podcasts, clickbait, selfies, blogs, and the like. It is the epistemological equivalent of Baudrillard's simulacra. The onslaught of information allows little time for critical reflection; to quote Neil Postman (1985, p. 66), "facts push other facts into and out of consciousness at speeds that neither permit nor require evaluation." In the attention economy, truth and post-truth are locked in a battle to the death.

Bowing to the new imperatives of the global information and attention economy, the media industry was restructured to fit its needs. Harsin (2015) holds that the proliferating regimes of post-truth reflect the increasingly anti-democratic character of neoliberalism by allowing the ruling class to use analytic knowledge to manipulate appearances and distract the public. In the process, neoliberal capitalism ushered in a "new temporality and spatiality of news production, circulation, and consumption" (p. 327). The gradual decline of trusted mainstream media sources, the closures of many newspapers, and the explosive growth of social media all attest to this transformation and the new landscapes of news production and consumption. The disintermediation of the media placed truth production in the hands of observers who seek and attain fame through social media outlets. Accordingly, variety of "truth markets" arose to serve varied audiences with widely divergent tastes. As once-dominant pillars of the mainstream media eroded, a variety of niche markets and filter bubbles arose and information became commodified. Clickbait reigns supreme. Accuracy gives way to shareability. In the process, the news media changed from providing useful content to affirming confirmation biases. To publics deprived of critical cognitive skills, fake news appears to be real. Herman and Chomsky (1988) famously warned decades ago that the media was skilled at manufacturing consent by relying heavily on elite sources for information; neoliberalism simply deepened, extended, and digitized the process in new ways.

There are other connections between neoliberalism and post-truth (Strassheim 2022). Attacks on experts and expertise are represented as the revolt of the masses against "elites," of common sense against useless book learning, a strategy that disempowers the intelligentsia and professionals. As social media has eroded trust in the public sphere, it has validated the private one: private ownership, private decisions. Truth becomes not a matter of norms and evidence but what serves one to be heard in the cacophony of the market. The disintegration of the social replaces the public good with a different version of freedom, a neo-liberal one: unregulated, individualized, and geared toward profit. Humans become, as a result, not social beings but data points, digital identities to be bought and sold. Moreover, post-truth and neoliberalism share a common contempt for democracy (Brown 2019; Farkas and Schou 2019; Van Dyk 2022), which is made evident in the new ways of manufacturing consent and manipulating public opinion.

European Landscapes of Post-Truth

> Who does not know the truth is simply a fool ...
> Yet who knows the truth and calls it a lie, is a criminal.
> Bertolt Brecht

Much like the United States, Europe too has experienced the travails of neoliberalism, rising income and spatial inequality, populist political movements, and a surge of post-truth in various forms. As with most of the world, Europe has been in the grip of relentless neoliberal assaults, mountains of fake news on social media, and right-wing populist movements.

While the broad contours between the two sides of the Atlantic are similar, there are also important differences. A varieties of capitalism approach to political economy emphasizes institutional differences among countries, acknowledging that capitalism means different things in different spatial contexts (Hancké 2009; Hall 2015). For example, unlike the U.S., Europe retained a powerful tradition of social democracies, generous public benefits, and influential labor unions. This literature need not be recapitulated here; suffice it to say that there are both similarities and differences between two of the world's largest and wealthiest regions.

Like the U.S., Europe too has witnessed a surge of populism, movements of people marginalized by neoliberalism (Mudde 2016). Many are united by Euroskepticism and a fear of mass immigration from Africa and the Middle East. Examples include the UK's Leave movement and the United Kingdom Independence Party, Germany's Alternative for Germany, France's National Rally, Spain's Partido Popular, and Victor Orban's Hungary. Right-wing parties have also recently come to power in Sweden and Italy.

Post-truth in Europe has emerged under somewhat different conditions than in the U.S. Several factors have mitigated its impacts there. While European media has some right-wing outlets, there is no Fox News, a major source of American fake news. However, Rupert Murdoch launched News UK TV in 2021 (Landler 2021), which is similar to Fox; he scaled it back to streaming platforms after concluding there was no market for the American-style network. In Britain, Boris

Johnson's advisor Dominic Cummings called the British Broadcasting Corporation (BBC) the "Brexit Bashing Corporation." The British media have become increasingly "Foxified" with the launch of Rupert Murdoch's News UK TV, launched in 2021, which is managed by a former Fox executive, David Rhodes (Landler 2021). News UK TV has an even more right-wing rival, GB News, which also engages in the continuous grievances found on the American right (Lewis 2021). In France there is CNews (Abdoul-Bagui 2021), and some digital outlets have styled themselves after Breitbart (Heft et al. 2020). Across Europe, conservative populist outlets have proliferated (Aalberg et al. 2016). In France, CNews closely resembles Fox News in tenor. Launched in 1999, it promotes the ideas of the extreme right, such as Marine LePen's National Rally (Abdoul-Bagui 2021). In the Netherlands and Belgium, right-wing populism has become mainstreamed through a variety of channels (Cammaerts 2018). Reactionary digital outlets have proliferated in Sweden, Denmark, Germany, and Austria (Heft et al. 2020). In Germany, outlets associated with or sympathetic to neo-Nazi movements such as Pegida and Alternative for Germany have flourished and launched attacks on immigrants and asylum-seekers (Baugut and Neumann 2019). Block (2018) details the ambivalent relationship between the truth and Spain's conservative Partido Popular. The rise of European post-truth has forced the continent's media to search for new norms of accountability (Eberwein et al. 2019; De Blasio and Selva 2021).

Other factors differentiate European from American post-truth. Most European countries offer free or low-cost university educations (Jongbloed 2004); in the cognitive-cultural capitalist economy, these people are less likely to be gullible and buy into conspiracy theories. Finally, Europeans tend to be more secular than Americans, more conversant in different languages, and often better informed. The result is that while there are certainly reactionary populist movements in Europe, post-truth has not found as fertile ground there.

Post-truth in Europe varies across its national landscapes. Brexit, of course, was the paramount example. But other instances reveal the depth to which the continent has succumbed. The French right, for example, has deployed post-truth strategies to attack the LGBT community (Harsin 2018). In Germany, neofascists mount post-truth electoral campaigns (Conrad 2022). In Italy, former Prime Minister Matteo Salvini spread post-truth lies in a series of tweets, a Europeanization of Trump's favorite tactic (Evolvi 2022). In Poland, the Law and Justice party has demonized immigrants using serial falsehoods; it also circulated conspiracy theories about the 2010 plane crash that killed President Lech Kaczynski.

Hungary's autocratic leader Viktor Orban has spewed forth a fountain of fake news, including lies about liberal billionaire George Soros and claims that the EU was supporting illegal immigration. Orban and his ruling party Fidesz used disinformation to force the relocation of the prestigious Central European University to

Vienna, promote an arch-conservative and authoritarian ideology, attempt a revisionist history of Hungary's role during the Holocaust, and justify Russian interventions. These media have spread disinformation during recent elections in attempts to discredit mainstream and liberal candidates.

Russian Fake News

Beyond the American right-wing mediasphere, the world's largest producer of post-truth, another large machine for the creation of fake news is the Russian government. It uses agents both officially tied to the Russian state and "gray" actors that are not, such as think tanks, pseudo-human rights groups, and non-governmental organizations. It has an array of media outlets at its disposal, including *Russia Today* (now *RT*), *Sputnik, Russia Insider,* and *Rossiya Segodnya.* Russia has cultivated a series of proxy sources, funded by the Kremlin, based in Western countries that keep a veneer of separation from the state to dupe readers that they are independent entities. Russian troll farms have been largely financed and organized by Yevgeny Prigozhin, also known as "Putin's cook." Russia also has a dedicated army of hacktivists whom Putin has called "patriotic hackers," whose actions have become an integral part of Russia's foreign military ventures. Russia's disinformation campaigns are relatively cheap and highly cost-effective.

Pro-Kremlin media have sought to discredit NATO, claimed various Western countries try to normalize homosexuality and pedophilia, portray U.S. allies as unwilling puppets, and justify Russia's sphere of influence as natural and necessary. The U.S. State Department (2022) identifies five dominant themes in Russian disinformation: Russia is a victim; the collapse of the West is immanent; historical revisionism; the "Color Revolutions" were U.S.-manufactured movements; and that reality is whatever the Kremlin says it should be. Russia has falsely claimed that the Ukrainian government banned the use of the Russian language, that Russia has no troops in Ukraine, and that the U.S. promised never to expand NATO. Russia has also spread lies about covid and the QAnon conspiracy.

Unlike the cold war, when Soviet propaganda was ideologically motivated, current Russian fake news appears to be aimed solely at sowing doubt and discord in the West, notably undermining liberal principles of governance. Nonetheless, the goal of Russian fake news resembles that of Soviet *agitprop* and *dezinformatsiya.* Soviet propaganda was stiff, boring, and unconvincing; in contrast, Russian disinformation is sleek, emotionally engaging, and believable. Russia has used a veritable army of bots, trolls, hacktivists, psy-ops, and other tools as forms of information warfare (*informatsionnaja wojna*) and the extension of "soft power." In the Russian view, disinformation is the extension of war by other means. Often the enormous volume of Russian fake news overwhelms Western attempts to confront it effectively.

While Russia's campaign began during its war with Georgia in 2008, it went into full swing following the annexation of Crimea in 2014. As Sukhankin (2019) writes, the post-2008 period was marked by a dramatic increase of 'black propaganda' – an outward vilification of the opponent with very little (if any) consideration for facts." One arm of its campaign is aimed at the "near abroad" (the Baltic states, Georgia, and Moldova), where it sows discord between ethnic Russians and their respective states, while another arm roams further afield, particularly in Western Europe and North America. Such efforts represent transnational cyber-authoritarianism in the service of fake news, or perhaps vice-versa.

One particularly active and virulent source of fake news is Russia's Internet Research Agency (IRA), a troll factory linked to Vladimir Putin and used by the Kremlin to promote its interests in many countries, mostly in Europe (especially Germany and Ukraine) or the U.S. Based in St. Petersburg, where it has more than 1,000 employees (Fig. 6.1), the IRA has become active in meddling in elections and peddling disinformation worldwide (Dawson and Innes 2019). Its goal is to foment mistrust of political leaders and spread propaganda favorable to Russia. It has updated old Soviet disinformation tactics to the digital age and is an integral part of Russia's hybrid warfare efforts. The IRA often leaks documents to Wiki-Leaks. The agency produces memes, tweets, Twitter bots, comments on news stories, and Facebook pages and groups. The agency spoofs personas by creating numerous false account profiles, engages in "follower fishing," and buys Twitter followers ($20 per 1,000). Managers "task" workers with targeting specific topics and countries. As Prier (2017, p. 77) notes, Russia

> has intelligence assets, hackers, cyber warrior trolls, massive bot networks, state-owned news networks with global reach, and established networks within the countries Russia seeks to attack via social media. Most importantly, the Russians have a history of spreading propaganda.

During the 2016 and 2020 U.S. presidential elections, Russia's Internet Research Agency (IRA) was active in spreading disinformation (Lukito et al. 2020). The IRA employs about 600 people as trolls and has a budget of $10 million (Al-Rawi and Rahman 2020); each employee is assigned specific targets. Its aim is specifically to spread disinformation and sow confusion. It is skilled at manipulating content-recommending algorithms to reach large audiences in an elaborate scheme of political astroturfing. The IRA is active on Twitter, Facebook, Instagram, Reddit, and 4chan, and adept at microtargeting audiences based on their age, ethnicity, gender, religion, and political beliefs (Al-Rawi and Rahama 2020). The IRA was par-

Figure 6.1: The Internet Research Agency building, St. Petersburg.

ticularly successful in having tweets from fake accounts appear in public opinion news summaries. It has close ties to right-wing commentators such as Alex Jones and Fox News's Tucker Carlson, and televises segments of his show regularly (e.g., about the Russian invasion of Ukraine).

For example, Russian disinformation likely played a role in Donald Trump's election in 2016 (Bastos and Farkas 2019). Robert Mueller's indictment of the IRA found that the agency "operated thousands of Twitter accounts posing as Americans to weigh in on US political discussions on social media between 2014 and 2017." Jensen (2018) holds that Russian tweets were primarily used to define the identities of Trump and Clinton rather than spread deceptive disinformation. For example, Russian tweets portrayed Clinton as beset by corruption and criminality, and Trump as a heroic figure taking on the political establishment.

The IRA also greatly exaggerated African-American support for Trump. It created a Facebook account called Blacktivist that focused on violent police arrest to sow outrage and discord, and included passionate denunciations of the criminal justice system (Isaac and Shane 2017). It also had pages called "Defund the 2nd" for gun-rights enthusiasts, LGBT United for gay rights proponents, and another for animal lovers. The IRA's Facebook page United Muslims of America highlighted discrimination against Muslim. Another, Being Patriotic, exaggerated the number of refugees being resettled and circulated stories from Alex Jones's Infowars; its posts were shared more than 750,000 times. Yet another, Secured Borders, circulated stories that Muslim men were collecting welfare for multiple wives. Such accounts were linked to Instagram and Twitter. Many of these sites were ultimately shut down by Facebook. The IRA also cribbed complaints about federal agents from conservative websites and edited YouTube videos to maximum effect (Confessore and Wakabayashi 2017). This form of "cultural hacking" illustrates a deft understanding of American politics.

The IRA has also been effective in spreading falsehoods to disrupt elections or spread rumors in Estonia, France, Ukraine, the Czech Republic, Georgia, and, most famously, the United States, where it actively promoted the candidacy of Donald Trump. During the 2016 presidential election, the IRA was very active spreading false stories promoting Donald Trump (Bastos and Farkas 2019). It urged Black voters to stay away from the polls, vote for third-party candidate Jill Stein, and spread the conspiracy theory that the Obama administration had wiretapped the Trump campaign. After the first presidential debate, the IRA started the #TrumpWon hashtag, which spread rapidly. In 2018 the IRA was indicted by Special Counsel Robert Mueller. Its disinformation blends seamlessly with alt-right websites such as Gateway Pundit and Breitbart. The IRA also spread lies about Western vaccines, a fictional chemical plant explosion in Louisiana started by ISIS, that refugees are terrorists, elections are rigged, and started a twitter hoax about racial violence at the University of Missouri. It has organized rallies designed to spread discord, such as Black Lives Matter, Blue Lives Matter, and "Safe Space for Muslims" outside the White House. The IRA also spread lies during the Brexit campaign. This tactic may involve the use of chat bots, or automated programs, to disseminate information virally, as well as fake accounts on social media networks such as Facebook, Twitter, Reddit, Instagram, and Tumblr. It has also promoted the neofascist group Alternative for Germany.

Another source of Russian disinformation is Russia Today, which purports to be a news network that offered coverage of the war in Ukraine, the annexation of Crimea in 2014, the Syrian civil war, Brexit, and U.S. presidential elections, exhibited unabashed "willingness to disseminate partial truths or outright fictions" (Yablokov 2015) in support of the Kremlin.

Russian disinformation also included Putin's ostensible rationale for invading Ukraine in 2022. Putin asserted that Ukraine was ruled by Nazis and thus in dire need of "denazification" (Troianovski 2022). He claimed that Ukrainian was not a different language than Russian. He also argued that Ukraine was an artificial product of the Soviet Union (Schwirtz et al. 2022). Thus is fake news used to justify illegal invasions and occupations in the 21st century.

The Spatiality of Post-Truth in Asia

Post-truth is not a uniquely Western phenomenon and has taken hold in Asia as well (Yee 2017). Adopting the varieties of capitalism approach, Asian post-truth often exhibits unique characteristics based on its historical experience (e. g., colonialism) and cultures, including numerous totalitarian governments that censor the media (e. g., China, Vietnam, North Korea), higher levels of trust in the media and government, a Confucian heritage that emphasizes education, and different norms concerning individualism and social conformity.

With the rapid economic growth of East Asia over the last four decades, many economies have shifted from low-wage manufacturing into services. Large Asian cities are often dynamic centers of capital accumulation with a heavy focus on finance, producer services, and information technology, including Seoul, Tokyo, Beijing, Shanghai, Hong Kong, Taipei, and Singapore. It is not coincidental that the creative class has flourished in Asia as elsewhere (Westlund and Calidoni 2010; Mellander et al. 2013).

The internet has grown rapidly in Asia, where penetration rates are often high, allowing fake news to circulate at the speed of light. Social media and messaging apps are popular, including Facebook, WhatsApp, and Twitter. Other examples include China's WeChat, with more than 860 million users, the instant messaging app LINE in Japan and Taiwan, and South Korea's KakaoTalk. Yet as elsewhere, Asia exhibits a rural-urban digital divide, which leaves rural populations vulnerable to conspiracy theories and fake news.

Asian fake news takes various forms. In Japan, net rightists (*neto-uyo*) have promoted revisionist histories of Japanese colonialism (Ogasawara 2019). Fake news also played significant roles in the 2018 election in Malaysia and the 2019 election in Indonesia (Jalli et al. 2019), and the 2017 election in South Korea (Go and Lee 2020). In Indonesia, doctored videos of the governor of Jakarta, Basuki Tjahaja Purnama ("Ahok") accused him of inviting a Chinese invasion and promoting communism, leading him to be jailed for blasphemy. In several countries, fake news has created covid vaccine hesitancy, including South Asia (Kanozia and Arya 2021) and Indonesia (Muzykant et al. 2021). In Bangladesh, fake news has led to attacks on the country's Hindu minority (Al-Zaman 2019).

Earthquake fake news is another variant of the phenomenon, and it played out during the 2018 Palu earthquake in Indonesia (Kwanda and Lin 2020), when rumors circulated that it was caused by the government and that logistical supplies were being hoarded. After Japan's 2011 earthquake and tsunami event, fake retweets on Twitter caused problems for users of social media.

Indian fake news has been propelled by the Hindutva fundamentalist movement (Iqbal 2019). Under Narendra Modi, the country's first "social media prime minister" and active Twitter user, and the Bharatiya Janata Party (BJP), media outlets have become politicized. Many are used to express overt and often xenophobic nationalism. Zee News and Star News serve as mouthpieces for right-wing Hindu nationalism (Thussu 2007). A social media app, NaMo, is dedicated to Modi and has spread lies. Fake news played an important role in India's 2019 election. Companies like the Srivastava Group have disseminated lies about Pakistan. In addition, Hindu nationalists have spread conspiracy theories, particularly about the country's Muslim minority (Sharma 2023). Rumors circulating on WhatsApp led to the lynchings of hundreds of Muslims (Al-Zaman 2021). Similarly, Facebook, Twitter, Reddit, and GitHub have become integral to what Farhat (2022) calls the "propaganda infrastructure of Hindutva." A common myth circulated by supporters of the BJP is the "love jihad," the notion that Muslim men try to convert Hindu women to Islam through seduction and marriage (Farokhi 2020); the falsehood has led to riots. Other hate speech has been directed at the *dalit*, who have been called termites and cockroaches. Hindutva activists even created a secret app called Tek Fog to propagate hate speech. Another rumor that circulated was that Donald Trump supported Modi.

More broadly, Modi and the BJP have attempted a comprehensive, post-truth discursive rescripting of India in the service of Hindutva (Ranganathan 20222). Elements of this strategy include rewriting India's history so that it appears as the story of a singularly Hindu nation, thus normalizing Hindu nationalism, a marked departure from the secular vision put forth by Gandhi and Nehru. Indeed, the legacy of Gandhi has not done well in the post-truth age (Mishra 2018). The BJP's goal is a greatly revised national memory. This approach ironically mirrors post-modernism's and post-structuralism's argument that history is little more than a set of discourses. Modi and company have also white-washed attacks against Muslims and lionized Nathuram Godse, Gandhi's assassin. This is post-truth in the service of neoliberal ethnic chauvinism.

Like the Spanish-American War, fake news can start other military conflicts: when the Pakistani Defense Minister read a fake story that claimed "Israeli Defense Minister: If Pakistan sends ground troops to Syria on any pretext, we will destroy their country with a nuclear attack," he threatened nuclear retaliation (quoted in McIntyre 2018, p. 111).

Fake news in China has exploded with the growth of social media such as the Facebook knock-off Sina Weibo and WeChat (Tang et al. 2021). In 2016, more than 30,000 fake news stories were posted each day (Cheng and Lee 2019). In a corrupt, totalitarian regime with few civil liberties, this is not surprising; China used stories of Western fake news to enhance internet censorship. The government has denounced stories about its human rights abuses as fake news. Long adept at censorship, the Chinese state is particularly sensitive about issues such as Tibet, Taiwan, and Falun Gong. It developed the notion of the "Three Warfares," psychological, legal, and media. The state-run media is a major source of rumors (Guo 2020) even as the state runs campaigns against fake news, although the country lacks extreme partisan outlets like Fox News. In 2011, in the wake of Japan's disastrous Fukushima accident, Chinese supermarkets ran out of salt after false rumors circulated that it protected against radiation poisoning. During the covid pandemic, social media circulated notions that alcohol consumption stopped the virus. These observations hint at the rise of what Cheng and Lee (2019) call a post-truth China, "where objective facts play a diminishing role, and Chinese people are losing their trust, despite the best efforts of organizations to deal with fake news in crises."

Fake news has been deployed to shape public opinion in the Korean peninsula (Oh et al. 2020). Asia's most extreme and ludicrous example of post-truth is North Korea. The most rigid, oppressive regime in the world, the last holdout of Stalinism, regularly resorts to lies and fake news about its Great Leader, Kim Jong Un. It represents an extreme case of how an authoritarian regime maintains consensus (Cathcart et al. 2014). According to North Korean state media, Kim Jong Un climbs mountains, is a world class composer who wrote six operas, and could drive a car when he was three (see Hem 2017). When he was born, new stars appeared in the heavens and winter instantly turned into spring. He learned to talk at three weeks and walk at eight weeks. The first time he played golf he got 11 holes-in-one (his father, Kim Jong Il, only got five in his first time). He never urinates or defecates. He can teleport and control the weather (Mercier 2020, pp. 128–145). This is post-truth elevated to the level of surrealism.

Often Asian governments also produce fake news. The Philippines' autocratic leader Duterte, for example, used the pretext that the country was a "narco-state" to justify a spate of extrajudicial killings. An on-line army of bloggers demonized the mainstream media, much as reactionaries have done in Europe and the U.S. Duterte waged a public war on media outlets, including revoking the operating license of the digital news site Rappler (Lees 2018). Rappler's director, Maria Ressa, subsequently shared the 2021 Nobel Peace Prize.

In Myanmar, fake news has been used to vilify the Muslim Rohingya minority (Kyaw 2019; Siddiquee 2020). The Rohingya have been portrayed as "illegal Bengali immigrants," Islamic extremists, and "pests" and dogs to erase their ethnicity and justify their mistreatment and expulsion. As with other kinds of fake news, such labels are designed to appeal to raw emotions, inflame hatred, and spread mistrust. Facebook was a favored tool of anti-Rohingya activists (Burrett 2021) and a major venue of hate speech. Buddhist radicals took to YouTube to post videos claiming that the Rohingya posed an existential threat. The Tatmadaw or military set up "Radio Free Myanmar," which spreads misinformation about the opposition National League for Democracy.

The Royal Thai Army used Twitter to spread lies about their political opposition. An account linked to the royal palace was suspended for violating Twitter's rules on spam and manipulation. Prominent Chinese-Indonesians have been targeted with fake videos; for example, the governor of Jakarta, Basuki Tjahaja Purnama, a Christian, was falsely portrayed as criticizing Muslims and lost his bid for re-election (Anwar 2021).

Neo (2022) notes that the governance of fake news in Asia is geographically uneven. He notes (p. 391) that "crackdowns on fake news occur more frequently in countries less affected by fake news." Those without broad media freedom tend to be the least affected. Some countries have securitized it, portraying as an existential crisis and using it as an excuse to curtail civil liberties. For example, in 2016, the Cyberspace Administration of China proclaimed that it was "forbidden to use hearsay to create news or use conjecture and imagination to distort the facts" (quoted in Yee 2017). In claiming to protect the country's social order, the government suppresses any information it deems dangerous. Other countries, such as Japan and South Korea, created agencies to detect and trace disinformation. Thailand formed an Anti-Fake News Center. Singapore imposes jail sentences and fines for Internet publishers who fail to correct "online falsehoods" that harm the public interest.

Posverdad: Latin America Grapples with Post-Truth

> Truth never penetrates an unwilling mind.
> Jorge Luis Borges

Latin America, too, has grappled with the epidemic of post-truth, although the topic has been studied far less in this context than elsewhere. In 2017, the neologism *posverdad* was included in the *Diccionario de la Lengua de Real Academia Española*, which defines it as "The deliberate distortion of a reality, which manipulates beliefs and emotions for the purpose of influencing public opinion and social attitudes." The evidence of a flood of post-truth is everywhere: government decisions that are not based on scientific evidence; fake news circulating with abandon; claims of election denial; vaccine denialism; and emotionally charged political circulating on social media.

Traumatized repeatedly by neoliberalism, Latin America has seen a surge of populist political movements on both the left and the right (Weyland 2003). Deep income inequality and years of IMF-sponsored restructuring programs have left vast swaths of people unhappy and resentful. The region has a long and tumultuous history of populism (Weyland 2001) that includes, most famously, Juan Peron's Argentina in the late 1940s and early 1950s. More recent examples include Evo Morales in Bolivia and Rafael Correa in Ecuador. These represent liberal populism, which is quite different from its right-wing counterpart.

As in other parts of the world, Latin American politics have become increasingly mediatized, and its media increasingly politicized. Many internet users in the developing world rely on their smart phones for internet access (Tombczyk et al. 2019). Popular leaders are often "tele-presidentes": Hugo Chavez launched a television show, *Aló, Presidente* and Luiz Inácio Lula gave hundreds of radio interviews on *Café com o Presidente.* The explosive growth of Latin American social media has also played a role in fertilizing the fields of post-truth. Many Latin American leaders are conversant on platforms such as Twitter (Waisbord and Amato 2017).

The changing corporate structure of Latin American media has also played a role in fomenting populist unrest. Given its traditional oligopolistic structure, in which television and radio companies colluded with the government, politicians only needed to woo a handful of executives to have access to large audiences (Boas 2013). Most television stations, for example, are owned by privately held rather than publicly-traded companies, which minimizes disclosure requirements. However, in the wake of the digital revolution, the media have become more decentralized. Many conservatives use the flattened hierarchies of the media to attack liberals and promote fearmongering and reactionary worldviews, including attacks on American liberals. The digital revolution has seen rapid increases in right-wing media outlets (Hedges 2016). Like elsewhere, Latin American netizens are prey to the algorithms that re-affirm confirmation biases and lock users into information bubbles where opposing views are unheard. For users who are marginally literate digitally, this poses especially severe problems (Vannini and Rega 2020). For example, many users believe Facebook *is* the internet. In addition, some outlets, such as the American-based Americano Media, serve as conduits between Latin American and U.S. Hispanics.

Not coincidentally, conservative populism, social media, and post-truth erupted in Latin America almost simultaneously (Siles et al. 2021). For example, Twitter enables the type of horizontal communications favored by right-wing rhetoric, avoiding oversite by gatekeepers. Locked into echo chambers and bubbles, social media users easily differentiate between in-groups and out-groups. In this environment, *noticias falsas* and *posverdad* flourish.

Latin American post-truth draws on the rich literary tradition of magical realism (Hart and Hart 2021). Literary tropes pioneered by the famed Colombian novelist Gabriel Garcia Marquez's *One Hundred Years of Solitude*, for example, position the reader as arbitrator of competing narratives. Spectral figures such as ghosts draw "attention to the now-you-see-me-now-you-don't dilemma of the Post-Truth universe" (Hart and Hart 2021, p. 161). Post-truth imitates magical mysticism's mystique, its romantic allure, the exciting hint of the mysterious. Both post-truth and magical mysticism operate at the level of affect, more concerned with feelings and emotions than fact and data.

Perhaps the most spectacular contemporary example of Latin American post-truth was Brazil's Jair Bolsonaro, the "Trump of the Tropics." He was elected in 2018 after Brazil right-wing media attacked his predecessor: Globo Media orchestrated the impeachment of President Dilma Roussef and strongly supported Bolsonaro (Van Dijk 2017). Rather than protect democracy as the "Fourth Estate," a view of the media widely popular in North America, some media segments actively worked against it (De Albuquerque 2019). After a campaign that heavily criticized mainstream media's "fake news," Bolsonaro "was elected president in large part based on a strategy of spreading huge amounts of lies through social media" (Perini-Santos 2020, p. 226). He became a world-famous figure for his dismissal of democracy, adulation of Brazil's military regime that ruled from 1964 to 1985, unparalleled support for the country's agribusiness sector, and enthusiastic endorsement of unlimited exploitation of the Amazon rainforest. Nicknamed "Captain Chainsaw," he blamed fires there on environmental groups. Perini-Santos (2020, p. 241) holds that like Trump, "He does not even seem to mind that his lies are so easily debunked, probably because most of his supporters do not care either."

For good reason do Fleury et al. (2022) call his regime a post-truth government, pointing to the Bolsonaro government's attacks on science, particularly that concerning climate change. Bolsonaro's post-truth included attacks on disciplines associated with critical thinking in the humanities and social sciences such as sociology and philosophy (de Oliveira Gomes 2021). His Education Ministry cut thousands of scholarships in both disciplines (Seabra and Vasconcellos *de Verçoza 2019*).

Brazilian post-truth has been enabled by its media. The traditional Brazilian media has long been highly oligopolized, and its right-wing owners have not been shy about using their outlets to promote fake news. For example, the country's leading newspaper, Folha de São Paulo published on its first page an invented, patently false criminal record of President Dilma Rousseff, and only corrected the information 20 days later, by which time the damage had been done (Perini-Santos 2020). The rise of post-truth in Brazil was also hastened by the creation of news deserts, which have popped up around the country in the wake of the oligopolization of the nation's media (da Silva and Pimenta 2020). The digital revolution clobbered small local outlets with independent editorial decision-making powers. Today, roughly 30 million Brazilians live in towns with no effective news service, creating fertile ground for conspiracy theories.

Like Trump, Bolsonaro weaponized covid disinformation (Ricard and Medeiros 2020), denying the virus's lethality, ignoring evidence about the effectiveness of masks and social distancing, and promoting fake cures like hydroxychloroquine. He falsely claimed of covid that "90% of people infected will not feel any symptoms" and "if I contracted COVID-19, because of my athletic background, I wouldn't feel anything or at most the symptoms of a gentle flu" (Ricard and Medeiros 2020). He bizarrely claimed that vaccines could turn people into crocodiles or bearded ladies (Zitser 2020). He refused to follow World Health Organization guidelines and claimed that covid was a form of "biological warfare." As a result of his disastrous response, Brazil suffered one of the highest covid caseloads in the world (Canineu and Muñoz 2021).

Like Trump in 2020, Bolsonaro lost his 2022 bid for re-election. Taking a page from Trump's playbook, he refused to concede, skipped his successor's inauguration, and threatened violence. Like Trump, he repeated claimed he lost because the election had been rigged (Nicas et al. 2022), casting Brazil's electronic voting machines into doubt. In this respect, he borrowed tactics and rhetoric straight from Trump, with whom he and his family have close ties (Kranish and Stanley-Becker 2023). The post-truth that emanated from him and his followers culminated in a mob storming federal government offices in Brasilia on January 8, 2023 in an unsuccessful attempt to reverse the election results, a revolt eerily similar to the January 6, 2021 attack on the U.S. Capitol building. More than 1,500 protestors were arrested, and the Brazilian Supreme Court initiated an investigation of Bolsonaro's role. Typically attempts to overthrow democracies in Latin America originate with a caudillo and the military, but this one was propelled by a mass guided by a delusion. Post-truth in the form of election denial raised its head again to threaten democracy. Notably, it reveals international ties, i. e., U.S. exports of election denial, indicating that post-truth is not static or place-bound, but fluid, mobile, and dynamic.

In the grip of left-wing populism, Venezuela is another example where post-truth has run rampant. Using the 2004 Law of Social Responsibility in Radio and Television, media outlets can be shut down for offenses such as showing "disrespect toward legitimate institutions and authorities." Under the administrations of both Hugo Chavez and Nicolas Maduro, the government has issued forth a steady stream of disinformation (del Mar Ramirez-Alvarado 2020). The Maduro regime blamed the U.S. for all of its problems and accused it of attempting to assassinate its president (Naim 2015). Critics of the regime argue it is hard to square the world's highest inflation and homicide rates with the country's enormous oil reserves. Given the long history of American intervention in Latin America, not all of the government's suspicions are necessarily untrue. In this case, the truth is caught between competing epistemic authorities: the Venezuelan example thus invites us to think about the shifting boundaries of post-truth, its fuzzy edges that encompass competing perspectives on reality.

Opponents of Venezuela's government have also resorted to mistruths, routinely calling its elected leaders "dictators" who only win through rigged elections As Dolack (2019) points out, "The U.S. government is in no position to point fingers, however, given its history in Latin America and the widespread voter suppression that is a regular feature of U.S. elections." Foreign press coverage of the country has also exaggerated its economic crisis, falsely claiming at times that it lacked essential supplies such as aspirin (Cook 2019). And for all the press coverage denouncing it as a dictatorship, opposition parties do score occasional electoral victories (Hawkins 2010).

Given the government's censorship and attempts to restrict news coverage it does not like, Venezuelans have largely taken to smart phones and social media to learn about their country's politics (Nalvarte 2016). Hence, debates about Venezuela often take place on Twitter (Farias 2018). Like other populist leaders, Chavez and Maduro represented themselves on Twitter as heroic figures combatting foreign regimes in the service of the masses, a Manichean struggle between good and evil. Despite their obvious political differences from Donald Trump, the rhetoric resembles that of the MAGA assemblage.

In Mexico, post-truth takes a different form. For decades, the ruling PRI exercised tight control over the media. In the 2000s, it began to experiment with more social media-driven forms of communication, including hackers, spamming, and paid social media commentators. For example, the Enrique Peña Nieto Administration (2012–2018) strategically deployed Peñabots, or automated social media accounts (botnets), to keep unfavorable news from being disseminated to the public (Leiferman and Khrushcheva 2019). Another example concerns the murder and disappearance of 43 students from Ayotzinapa teachers' college in Guerrero in 2014, which went largely unreported for some time until it leaked and provoked a national outrage. Nonetheless, not a single person was held responsible and no bodies were ever found. The same year, when news broke that the First Lady was gifted a mansion by contractors in the Estado de México region when Peña Nieto was Governor, a presidential crony was put in charge of investigating and no charges of corruption were filed. In 2017, it came to light that the Mexican government used surveillance software to hack the smartphones of journalists, activists, and political opponents. In addition, covid disinformation circulated widely in Mexico during the pandemic (Galarza Molina 2022).

In Argentina, post-truth has been used to cast doubt on the number of *desaparecidos*, people murdered by the dictatorship between 1976 and 1983 (Feierstein 2020; Gudonis and Jones 2020). *Clarin*, the country's leading newspaper, has lamented electoral uncertainty, even though, as Pecheny 2019) notes, "Electoral uncertainty is what makes democracy a democracy." Argentine conservatives have effectively deployed social media to challenge conventional political norms and advance highly nationalist explanations of the country's economic crises (Armony and Armony 2005). Conservative bloggers have thrived: for example, Agustin Laje is a right-wing Argentine commentator with 800,000 Twitter followers (Gavozzo 2022).

آخر الحقيقة: Post-truth in the Middle East

> Lying is a disease and truth is a cure.
> Arabic proverb

In the complex and often violent maelstrom of Middle Eastern geopolitics, post-truth has taken several forms. Unlike in the West, in which the producers of post-truth tend to be private bodies, in this region post-truth is often manufactured by the state. The Middle East and North Africa, with a few exceptions, are governed by autocratic regimes that strictly control the media in what might be called "networked authoritarianism." This form of governance is highly conducive to post-truth. For example, disinformation campaigns using social media are one of the most visible dimensions of post-truth politics (Benkler et al. 2018). The Arab Spring uprisings of 2011 allowed social media to shine new light on government actions; unfortunately, the same media allowed post-truth to flourish, particularly when social media was repurposed for government propaganda (Webb and Emam 2021).When it comes to fake news, the boundaries between government-owned and private media are often blurry: Alsridi et al. (2018) claim that "some well-known mainstream media, such as Al-Jazeera TV and Al-Arabiya TV, have recently produced false information through deliberately made-up news stories to divert the public for various reasons, especially during and after the 2011 Arab uprisings."

Fake news in the Middle East is spread either through bots, software programs that mimic human actions online, or by human beings; many governments use cybermilitias or electronic armies (Deibert 2015; Abrahams and Leber 2021), typically people using false names who participate in online forums. Examples of the latter include Iraq's Popular Mobilization Forces and Syria's Electronic Army. The Algerian and Sudanese governments have similar outfits (Schaer 2021). Such forces are used to discredit and intimidate journalists and opposition figures,

Across the Muslim and Arab world, post-truth has reared its ugly head in both democracies and dictatorships alike (Douai 2019). Truth became weaponized in many countries following the Arab Spring of 2011, in which innovations such as citizen journalism popped up in the region. Authoritarian regimes in the region have long spouted disinformation at copious rates. As Douai (2019) puts it,

> Despite apparent rich diversity, the Arab media landscape remains dominated by authoritarian governments hostile to press freedom. ... Conspiracy theories about the machinations of Israel, the Jewish Lobby, and the US and Western quest against Arabs routinely find air and credence in Arab audiences and media outlets.

Social media has led to cyberwars across the Middle East (Al-Rawi 2021). For example, when Qatar's Official News Agency was hacked on April 19, 2017 and a false story posted about a non-existent speech by the emir praising Iran, Hezbollah, and Hamas, it drew intense condemnation from Saudi Arabia, Bahrain, Egypt, and the United Arab Emirates. The event led to a blockade of Qatar and severing of diplomatic and trade relations. In the ensuing public relations battle, Saudi trolls claimed that Qatar was conniving with Al Qaeda, and the Qatari-owned Herrods' department store was collecting names and credit card information from shoppers originating from countries that opposed the country (Cherkaoui 2018). In the aftermath, Twitter removed more than 4,200 Twitter accounts from the United Arab Emirates that were directed against Qatar (Leber and Abrahams 2019).

The Syrian government has long maintained an electronic army to promote its view of the world (Al-Rawi 2014) and used it to great effect. A propaganda campaign waged by the Assad regime on social media found enthusiastic backers. These efforts were greatly assisted by Russian cyberoperatives. The Syrian regime waged a disinformation campaign against the White Helmets, a humanitarian group that claims no political affiliation but documented human rights abuses during the civil war (Cosentino and Alikasifoglu 2019). The group was accused of staging attacks and fabricating evidence to cater to the Western media, part of an alleged plot to promote regime change. They were also portrayed as supporting jihadists, and thus not worthy of humanitarian protection.

Following the Saudi government's 2018 murder of *Washington Post* journalist Jamal Khashoggi in its consulate in Istanbul, it attempted to combat negative publicity by saying its officials there were simply "tourists," even though they arrived in the middle of the night armed with bone saws, a narrative met with widespread skepticism. Saudi trolls attacked Khashoggi's credibility, claiming he was killed by Turkey or Qatar, that he had ties to extremist Muslim groups, and that his fiancé is a Turkish spy (Al-Rawi 2021).

In Egypt, fake news played a central role in the 2013 coup against President Morsi, when it was used to announce implausibly large crowds of protestors in favor of the democratic government's overthrow, numbers falsely attributed to CNN and BBC (Shafick 2021). Under Abdel Fattah al-Sisi, yet another autocrat in the service of neoliberalism, the government has greatly restricted freedom of the press and blocked several media outlets. Under al-Sisi, the Egyptian government began a legal crackdown on "fake news" (Khaled 2019). When a young, female Polish tourist, Magdalena Zuk, died on holiday in Egypt in 2017, fake news stories that she was murdered circulating on social media caused immense damage to the country's tourism sector and straining relations between Egypt and Poland. Post-truth has also contaminated the Middle Eastern geopolitics of water (Wheeler and Hussein 2021): for example, Egyptian authorities, upset about the Grand Ethiopia Renaissance Dam on the Nile River and its potential to affect downstream flows, asserted baselessly that it was poorly designed and likely to collapse.

In the ostensible democracy of Turkey, President Recep Tayyip Erdoğan has exercised strict control over the media in an increasingly authoritarian regime, one of many promoted by neoliberalism worldwide. Following the 2013 Gezi Park protests, social media became a vehicle for manipulating public opinion and spreading pro-government disinformation. The ruling party, the AKP, developed a semi-official "Twitter army" called the AKtrolls toward this end with an estimated 13,000 trolls, a *de facto* propaganda wing of the state (Saka 2018; Cosentino and Alikasifoglu 2019). Turkish post-truth witnessed another surge following the abortive coup attempt on July 15, 2016, which was mercilessly crushed. Turkish officials called it a "Gülenist putsch-in-the-making" (Tas 2018) after the exiled social critic and activist Fethullah Gülen, Erdoğan's nemesis. The president blocked normal investigative channels and exercised state authority to control the narrative around the event, inundating the media with false claims. Its arguments were emotive rather than factual, drawing on Ottoman and religious notion in an appeal to its nationalist base. It claimed the coup attempt was sponsored by NATO to enforce regime change; that American generals were behind the event; that Gülen was a Jewish agent of the Vatican, or he was a Christian priest leading a crusade against the country; and that the coup was part of a broader Western assault to stifle Turkey's economic growth. Erdoğan himself "described the post-coup repression as "a clash between the cross and the crescent" (Tas 2018, p. 8). Opposition political figures with no ties to Gülen were accused of being his co-conspirators. Gülen was even accused of manufacturing earthquakes to destroy the country! In this climate, any criticism of Erdoğan or the government was portrayed as an attack on the entire nation. Conversely, Erdoğan was portrayed as restoring the lost glory of the Ottomans.

As Farzani (2016) points out, "In Iran, post-truth news is old hat." Iranian state-run television reports that all of the country's problems are the fault of the Great Satan, the U.S. Thus, the Sept. 11, 2001 attacks on the World Trade Center were initiated by Americans themselves to justify the invasions of Afghanistan and Iraq. Later, this narrative shifted to blame Saudi Arabia. Farzani (2016) notes that

"Iranian state TV never covers conflicts that are too complex for a post-truth snap-shot." Fake news spread anxieties about covid vaccines. The Iranian Twittersphere has served both the mullah regime and its opponents. False allegations against protestors flourished after the demonstrations began in 2022, claiming that they were atheists, murdered police officers, and threatened national security (Dehghan and Glazunova 2021; Rahmanian 2021).

Finally, post-truth has appeared in Israel as well. Critics of Zionism aptly dismiss its lies about Palestine, such as the oft-cited phrase "a land without people for a people without land." The phrase actually originated with 19th century Christian writers (Muir 2008). Palestine was home to hundreds of thousands of Palestinians before the creation of Israel in 1948, many of whom fled in the ensuing *nakba* or disaster.

Post-truth continues to haunt Israel. In the 2019 election, false tweets circulated that the politician Avigdor Liberman wanted to ban the Jewish commandment of circumcisions. Like Donald Trump, Benjamin Netanyahu rode a wave of populist anger into power; like Trump, he regularly dismisses media coverage with which he disagrees as "fake news" (Heller 2019). Allegations of corruption against him are a "witch hunt." The rise of Likud represents the triumph of neoliberalism in Israel; fake news is its favorite weapon to legitimize its political agenda. Likud leaders have circulated stores that Labor Party politicians were secretly Arabs hiding their ethnicity, that all Palestinians are a threat to national security, and that Jews opposing the occupation of the West Bank are traitors. Zionists regularly engage in blatant anti-Muslim tactics by demonizing Palestinians. They claim to want a solution to the very predicament that put them in power. Israeli scholars have blamed Palestinians for their water shortages, overlooking the deep distributional inequalities in the region (Wheeler and Hussein 2021). Even worse, Israeli settlers on the West Bank have dismissed violence against Palestinians as "fake news" despite video evidence to the contrary (Stein 2021).

Like Israel, the Palestinians have confronted a viral wave of fake news. Most are highly distrustful of Israeli authorities, which they dismiss as spreading Zionist propaganda. The corrupt and incompetent Palestinian Authority has little credibility and is often charged with promulgating falsehoods; Hamas fares little better. Marshaqa (2020) notes

> fake news in Palestine is also influenced by additional factors specific to the Palestinian context, such as the ongoing unlawful Israeli occupation of the Palestinian territory, political division, weak governance structure and the absence of relevant laws.

Post-Truth with African Characteristics

> The truth is the world's secret.
> Zulu proverb

Post-truth may have originated in the global North, but it has invaded the South with a vengeance. Africa offers examples. In this case, post-truth assumes forms shaped by the colonial legacy, tribal conflicts, and other forces unique to the African continent. Africa has a long history of fake news, where "truth regimes remain both loose and contested" (Ogola 2017). Fake news and post-truth have flourished in the wake of electoral crises, civil wars, economic instability, and state-run media that often propagate half-truths. As elsewhere, African political leaders often manipulate news to mobilize mass support. As Prinanda (2019) points out, African post-truth varies across the continent depending on local circumstances, cultures, and political assemblages.

While internet penetration rates in Africa are not as high as in most of the world, nonetheless social media there has grown rapidly, creating fertile fields for post-truth to flourish. In 2022, 43% of the continent accessed the Internet, and 21% used Facebook. As in other parts of the world, this trend has undermined traditional media outlets and given rise to a wide variety of voices, some of which propagate fake news.

Fake news has eroded media trust in various parts of Africa (Wasserman and Madrid-Morales 2019; Wasserman 2020), plunging parts of that continent into the post-truth era (Okoro and Emmanuel 2018). For example, in Cameroon in 2017, false stories circulated on Facebook supporting the Anglophone secessionist movement (Nounkeu 2020), an event that entered into the country's electoral politics. Indeed, across the African continent secessionist movements have effectively deployed post-truth as a political weapon (Barlow 2020).

In Uganda, Trotter and Maconachie (2018) note that "Fact-checking recent governmental speeches and policies reveals a hefty presence of post-truth politics in Uganda's energy sector." In this case, post-truth took the form of overly optimistic proclamations about the country's electricity planning and prices, However, they point out that for the most part, post-truth failed when confronted with the observable reality of Uganda's energy poverty.

African elections have been tarred by fake news. In Nigeria, politicians employ "propaganda secretaries" to shape political discourses (Hassan and Hitchen 2019). In Kenya, Twitter, Facebook and WhatsApp were used to spread disinformation during the 2017 election (Sambuli 2017; Maweu 2019). During the 2018 Zimbabwean election, both ZANU and its opposition, the Movement for Democratic Change, resorted to cyber-propaganda (Ncube 2019). Similarly, fake news arose during elections in the Ivory Coast in 2010.

Sometimes African fake news is simply silly. In 2016 in Eritrea, fake Twitter posts claimed that the government mandated that all men to marry two women to raise the country's birth rate (Evon 2016). Other interventions are more serious. Some African governments have turned fake news on its head, using it to punish political opponents. In Tanzania, President Magufuli closed the newspaper *Daima* because it allegedly spread "false information."

Fake news has particularly prevalent in South Africa. Economists there worry about post-truth "fakenomics" (Keeton 2018). Post-truth has been used to foster xenophobia (Chenzi 2020), where it has incited violence between nationals and immigrants. As the economic hub for the southern part of the continent, South Africa attracts many workers from other countries. Fake news demonizes them and reduces them to criminals. In South Africa, satirical "news" programs parody the real thing, undermining official narratives, but has also been used to defend corrupt politicians such as Jacob Zuma as the victims of White racism (Wasserman 2020). The Guptas, an influential family in South Africa, deployed bots to deflect criticisms that they had engaged in state capture (Mare and Matsilele 2020).

In post-apartheid South Africa, historiography has become the center of heated debates that often flirt with post-truth (Bam-Hutchinson 2020). Often these controversies unfold in universities (Horsthemke 2017, 2022). At the University of Cape Town, the 2015 "Rhodes Must Fall" movement, which started as an effort to take down a stature of the famous colonialist, erupted into a broader attempt to decolonize the curriculum; in its wake, ferocious debates broke out about the "true" meaning of history, a subject of continuous and inevitable disagreement. Horsthemke (2022, p. 115) notes that in this context, "The intercultural imperative of accommodation and acceptance has entailed a radical reconsideration of truth." Similar protests and debates occurred in other South African universities as well as in the United Kingdom and the United States.

Sometimes lies told by opportunistic politicians have devastating effects. For example, South African president Thabo Mbeki claimed that anti-retroviral drugs used to treat AIDS were part of a Western plot, and that the disease could be cured with garlic and lemon juice, leading to the deaths of 300,000 people (Boseley 2008). AIDS denialism was compounded by quacks, who sold "cures" such as *ubhejane*, Zulu for "black rhinoceros" and promoted fears of antiretroviral drugs, which do work (Specter 2007). Similarly, Mbeki and his health minister, Tshabalala-Msimang, promoted useless remedies such as Virodene, an industrial solvent, and Secomet V, which is made from clover. Denial that AIDS is spread by HIV led men who infected partners to deny that they were responsible. As a result, South Africa has the world's largest population of HIV-infected people.

During the covid pandemic, fake news in Africa led to widespread disinformation (Ahinkorah et al. 2020; Bangalee and Bangalee 2021), often leading the public to reject scientific claims and embrace unscientific ones about how to stop the spread of the virus. Social media has been central to the propagation of covid falsehoods. As Ahinkorah et al. (2020) note, "various conspiracy theory on COVID-19 range from the creation of a biological weapon to break the economic power of China against other economically endowed nations like the US to the use of local herbs or products (e.g., coconut oil, ginger, garlic) to cure the virus have been asserted on various media platforms." Similarly, Schmidt et al. (2020) "found that false information circulated on social media not only instigated confusion, fear and panic, but also contributed to the construction of misconceptions, othering and stigmatizing responses to Covid-19." In some cases, the geography of African vaccine hesitancy and denialism was shaped by the earlier history of AIDS denialism (Jaiswal 2020).

Chapter Conclusion

The geographies of post-truth unfold across the world at multiple scales and in a variety of national and local contexts. For this reason, post-truth means different things in different places.

Driving the global surge of post-truth has been neoliberalism. Because it promotes highly unpopular political policies, neoliberalism must disguise itself: post-truth is the cloak that hides the ugly reality of privatization, deregulation, and tax cuts for the wealthy and corporations. Instead, populist supporters of neoliberalism foreground culture wars that put the onus of blame on immigrants, mythologized "elites," and demonized progressives. Thus, the contours of digitized, information-intensive, and globalized neoliberalism are clear across the globe.

All over the world, the conservative mediaverse has fuelled the rise of right-wing populism (Tumber and Waisbord 2021). Unfortunately, fake news is not only an American or even Western phenomenon. It has sprouted up in a variety of contexts, particularly in countries ruled by autocratic politicians. Just as truth is the first casualty of war, so too is it the first casualty of dictators who manipulate news to mold public opinion. Closely intertwined with this phenomenon is the fabrication of post-truth geographies of various sorts, such as those associated with immigrants, the coronavirus pandemic, vaccines, and climate change denial.

Fake news varies as well among the world's major regions. In Europe, post-truth often resembles that in the U.S., with a well-educated, urbanized creative class and lagging rural areas. Conservative British tabloids perhaps most closely mirror the frequent deceptions issued by Fox News, and helped to pave the way for the disaster that is Brexit. Russia is a major exporter of post-truth through its Internet Research Agency, which has propagated falsehoods across the West. In Asia, post-truth can be found in a variety of different national contexts, where it has interfered with elections, earthquake recovery, and attempts to address the covid pandemic. Indian post-truth in the service of Hindutva is particularly venomous, as are the anti-Muslim falsehoods directed against the Rohingya in Myanmar. In Latin America, *posverdad* has flourished in the wake of populist movements, notably in Brazil, where Bolsonaro is a leading practitioner. In the Middle East, governments have wielded post-truth like a cudgel against political opponents, as illustrated by the lies spread by the Iranian regime, Turkey's Erdoğan, and Saudi attempts to vilify Khashoggi after they murdered him. Finally, in Africa, post-truth has interfered with elections and strategies to contain the AIDS epidemic there.

All of these examples serve to illustrate that post-truth is not some abstract academic debate among a small group of esoteric philosophers. On the contrary, post-truth has serious social origins and social consequences. The spatiality of post-truth – its urban-rural differences, national variations – is essential to comprehending where, how, and why it emerges, and its differential impacts. Perhaps its geographic variability undermines the very coherence of the notion: there is not *one* post-truth, but many, each tailored to its concrete temporal and social circumstances.

Chapter 7
Conclusions: Contours of Geography in the Age of Fake News

> Beware of false knowledge: it is more dangerous than ignorance.
> George Bernard Shaw

Life on the moon. Non-existent weapons of mass destruction. Covid vaccination hesitancy. Brexit. Macedonian teenagers spreading lies. Election denial. A fake border wall with Mexico. Climate change denial. Rumor bombs. Deepfake videos. Rumor bombs. These diverse examples not only illustrate the multiple forms of fake news, but also point to how resoundingly spatial the post-truth world can be. Knowledge, including truth, is never free of its historical and geographic contexts; the same is true of post-truth.

As we have seen, "truth" has multiple definitions. By far the most popular, and the one that underpins science and most everyday interpretations, is the correspondence theory, which holds that truth arises from an isomorphic mapping of statements onto facts. This notion, which arose during the Enlightenment, places a premium on data and evidence, and underpins epistemologies such as empiricism and positivism. This notion of truth has been essential to modern science.

But, alas, facts are not quite what they seem to be. Facts have a history, and their boundaries are often fuzzy. Take, for example, Mandelbrot's (1967) famous dissection of the British coastline, which introduced fractals. The given "fact" of the length of the coast depends heavily on how fine a measure one uses. Are "facts" then products of how we measure and understand reality rather than simply reality unproblematically presenting itself to us? Moreover, the facts never speak for themselves; they are always interpreted. There certainly exists an objective reality, but we only know it subjectively. For this reason, the strict separation of facts from values is problematic. Both phenomenology and the pragmatist theory of truth grounded the notion in everyday life: experience comes before knowledge. Truth is mediated through language and rooted in our assumptions about how the world functions. To socialize truth is to view it as partial, selective, and embodied. Truth is a story we tell about the world, and ourselves, to convince others and get things done.

All of these comments point to the notion that truth is not some given object "out there," but produced, and, thus, always a reflection of its social circumstances. What is assumed or taken to be true has varied over time and space. An enormous body of thought that arguably began with Nietzsche has relativized truth, knocking it off its perch of objectivity and revealing that truth hides its social origins. Truth

https://doi.org/10.1515/9783110749847-008

may serve one class and not another; truth is gendered; false "truths" such as racism are obviously dehumanizing. This line of thought need not lead one into endless – and unproductive – relativism, such as that unleashed by postmodernism. Rather, it forces us to resituate truth from an abstract Platonic realm of pure ideals into the messy world of social reality. Moreover, as Foucault so powerfully showed, truth is always linked to power: its purpose is to further an interest. Once we let go of the idea that truth is a set of beliefs grounded in facts and objective reality, we enter a world in which truth is slippery, changes over time, varies over space, and reflects the circumstances of its making. There is not one, single truth, but many. In short, we must see truth(s) as a social construction.

The rise of post-truth reflects a long, fascinating but sordid history of lies and propaganda. The use of deceit is, of course, as old as humanity. Fake news erupted periodically in Western history, often to sensationalize news stories (e.g., yellow journalism and contemporary tabloids) or to spread propaganda. Religion and racism are two of the greatest forms of fake news in world history. Political propaganda has legitimized one vicious regime after another, such as the Nazis and Soviet agitprop. Militaries have frequently used propaganda in the weaponization of truth. Corporations have used false advertising in the service of enhancing profits, commercializing post-truth. Even photography and video can be manipulated to distort reality.

Fake news has been repeatedly deployed by racists and nativists against immigrants and the politically weak. It has been weaponized against people of color, the LGBT community, and a vast assortment of "others." Notably, post-truth almost never "punches up," i.e., engages in critiques of wealth and power. Only the absurd conservative rejection of "elites" and expertise even begins to approximate this trend. The class bias of post-truth reveals it to be a wholesale assault on Enlightenment values and democracy itself.

On top of this history of fake news, a perfect storm of circumstances catapulted post-truth to the forefront of social and philosophical analysis in the late 20th and early 21st centuries. Post-truth arose under historically-specific conditions, notably the rise of digitized, globalized, neoliberal capitalism. Because knowledge always reflects the social circumstances of its creation, post-truth emerged hand-in-hand with an information-intensive type of capitalism that has commodified consciousness, and everything else, to an unprecedented degree. Neoliberalism's enhancement of class, racial, and geographic inequalities in turn created enormous political polarization, and post-truth has fueled the flames of conflict, undermining trust and threatening democracy. In such a climate, the truth becomes highly politicized: one party's self-evident truths are another's obvious lies and falsehoods. In short, truth serves one tribe and not another.

The explosion of the internet, and with it, algorithms and filter bubbles, led to the endless multiplication of confirmation biases as ever-larger numbers of people sought information from within their own echo chambers. The post-truth era is characterized by loss of control over who determines what is truth and distrust of established media outlets, a fear fanned by right-wing politicians the world over. Once naively celebrated as the harbinger of a new age in which information would be cost-free, the internet instead gave rise to a cacophony that devalued truth itself, a tsunami of "truth decay" (Kavanagh and Rich 2018). The overabundance of news sources allows users to avoid conflicting opinions and obtain information only from sources they like. In essence, social media turbocharged post-truth, replacing the traditional hierarchy of news organizations with an unregulated wilderness in which any opinion is as good as any other. Fake news, predictably, exploded. In this context, fringe views become normalized. The internet and social media have elevated fake news to new heights: think of it as fake news on steroids. Under cognitive-cultural capitalism, the struggle over power centers on the production and consumption of information, including the media, advertising, news, and education.

Postmodernists, among others, long celebrated the death of the Enlightenment, the rise of perspectivalism and the downfall of positivism. In the void that followed, identity politics mushroomed. Yet this triumph is Pyrrhic at best: in such a world, facts and objectivity have become disdained as Western, white, male biases. This is absurd. As Pinker (2018) argues, it is time for a robust defense of Enlightenment values, which have led to major, sustained progress in the human condition worldwide. While the Western world long took Enlightenment values for granted, it has become painfully clear that these must be reasserted and defended strenuously and continuously.

In sharp contrast to Enlightenment values such as objectivity (yes, arguing one is value-free is itself a value), post-truth relies exclusively on emotion and affect. "Post-truth is, first and foremost, an emotional phenomenon" (D'Ancona 2017, p. 126). Appeals to emotions elevate feelings over facts and data. As Tas (2018, p. 14) puts it, "Post-truth politics relies on the propensity of individuals to believe in what feels plausible and intuitively true." One does not have to subscribe to the correspondence theory of truth to be alarmed by this trend, which devalues all forms of empirical evidence. Uncoupling arguments from data opens the door to unfounded allegations and conspiracy theories.

The widespread dissemination of post-truth under neoliberalism did not happen by itself, nor was it a coincidence. Post-truth is produced, by actors with intentions and capabilities. Specifically, it largely arose due to the vast right-wing propaganda machine that emerged in the service of neoliberalism. Faced with an unpopular political agenda, conservatives masked their goals with culture wars, stoking resentment, outrage, indignation, and anger, the primary emotions associated with post-truth. They drew on widespread anti-intellectualism to do so, combining ignorance of history and science with hostility toward the well-educated. Science denialism spread from evangelical circles to become a badge of honor on the right, leading to disastrous movements opposed to vaccines, evolution, and attempts to curb climate change. In the U.S., these efforts were at every turn abetted by the Republican Party and wealthy corporate campaign donors.

More egregiously, the machinery for the manufacture of post-truth included an enormous reactionary mediasphere. Front and center in this infrastructure is Fox News, a wildly popular outlet on the right that is arguably the single greatest source of media lies in the world today. As the propaganda wing of an increasingly reactionary Republican Party, Fox became the model for similar outlets elsewhere, leading to the Foxification of news in Europe and Australia. Innumerable right-wing websites (Breitbart), newspapers (*Washington Times*) and radio programs (Clear Channel, Rush Limbaugh), some even more extreme than Fox, also flourished in this environment. Conservative media has created an alternative universe in which truth, data, facts, evidence, and reason are largely dismissed as constructs of the "lamestream media." For large numbers of people who pay minimal attention to the news, especially the gullible, aliterate, and marginally literate, fake news poses a very real danger. The explosion of right-wing media has created a vast echo chamber in which vast numbers of people willfully subscribe to the falsehoods perpetuated by professional political liars, grifters, and frauds. The result is the construction of multiple, simultaneous alternative realities, each defined by the filter bubbles deployed by different groups. Manjoo (2008, p. 219) asks poignantly, "If you've set up a whole reality that says something false is true, and if so many people have bought into that reality and even defending it – one has to ask, Is it really even a lie anymore?"

Given that millions of people obtain their news this way, it is utterly unsurprising that reactionary conspiracy theories have flourished. Witness the enormous popularity of QAnon, that holds a cabal of Democratic politicians are pedophile baby-eaters. Other conspiracies focus on Jews (George Soros, the Rothschilds, Jewish space lasers), the New World Order, immigrants, and 5G internet. Such falsehoods seamlessly slip into the political domain, generating endless claims about stolen elections by reactionaries who lost them. Donald Trump rode this tidal wave of post-truth to become the greatest prevaricator in world history, telling tens of thousands of boldfaced lies that were enthusiastically repeated by sympathetic conservative media outlets.

The consequences of such rhetoric can be deadly, as in the January 6, 2021 storming of the U.S. capitol building and the 2023 storming of the Brazilian capital by election denialists. Covid vaccine denialism led to the unnecessary deaths of hundreds of thousands of people in the U.S., and likely millions the world over. In Britain, falsehoods and fake news played a central role in the success of Brexit, which has had deleterious effects on the British population. In short, post-truth is no trifling matter. It has hampered the battle against climate change. It encourages racism, sexism, anti-intellectualism, and hatred of immigrants. Post-truth, in short, is a malignant cancer on the world's body politic.

A post-truth world did not emerge out of a vacuum. This state of affairs reflects very real and deep ontological realities of the contemporary world. The triumph of global neoliberalism, the popularity of reactionary ethno-nationalism, and the low barriers to entry afforded by the internet have combined in a perfect storm to unleash a tsunami of lies upon the world, mostly by reactionary political forces. The place where post-truth society has emerged the most quickly and vehemently is the United States; this is no accident, but a reflection of American exceptionalism, the unique combination of historical factors such as a high degree of religiosity, anti-intellectualism, sense of entitlement, and lack of social democracy that typifies U.S. society.

The rise of cognitive-cultural capitalism in the late 20th century set the stage for one of the more important dimensions of the geography of post-truth, the urban-rural divide. All over the world, the growth of financial and producer services generated a series of globalized metropolitan areas linked to one another through vast networks of information, capital, goods, and people. National labor markets reflect this process in the dichotomy between prosperous cities and lagging rural areas. In metropolitan regions, college-educated workers – the creative class – enjoy the fruits of information-intensive capitalism. Their educations tend to predispose them to be less gullible about the lies and conspiracy theories that form the core of post-truth. In contrast, in many rural areas and small towns, gutted by deindustrialization and the flight of the young to cities, post-truth tends to rampage unchecked and confirmation biases are unchallenged. The problem is compounded by the restructuring of the media industry and the rise of news deserts.

Globally, post-truth flourished in the wake of neoliberalism. What does the structure of the world-system have to do with post-truth geographies? Well, actually quite a bit. Globalized, neoliberal, digitized capitalism has set the stage for a post-truth world. To advance unpopular political agendas, including tax cuts for the wealthy and budget cuts for everyone else, right-wing politicians have weaponized truth and turned to boldfaced lies. If they lose an election, it is because it is rigged. Everywhere, neoliberalism has generated enormous income and spatial inequalities. Rural areas and small towns in particular have been marginalized even as the creative class in large cities thrives. The process has generated large pools of disenfranchised, resentful people who are ready, gullible victims of post-truth politics, blaming immigrants, liberals, "elites," experts, scientists, and marginalized groups such as women and ethnic and sexual minorities.

Across the planet, post-truth rages over landscapes unevenly globalized, terrorized by neoliberalism, and exhibiting a vast range of cultural and political contexts. Autocrats in places such as Saudi Arabia, Hungary, Turkey, Egypt, Brazil, and the Philippines seized onto post-truth with enthusiasm. Hindutva reactionaries in India deploy it to great effect. Russia has become the world's largest exporter of post-truth, using it to sow discord and undermine faith in elections in Europe and the U.S. The globalization of post-truth has led to a multiplicity of national variations.

Even worse, post-truth undermines the glue that holds democracies together. Much as neoliberalism poses a direct threat to democracies (Giroux 2018), so too does post-truth. Levitsky and Ziblatt (2018), in their well-received volume *How Democracies Die*, point out that democratic governments are endangered when one side does not play by the rules of fair governance. Fake news and conspiracy theories have become staples of the global right, including Trump, Bolsonaro, Orban, Modi, Erdogan, and others. Election denial has become ubiquitous. Autocrats use post-truth to squash movements for democratic reform. For good reason, historian Timothy Snyder (2017, p. 70) warns that "post-truth is pre-fascism."

Because social processes inevitably play out on the ground, fake news generates numerous post-truth geographies. The denial of climate change is perhaps the most pernicious and destructive. False stories about immigrants, human rights activists, journalists, environmentalists, Muslims, and ethnic minorities are all forms of post-factual spatialities. Because fake news has such pernicious effects, feeding off of and contributing to geographical ignorance, identifying and combatting it are a pressing issue. Attacks on truth and the rise of a post-truth world are not some abstract intellectual concern, but very real political problems. For geographers concerned about research and pedagogy, discerning the difference between truth and falsehood is more important than ever.

There has been much hand-wringing about what to do about post-truth. Various strategies including more widespread fact-checking, holding social media giants accountable, encouraging media literacy in the schools, and higher standards for truth-telling in the media. Yet none of these will work in the absence of a broad-based, global movement for democracy. Dery (2021) notes pithily:

> Circling the wagons around the Enlightenment virtues of skeptical inquiry, evidence-based argument and disinterested science isn't a winning strategy in a post-truth moment. ... Sternly instructing the masses that they've got their facts wrong – "profsplaining," let's call it – is only going to play into popular perceptions of academics as ivory-tower elitists defending their cultural authority against the unlettered rabble.

Moreover, combatting post-truth will require tactics appropriate to varying spatial contexts. In this sense, geography is not simply fundamental to understanding post-truth, but to overcoming it as well.

> Tell a hundred lies a day and it sounds like the truth.
> Barney Warf

References

Aalberg T., F. Esser, C. Reinemann, J. Strombac, and C. De Vreese (eds.) 2016. *Populist Political Communication in Europe.* Routledge.

Abdoul-Bagui, A. 2021. Media and the rise of right-wing populism: gauging the role of CNews in promoting far-right ideology in France. *Open Journal of Political Science* 11(4):752–769.

Abernathy, P. 2016. *The Rise of a New Media Baron and the Emerging Threat of News Deserts.* University of North Carolina Press.

Abernathy, P. 2018. The Expanding News Desert. University of North Carolina Center for Innovation and Sustainability in Local Media. https://www.cislm.org/wp-content/uploads/2018/10/The-Expanding-News-Desert-10_14-Web.pdf

Abrahams, A. and A. Leber. 2021. Electronic armies or cyber knights? The sources of pro-authoritarian discourse on Middle East Twitter. *International Journal of Communication* 15:27.

Abreu, M. and O. Öner. 2020. Disentangling the Brexit vote: the role of economic, social and cultural contexts in explaining the UK's EU referendum vote. *Environment and Planning A: Economy and Space* 52:1434–1456.

Agassi, J. 1991. Popper's demarcation of science refuted. *Methodology and Science* 24:1–7.

Ahearn, C., J. Brand, and X. Zhou. 2022. How, and for whom, does higher education increase voting? *Research in Higher Education* 63:1–24.

Ahinkorah, B., E. Ameyaw, J. Hagan Jr., A. Seidu, and T. Schack. 2020. Rising above misinformation or fake news in Africa: Another strategy to control COVID-19 spread. *Frontiers in Communication* 5. https://www.frontiersin.org/articles/10.3389/fcomm.2020.00045/full

Ahinkorah, B., E. Ameyaw, J. Hagan Jr., A. Seidu, and T. Schack. 2020. Rising above misinformation or fake news in Africa: another strategy to control COVID-19 spread. *Frontiers in Communication* 5:45.

Alba, D. 2020. 'Release the kraken,' a catchphrase for unfounded conspiracy theory, trends on Twitter. *New York Times* (Dec. 17). https://www.nytimes.com/2020/11/17/technology/release-the-kraken-a-catchphrase-for-unfounded-conspiracy-theory-trends-on-twitter.html

Alexander, J., E. Butler Breese, and M. Luengo. 2016. *The Crisis of Journalism Reconsidered: Democratic Culture, Professional Codes, Digital Future.* Cambridge University Press.

Ali, C. 2020. The politics of good enough: rural broadband and policy failure in the United States. *International Journal of Communications* 14:5982–6004.

Allcott, H. and M. Gentzkow. 2017. Social media and fake news in the 2016 election. *Journal of Economic Perspectives* 31(2):211–236.

Al-Rawi, A. 2014. Cyber warriors in the Middle East: the case of the Syrian electronic army. *Public Relations Review* 40(3):420–428.

Al-Rawi, A. 2021a. *Cyberwars in the Middle East.* Rutgers University Press.

Al-Rawi, A. 2021b. Disinformation under a networked authoritarian state: Saudi trolls' credibility attacks against Jamal Khashoggi. *Open Information Science* 5(1):140–162.

Al-Rawi, A. and A. Rahman. 2020. Manufacturing rage: The Russian Internet Research Agency's political astroturfing on social media. *First Monday* 25(9). https://firstmonday.org/ojs/index.php/fm/article/download/10801/9723

Alsridi, H., M. Elareshi, and A. Ziani. 2018. News sites and fake news in the Egyptian political transformation 2013–2014: Aljazeera. net case study. *KnE Social Sciences*, pp.1–14.

Alterman, E. 2004. *When Presidents Lie: A History of Official Deception and its Consequences.* Viking.

https://doi.org/10.1515/9783110749847-009

Al-Zaman, M. 2019. Digital disinformation and communalism in Bangladesh. *China Media Research* 15(2):68 – 76.

Al-Zaman, M. 2021. Social media fake news in India. *Asian Journal for Public Opinion Research* 9(1):25 – 47.

Anwar, S. 2021. The need for improvement of digital literacy to fighting against fake news in Indonesia. *Webology* 18. http://mail.webology.org/data-cms/articles/20211102103854amWEB18251.pdf

Araki, S. 2020. Educational expansion, skills diffusion, and the economic value of credentials and skills. *American Sociological Review* 85:128 – 175.

Arendt, H. 1951. *The Origins of Totalitarianism.* Harcourt, Brace.

Arendt, H. 1968. Truth in politics. In H. Arendt (ed.) *Between Past and Future: Eight Exercises in Political Thought.* pp. 223 – 259. Penguin.

Arendt, H. 1972. Lying in politics. In *Crises of the Republic.* Harcourt Brace.

Armony, A., and V. Armony. 2005. Indictments, myths, and citizen mobilization in Argentina: A discourse analysis. *Latin American Politics and Society* 47(4):27 – 54.

Ashworth, J. and T. Ransom. 2019. Has the college wage premium continued to rise? Evidence from multiple US surveys. *Economics of Education Review* 69:149 – 154.

Atkinson, C. 2019. Fake news can cause 'irreversible damage' to companies – and sink their stock price. *NBC News* (April 25). https://www.nbcnews.com/business/business-news/fake-news-can-cause-irreversible-damage-companies-sink-their-stock-n995436

Atkinson, C. 2019. Fox News apologizes for graphic about '3 Mexican countries.' *NBC News* (April 1). https://www.nbcnews.com/business/business-news/fox-news-apologizes-graphic-about-3-mexican-countries-n989526

Baggini, J. 2017. *A Short History of Truth: Consolations for a Post-Truth World.* Quercus.

Bakir, V. and A. McStay. 2018. Fake news and the economy of emotions: problems, causes, solutions. *Digital Journalism* 6(2):154 – 175.

Ball, J. 2018. *Post-Truth: How Bullshit Conquered the World.* Biteback.

Bam-Hutchison, J. 2020. Decolonising historiography in South Africa: reflecting on 'post-truth' relevance 25 years since Mandela. In M. Gudonis and B. Jones (eds.) *History in a Post-Truth World.* pp. 235 – 250. Routledge.

Bangalee, A. and V. Bangalee. 2021. Fake news and fallacies: Exploring vaccine hesitancy in South Africa. *South African Family Practice* 63(1).

Barbour, K. 2018. Embodied ways of knowing: Revisiting feminist epistemology. In L. Mansfield, J. Caudwell, B. Wheaton, and B. Watson (eds.) *The Palgrave Handbook of Feminism and Sport, Leisure and Physical Education.* pp. 209 – 226. Palgrave Macmillan.

Barclay, D. 2018. *Fake News, Propaganda, and Plain Old Lies: How to Find Trustworthy Information in the Digital Age.* Rowman & Littlefield.

Barker, D., R. Detamble, and M. Marietta. 2021. Intellectualism, anti-intellectualism, and epistemic hubris in red and blue America. *American Political Science Review* 115:1 – 16.

Barlow, E. 2020. Secession in the post-truth, post-order world: a view from Africa. In M. Riegl and B. Dubos (eds.) *Perspectives on Secession: Theory and Case Studies.* pp. 31 – 44. Springer.

Barnes, B. 1982. *T.S. Kuhn and Social Science.* Macmillan.

Barros, A. and S. Taylor. 2020. Think tanks, business and civil society: The ethics of promoting pro-corporate ideologies. *Journal of Business Ethics* 162:505 – 517.

Barstow, D. and R. Stein. 2005. Under Bush, a new age of prepackaged TV news. *New York Times* (March 13). https://www.nytimes.com/2005/03/13/politics/under-bush-a-new-age-of-pre packaged-tv-news.html

Bastos, M. 2016. Digital journalism and tabloid journalism. In B. Franklin and S. Eldridge (eds.) *The Routledge Companion to Digital Journalism Studies.* pp. 217–225. Routledge.

Bastos, M. and D. Mercea. 2019. The Brexit botnet and user-generated hyperpartisan news. *Social Science Computer Review* 37(1):38–54.

Bastos, M. and J. Farkas. 2019. "Donald Trump is my president!": The Internet Research Agency propaganda machine. *Social Media + Society* 5(3):2056305119865466.

Baudrillard, J. 1981/1994. *Simulacra and Simulation.* University of Michigan Press.

Baudrillard, J. 1983. *Simulations.* Semiotexte. http://www.kareneliot.de/downloads/ JeanBaudrillard_Simulations_and_Simulacra.pdf

Baudrillard, J. 1986. *America.* Verso.

Baudrillard, J. 1995. *The Gulf War Did Not Take Place.* Indiana University Press.

Baugut, P. and K. Neumann. 2019. How right-wing extremists use and perceive news media. *Journalism & Mass Communication Quarterly* 96(3):696–720.

Beer, T. 2020. Trump predicted 'covid, covid, covid' would end after the election. It's worse than ever. *Forbes* (Nov. 11). https://www.forbes.com/sites/tommybeer

Belsey, C. 2002. *Poststructuralism: A Very Short Introduction.* Oxford University Press.

Benkler, J., R. Faris, and H. Roberts. 2018. *Network Propaganda. Manipulation, Disinformation, and Radicalization in American Politics.* Oxford University Press.

Benkler, Y., R. Faris, H. Roberts, H., and E. Zuckerman. 2017. Breitbart-led right-wing media ecosystem altered broader media agenda. *Columbia Journalism Review* (March 3). https:// www.cjr.org/analysis/breitbart-media-trump-harvard-study.php

Bennett, W. and S. Livingston. 2018. The disinformation order: disruptive communication and the decline of democratic institutions. *European Journal of Communication* 33(2):122–139.

Bennhold, K. 2017. To understand 'Brexit,' look at Britain's tabloids. *New York Times* (May 2). https:// www.nytimes.com/2017/05/02/world/europe/london-tabloids-brexit.html

Bensinger, G. 2021. Social media is polluted with climate denialism. *New York Times* (Nov. 12). https:// www.nytimes.com/2021/11/12/opinion/climate-change-facebook-glasgow.html

Bergen, P. 2018. Trump's terrorism argument for border wall is bogus. *CNN* (Dec. 13). www.cnn.com/ 2018/12/11/opinions/trump-southern-border-terrorists-opinion-bergen/index.html

Berlet, C. and S. Sunshine. 2019. Rural rage: the roots of right-wing populism in the United States. *Journal of Peasant Studies* 46(3):480–513.

Bernstein, J. 1995. *Recovering Ethical Life: Jürgen Habermas and the Future of Critical Theory* Routledge.

Best, S. 1991. *Postmodern Theory: Critical Interrogations.* Macmillan.

Billing, D. 2003. Generic cognitive abilities in higher education: An international analysis of skills sought by stakeholders. *Compare: A Journal of Comparative and International Education* 33(3):335–350.

Binelli, Chiara, and Matthew Loveless. 2016. The urban–rural divide: perceptions of income and social inequality in Central and Eastern Europe. *Economics of Transition* 24(2):211–231.

Binnie, J., J. Holloway, S. Millington, and C. Young (eds). 2006. *Cosmopolitan Urbanism.* Routledge.

Birulin, O., V. Smirnov, and A. Wait. 2020. The evolving nature of the college wage premium. *Economic Modelling* 93:474–479.

Björnberg, K., M. Gilek, and S. Hansson. 2017. Climate and environmental science denial: A review of the scientific literature published in 1990–2015. *Journal of Cleaner Production* 167:229–241.

Blake, A. 2017. Donald Trump is rekindling one of his favorite conspiracy theories: Vaccine safety. *Washington Post* (Jan. 10). www.washingtonpost.com/news/the-fix/wp/2017/01/10/donald-trump-is-rekindling-one-of-his-favorite-conspiracy-theories-vaccine-safety/

Blake, A. 2020. Trump blames hospitals for mask and ventilator shortages. *Washington Post* (March 29). https://www.washingtonpost.com/politics/2020/03/29/trump-bizarrely-blames-hospitals-mask-ventilator-shortages/

Bloch, M. 1921/2013. Reflections of a historian on the false news of the war. *Michigan War Studies Review* (July 1). http://miwsr.com/2013-051.aspx

Block, D. 2018. *Post-Truth and Political Discourse.* Springer.

Bloomfield, E. and D. Tillery. 2019. The circulation of climate change denial online: Rhetorical and networking strategies on Facebook. *Environmental Communication* 13(1):23 – 34.

Boas, T. 2013. Mass media and politics in Latin America. In J. Dominguez and M. Shifter (eds.) *Constructing Democratic Governance in Latin America.* pp. 48 – 77. John Hopkins University Press.

Bodner, J., W. Welch, I. Brodie, A. Muldoon, D. Leech, and A. Marshall. 2020. *COVID-19 Conspiracy Theories: QAnon, 5G, the New World Order and Other Viral Ideas.* McFarland.

Boisjoly, J., G. Duncan, M. Kremer, D. Levy, and J. Eccles. 2006. Empathy or antipathy? The impact of diversity. *American Economic Review* 96(5):1890 – 1905.

Boler, M., and E. Davis. 2018. The affective politics of the "post-truth" era: feeling rules and networked subjectivity. *Emotion, Space and Society* 27:75 – 85.

Borchard, G. 2018. Yellow journalism: Pulitzer and Hearst battle for readers. In G. Borchard (ed.) *A Narrative History of the American Press.* pp 147 – 166. Routledge.

Boschma, R. and M. Fritsch. 2009. Creative class and regional growth: empirical evidence from seven European countries. *Economic Geography* 85(4):391 – 423.

Boseley, S. 2008. Mbeki AIDS denial 'caused 300,000 deaths'. *The Guardian* (Nov. 26). https://www.theguardian.com/world/2008/nov/26/aids-south-africa

Boudry, M., S. Blancke, and M. Pigliucci. 2015. What makes weird beliefs thrive? The epidemiology of pseudoscience. *Philosophical Psychology* 28(8):1177 – 1198.

Bouie, J. 2018. The Enlightenment's dark side: how the Enlightenment created modern race thinking, and why we should confront it. *Slate* (June 5). https://www.bunkhistory.org/resources/2681

Boycoff, M. and J. Boycoff. 2004. Balance as bias: global warming and the US prestige press. *Global Environmental Change* 14(2):125 – 136.

Branch, G. 2020. Anti-intellectualism and anti-evolutionism: lessons from Hofstadter. *Phi Delta Kappan* 101(7):22 – 27.

Branton, R. and B. Jones. 2005. Reexamining racial attitudes: the conditional relationship between diversity and socioeconomic environment. *American Journal of Political Science* 49(2):359 – 372.

Braun, K. 2019. Unpacking post-truth. *Critical Policy Studies* 13(4):432 – 436.

Brennen, J., F. Simon, P. Howard, and R. Nielsen. 2020. Types, sources, and claims of COVID-19 misinformation. University of Oxford. https://ora.ox.ac.uk/objects/uuid:178db677-fa8b-491d-beda-4bacdc9d7069/download_file?safe_filename=Brennen%2520-%2520COVID%252019%2520Misinformation%2520FINAL.pdf&file_format=pdf&type_of_work=Record

Briggs, C. and C. Mantini-Briggs. 2003. *Stories in the Time of Cholera: Racial Profiling During a Medical Nightmare.* University of California Press.

Broad, J. 2017. Early modern feminism and Cartesian philosophy. In A. Garry, S. Khader, and A. Stone (eds.) *The Routledge Companion to Feminist Philosophy.* pp. 71 – 81. Routledge.

Broad, W. and D. Levin. 2020. Trump muses about light as remedy, but also disinfectant, which is dangerous. *New York Times* (April 24). https://www.nytimes.com/2020/04/24/health/sunlight-coronavirus-trump.html

Broaddus, M., M. Harmon, and K. Mounts. 2011. VNRs: Is the news audience deceived? *Journal of Mass Media Ethics* 26(4):283–296.

Brock, D. and A. Rabin-Havt. 2012. *The Fox Effect: How Roger Ailes Turned a Network into a Propaganda Machine.* Anchor.

Broniatowski, D., A. Jamison, S. Qi, L. AlKulaib, T. Chen, A. Benton, S. Quinn, and M. Dredze, 2018. Weaponized health communication: Twitter bots and Russian trolls amplify the vaccine debate. *American Journal of Public Health* 108(10):1378–1384.

Brown, K. 2011. *Foul Bodies.* Yale University Press.

Brown, R. and Miles H. 2006. An integrative theory of intergroup contact. *Advances in Experimental Social Psychology* 37:255–343.

Brown, W. 2019. *In the Ruins of Neoliberalism: The Rise of Antidemocratic Politics in the West.* Columbia University Press.

Bruni, F. 2020. Donald Trump is the best ever president in the history of the cosmos. *New York Times* (July 25). https://www.nytimes.com/2020/07/25/opinion/sunday/trump-lies.html

Bruns, A., E. Hurcombe, and S. Harrington. 2021. Covering conspiracy: approaches to reporting the COVID/5G conspiracy theory. *Digital Journalism* 1–22. https://snurb.info/files/2021/Covering%20Conspiracy%20(preprint).pdf

Bump, P. 2018. Trump has a new go-to political foil: An imaginary version of California. *Washington Post* (Oct. 23). www.washingtonpost.com/politics/2018/10/23/trump-has-new-go-to-political-foil-an-imaginary-version-california/

Bump, P. 2019. Trump claims that wind farms cause cancer for very Trumpian reasons. *Washington Post* (April 3). www.washingtonpost.com/politics/2019/04/03/trump-claims-that-wind-farms-cause-cancer-very-trumpian-reasons/

Bump, P. 2020. Trump's repeated insistences that coronavirus is under control have reached a critical moment. *Washington Post* (March 16). https://www.washingtonpost.com/politics/2020/03/16/trumps-repeated-insistences-that-coronavirus-is-under-control-have-reached-critical-moment/

Burkhardt, J. 2017. History of fake news. *Library Technology Reports* 53(8):5–9.

Burrett, T. 2021. Journalism in Myanmar: freedom, Facebook and fake news. In J. Morrison, J. Birks, and M. Berry (eds.) *The Routledge Companion to Political Journalism.* pp. 131–141. Routledge.

Byrnes, J. 2015. Trump: refugees "pouring into" US could be ISIS. *The Hill* (Nov. 17). https://thehill.com/blogs/blog-briefing-room/news-campaigns-presidential-campaigns/260420-trump-refugees-pouring-into-us

Byun, S.-Y., M. Irvin, and J. Meece. 2015. Rural/nonrural differences in college attendance patterns. *Peabody Journal of Education* 90(2): 263–279. https://www.ncbi.nlm.nih.gov/pmc/articles/PMC4430117/

Calcutt, A. 2016. The surprising origins of 'post-truth' – and how it was spawned by the liberal left. *The Conversation.* http://theconversation.com/thesurprising-origins-of-post-truth-and-how-it-was-spawned-by-the-liberal-left-68929

Calhoun, C. 1992. *Habermas and the Public Sphere.* MIT Press.

Calvillo, D., A. Rutchick, and R. Garcia. 2021. Individual differences in belief in fake news about election fraud after the 2020 US election. *Behavioral Sciences* 11(12):175–183.

Cameron, C. 2019. Trump repeats a false claim that doctors "execute" newborns. *New York Times* (April 28). www.nytimes.com/2019/04/28/us/politics/trump-abortion-fact-check.html

Cammaerts, B. 2018 The mainstreaming of extreme right-wing populism in the Low Countries: What is to be done? *Communication Culture & Critique* 11(1):7 – 20.

Campbell, W. 2001. *Yellow Journalism: Puncturing the Myths, Defining the Legacies.* Praeger.

Canineu, M. and C. Muñoz. 2021. The toll of Bolsonaro's disastrous covid-19 response. Human Rights Watch (Oct. 27). https://www.hrw.org/news/2021/10/27/toll-bolsonaros-disastrous-covid-19-response

Carey, C. 2016. Breaking the news: telegraphy and yellow journalism in the Spanish-American war. *Periodicals: A Journal of History & Criticism* 26(2):130 – 148.

Carlson, L. 1981. *Indians, Bureaucrats, and Land: The Dawes Act and the Decline of Indian Farming.* Greenwood Press.

Carpenter, A. 2018. *Gaslighting America: Why We Love It When Trump Lies to Us.* Broadside Books.

Carr, P. and M. Kefalas. 2009. *Hollowing out the Middle: The Rural Brain Drain and what it Means for America.* Beacon Press.

Case, A. and A. Deaton. 2022. The great divide: education, despair, and death. *Annual Review of Economics* 14:1 – 21.

Cassino, D. 2016. *Fox News and American Politics: How One Channel Shapes American Politics and Society.* Routledge.

Cathcart, A., C. Green, and S. Denney. 2014. How authoritarian regimes maintain domain consensus: North Korea's information strategies in the Kim Jong-un era. *Review of Korean Studies* 17(2):145 – 178.

Cawalladr, C. 2017. Daniel Dennett: 'I begrudge every hour I have to spend worrying about politics'. *The Observer* (Feb. 12). http://www.theguardian.com/science/2017/feb/12/daniel-dennett-politics-bacteria-bach-back-dawkins-trump-interview

Centola, D. 2020. Why social media makes us more polarized and how to fix it. *Scientific American* (Oct. 15). www.scientificamerican.com/article/why-social-mediamakes-us-more-polarized-and-how-to-fix-i

Cermak, I. 2021. Jumping the shark: White shark representations in great white serial killer lives—The fear and the (pseudo-)science. *Journalism and Media* 2(4):584 – 604.

Cheng, Y. and C.J. Lee. 2019. Online crisis communication in a post-truth Chinese society: evidence from interdisciplinary literature. *Public Relations Review* 45(4):101826.

Chenzi, V. 2020. Fake news, social media and xenophobia in South Africa. *African Identities* 18:1 – 20.

Cheregi, B. 2015. The media construction of anti-immigration positions: the discourse on the Romanian immigrants in the British press. *Revista Romana de sociologie* 26(3/4):279 – 298.

Cherkaoui, T. 2018. A new kind of information warfare? Cyber-conflict and the Gulf crisis 2010 – 2017. *Political Economy of Communication* 6(1):3 – 35.

Chesney, R. and D. Citron. 2019. Deepfakes and the new disinformation war: the coming age of post-truth geopolitics. *Foreign Affairs* 98:147 – 155.

Chidester, D. 2003. Fake religion: ordeals of authenticity in the study of religion. *Journal for the Study of Religion* 16(2):71 – 97.

Chinn, C., S. Barzilai, and R. Duncan. 2021. Education for a "post-truth" world: new directions for research and practice. *Educational Researcher* 50(1):51 – 60.

Chiu, A. 2020. Rush Limbaugh on coronavirus: 'The common cold' that's being 'weaponized' against Trump. *Washington Post* (Feb. 25). https://www.washingtonpost.com/nation/2020/02/25/limbaugh-coronavirus-trump/

Cianciotto, J. and S. Cahill. 2007. Anatomy of a pseudo-science. *Gay & Lesbian Review Worldwide* 14(4):22 – 25.

Clifton, N. 2008. The "creative class" in the UK: an initial analysis. *Geografiska Annaler: Series B, Human Geography* 90(1):63 – 82.

Coady, D. 2020. The fake news about fake news. In S. Bernecker, A. Flowerree, and T. Grundmann (eds.) *The Epistemology of Fake News.* pp. 68 – 81. Oxford University Press.

Cohn, N. 2021. How educational differences are widening America's political rift. *New York Times* (Sept. 8). https://www.nytimes.com/2021/09/08/us/politics/how-college-graduates-vote.html

Collins, J. 2019. "The facts don't work": the EU referendum campaign and the journalistic construction of 'post-truth politics.' *Discourse, Context & Media* 27:15 – 21.

Conboy, M. 2002. *The Press and Popular Culture.* Sage.

Confessore, N. and D. Wakabayashi. 2017. How Russia harvested American rage to reshape U.S. politics. *New York Times* (Oct. 9). https://www.nytimes.com/2017/10/09/technology/russia-election-facebook-ads-rage.html

Conrad, M. 2022. A post-truth campaign? The Alternative for Germany in the 2019 European Parliament elections. *German Politics and Society* 40(1):58 – 76.

Conway, M., M. Grabe, and K. Grieves. 2007. Villains, victims and the virtuous in Bill O'Reilly's "no-spin zone." Revisiting world war propaganda techniques. *Journalism Studies* 8(2):197 – 223.

Cook, M. 2019. Venezuela Coverage Takes Us Back to Golden Age of Lying About Latin America. Fairness and Accuracy in Reporting (Feb. 22). https://fair.org/home/venezuela-coverage-takes-us-back-to-golden-age-of-lying-about-latin-america/

Corasaniti, N., R. Epstein, and J. Rutenberg. 2020. The Times called officials in every state: No evidence of voter fraud. *New York Times* (Nov. 10). https://www.nytimes.com/2020/11/10/us/politics/voting-fraud.html

Cormier, H. 2000. *The Truth is what Works: William James, Pragmatism, and the Seed of Death.* Rowman & Littlefield.

Cortada, J. and W. Aspray. 2019. *Fake News Nation: The Long History of Lies and Misinterpretations in America.* Rowman & Littlefield.

Cosentino, G. and B. Alikasifoglu. 2019. Post-truth politics in the Middle East: the case studies of Syria and Turkey. *Artnodes* 24:91 – 100.

Cosgrove, D. 2012. *Geography and Vision: Seeing, Imagining and Representing the World.* Bloomsbury Publishing.

Cox, C. 1999. *Nietzsche: Naturalism and Interpretation.* University of California Press.

Cramer, K. 2016. *The Politics of Resentment: Rural Consciousness in Wisconsin and the Rise of Scott Walker.* University of Chicago Press.

Crisp, R. and R. Turner. 2011. Cognitive adaptation to the experience of social and cultural diversity. *Psychological Bulletin* 137(2):242 – 266.

Crombie, A. 1980. Science and the arts in the Renaissance: The search for truth and certainty, old and new. *History of Science* 18(4):233 – 246.

Cronin, T. 2008. *On the Presidency: Teacher, Soldier, Shaman, Pol.* Routledge

Culloty, E. and J. Suiter. 2021. Anti-immigration disinformation. In H. Tumber and S. Waisbord (eds.) *The Routledge Companion to Media Disinformation and Populism.* pp. 221 – 230. Routledge.

Cunningham, S. 2002. *The Idea of Propaganda: A Reconstruction.* Greenwood.

D'Ancona, M. 2017. *Post-Truth: The New War on Truth and How to Fight Back.* Ebury Press.

Da Silva, C. 2018. Trump claims asylum seekers bring 'large scale crime and disease' to U.S. *Newsweek* (Dec. 11). https://www.newsweek.com/donald-trump-says-migrants-bring-large-scale-crime-and-disease-america-1253268 da Silva, C. and A. Pimenta. 2020. Local news deserts in Brazil: historical and contemporary perspectives. In A. Gulyas and D. Baines (eds.) *The Routledge Companion to Local Media and Journalism*. pp. 44–53. Routledge.

Daly, G. 2008. Ology schmology: a post-structuralist approach. *Politics* 28(1):57–60.

Darnton, R. 2017. The true history of fake news. *New York Review of Books* (Feb. 13). https://www.ny books.com/daily/2017/02/13/the-true-history-of-fake-news/

David, M. 2002. The correspondence theory of truth. In E. Zalta (ed.) *Stanford Encyclopedia of Philosophy*. https://plato.stanford.edu/entries/truth-correspondence/#1

Davis, E. 2018. *Post-Truth: Why We have Reached Peak Bullshit and what We Can Do about It*. Little, Brown.

Dawsey, J., D. Paletta, and E. Werner. 2018. In fundraising speech, Trump says he made up trade claim in meeting with Justin Trudeau. *Washington Post* (March 15). www.washingtonpost.com/news/post-politics/wp/2018/03/14/in-fundraising-speech-trump-says-he-made-up-facts-in-meeting-with-justin-trudeau/

Dawson, A. and M. Innes. 2019. How Russia's Internet Research Agency built its disinformation campaign. *Political Quarterly* 90(2):245–256.

De Albuquerque, A. 2019. Protecting democracy or conspiring against it? Media and politics in Latin America: a glimpse from Brazil. *Journalism* 20(7):906–923.

De Blasio, E. and D. Selva. 2021. Who is responsible for disinformation? European approaches to social platforms' accountability in the post-truth era. *American Behavioral Scientist* 65(6):825–846.

de Oliveira Gomes, C. 2021. Brazilian educational system under attack: the reforms proposed after the 2016 coup and their sociological contexts. *European Journal of Education* 4(2):1–11.

De Vries, C. 2018. The cosmopolitan-parochial divide: changing patterns of party and electoral competition in the Netherlands and beyond. *Journal of European Public Policy* 25:1541–1565.

Dehghan, E. and S. Glazunova. 2021. 'Fake news' discourses: an exploration of Russian and Persian Tweets. *Journal of Language and Politics* 20(5):741–760.

Deibert, R. 2015. Authoritarianism goes global: cyberspace under siege. *Journal of Democracy* 26(3):64–78.

del Mar Ramirez-Alvarado, M. 2020. Post-truths and fake news in disinformation contexts: the case of Venezuela. In *Handbook of Research on Transmedia Storytelling, Audience Engagement, and Business Strategies*. pp. 306–320. IGI Global.

Del Vicario M., F. Zollo, G. Caldarelli, A. Scala, and W. Quattrociocchi. 2017. Mapping social dynamics on Facebook: the Brexit debate. *Social Networks* 50:6–16.

Deleuze, G. and F. Guattari. 2000. *A Thousand Plateaus*. Athlone Press.

DellaVigna, S. and E. Kaplan. 2007. The Fox News effect: media bias and voting. *Quarterly Journal of Economics* 122(3):1187–1234.

Derrida, J. 1967/2016. *Of Grammatology*. G. Spivak (trans.) Johns Hopkins University Press.

Dery, M. 2021. Profsplaining and other disorders. *Chronicle of Higher Education* (Nov. 26): 20–22.

DeStefano, F. 2007. Vaccines and autism: evidence does not support a causal association. *Clinical Pharmacology & Therapeutics* 82(6):756–759.

Deutsch, D. 2011. *The Beginning of Infinity: Explanations that Transform the World*. Penguin.

Diamond, D., H. Knowles, and T. Pager. 2021.Vaccine hesitancy morphs into hostility, as opposition to shots hardens. *Washington Post* (July 15). https://www.washingtonpost.com/politics/covid-vac cines-biden-trump/2021/07/15/adaf6c7e-e4bd-11eb-a41e-c8442c213fa8_story.html

Dijkstra, L., H. Poelman, and A. Rodríguez-Pose. 2020. The geography of EU discontent, *Regional Studies* 54:737–753.

Dillet, B. 2017. What is poststructuralism? *Political Studies Review* 15(4):516–527.

DiResta, R. 2021. The misinformation campaign was distinctly one-sided. *The Atlantic* (March 15). https://www.theatlantic.com/ideas/archive/2021/03/right-wing-propagandists-were-doing-something-unique/618267/

Doctor, K. 2019. By selling to America's worst newspaper owners, Michael Ferro ushers the vultures into Tribune. *Neimanlab* (Nov. 20). https://www.niemanlab.org/2019/11/newsonomics-by-selling-to-americas-worst-newspaper-owners-michael-ferro-ushers-the-vultures-into-tribune/

Dolack, P. 2019. Sorting through the lies about Venezuela. *Counterpunch* (Feb. 1). https://www.counterpunch.org/2019/02/01/sorting-through-the-lies-about-venezuela/

Doms, M., T. Dunne, and K. Troske. 1997. Workers, wages, and technology. *Quarterly Journal of Economics* 112(1):253–290.

Douai, A. 2019. Global and Arab media in the post-truth era: globalization, authoritarianism and fake news. *IEMed: Mediterranean Yearbook 2019.* pp.124–132. Dialnet.

Douglas, L. 2017. Donald Trump's dizzying *Time* magazine interview was 'Trumpspeak' on display. *The Guardian* (March 24). https://www.theguardian.com/commentisfree/2017/mar/24/donald-trumps-dizzying-time-magazine-interview-trumpspeak

Dovidio, J., S. Gaertner, and K. Kawakami. 2003. Intergroup contact theory: The past, present, and the future. *Groups Processes and Intergroup Relations* 6(1):5–21.

Drobnic Holan, A. 2016. 2016 Lie of the Year: Fake News. *PolitiFact* (Dec. 13). www.politi fact.com/truth-o-meter/article/2016/dec/13 /2016-lie-year-fake-news/

Dunlap, R. and A. McCright. 2010. Climate change denial: sources, actors and strategies. In C. Levery-Tracy (ed.) *Routledge Handbook of Climate Change and Society.* pp. 240–259. Routledge.

Dunlap, R. and P. Jacques. 2013. Climate change denial books and conservative think tanks: exploring the connection. *American Behavioral Scientist* 57:1–33.

Dzwonczyk, E. 2020. Clusters of nonmedical exemptions to vaccination in Illinois K-12 schools. *Professional Geographer* 72(1):22–36.

Eberwein, T., S. Fengler, and M. Karmasin (eds.) 2019. *Media Accountability in the Era of Post-truth Politics: European Challenges and Perspectives.* Routledge.

Edelman, M. 2001. *The Politics of Misinformation.* Cambridge University Press.

Edelman, M. 2021. Hollowed out Heartland, USA: How capital sacrificed communities and paved the way for authoritarian populism. *Journal of Rural Studies* 82:505–517.

Egan, L. 2020. Trump calls coronavirus Democrats' 'new hoax'. NBCNews (Feb. 28). https://www.nbcnews.com/politics/donald-trump/trump-calls-coronavirus-democrats-new-hoax-n1145721

Egan, T. 2015. Exxon Mobil and the G.O.P.: fossil fools. *New York Times* (Nov. 5). https://www.nytimes.com/2015/11/06/opinion/fossil-fools.html

Eisenstein, E. 1979. *The Printing Press as an Agent of Change.* Cambridge University Press.

Ekman, M. 2019. Anti-immigration and racist discourse in social media. *European Journal of Communication* 34(6):606–618.

Ellenbogen, S. 2003. *Wittgenstein's Account of Truth.* State University of New York Press.

Ellinas, A. 2010. *The Media and the Far Right in Western Europe.* Cambridge University Press.

Engelland, C. 2020. *Phenomenology.* MIT Press.

Erlaine, D. 2020. The culture of flat earth and its consequences. *Journal of Science & Popular Culture* 3(2):173–193.

Esser, F. and H. Brosius. 1996. Television as arsonist? The spread of right-wing violence in Germany. *European Journal of Communication 11*(2):235–260.

Esslin, M. 1982. *The Age of Television*. W.H. Freeman.

Europol. 2022. Facing reality? Law enforcement and the challenge of deepfakes. https://www.euro pol.europa.eu/cms/sites/default/files/documents/Europol_Innovation_Lab_Facing_Reality_Law_En forcement_And_The_Challenge_Of_Deepfakes.pdf

Evolvi, G. 2022. "Europe is Christian, or it is not Europe": post-truth politics and religion in Matteo Salvini's tweets. In M. Conrad, G. Hálfdanarson, A. Michailidou, C. Galpin, and N. Pyrhönen (eds.) *Europe in the Age of Post-Truth Politics: Populism, Disinformation and the Public Sphere.* pp. 129–148. Springer.

Evon, D. 2016. FALSE: Eritrean men are being forced to marry multiple women. Snopes https://www.snopes.com/fact-check/eritrea-multiple-wives/

FAIR. 1995. *The Way Things Aren't: Rush Limbaugh's Reign of Error.* New Press.

Fallou, L., M. Marti, I. Dallo, and M. Corradini. 2022. How to fight earthquake misinformation: a communication guide. *Seismological Research Letters 93*(5):2418–2422.

Farhat, L. 2022. Inside India's digital hate space. *Focus.* http://irs.org.pk/Focus/05FocusMay22.pdf

Farias, A. 2018. Twitter and institutional change: Insights from populist and pluralist discourses in Venezuela. *Potentia: Journal of International and Public Affairs* 9:79–96.

Farkas, J. and J. Schou. 2019. *Post-Truth, Fake News and Democracy: Mapping the Politics of Falsehood.* Routledge.

Farokhi, Z. 2020. Hindu nationalism, news channels, and "post-truth" Twitter: A case study of "love jihad". In M. Boler and E. Davis (eds.) *Affective Politics of Digital Media.* pp. 226–244. Routledge.

Farrell, H. 2012. The consequences of the internet for politics. *Annual Review of Political Science* 15(1):35–52.

Farzani, F. 2016. In Iran, post-truth news is old hat. *Iranwire* (Nov. 21). https://iranwire.com/en/blogs/64209/

Feierstein, D. 2020. Post-truth and the construction of representations of the past: the theory of the two demons and the case of Argentina. In M. Gudonis and B. Jones (eds.) *History in a Post-Truth World.* pp. 142–158. Routledge.

Fenster, M. 2008. *Conspiracy Theories: Secrecy and Power in American Culture.* University of Minnesota Press.

Ferrara, E. 2017. Disinformation and social bot operations in the run up to the 2017 French presidential election. *First Monday* 22:8. https://arxiv.org/ftp/arxiv/papers/1707/1707.00086.pd

Ferraro, M. and J. Chipman. 2019. Fake news threatens our businesses, not just our politics. *Washington Post* (Feb. 8). https://www.washingtonpost.com/outlook/fake-news-threatens-our-businesses-not-just-our-politics/2019/02/08/f669b62c-2b1f-11e9-984d-9b8fba003e81_story.html

Feuer, W. 2020. Donald Trump Jr. dismisses covid deaths as 'almost nothing' even as U.S. averages 800 deaths per day. CNBC (Oct. 30). https://www.cnbc.com/2020/10/30/donald-trump-jr-dis misses-covid-deaths-as-almost-nothing-even-as-us-averages-800-deaths-per-day.html

Feyerabend, P. 1975. *Against Method: Outline of an Anarchistic Theory of Knowledge.* New Left Books.

Fineman, M. 2012. *Faking It: Manipulated Photography before Photoshop.* Metropolitan Museum of Art.

Fischer, F. 2019. Knowledge politics and post-truth in climate denial: on the social construction of alternative facts. *Critical Policy Studies* 13(2):133–152.

Fishel, B. 2006. Limbaugh claimed Democratic Party is inviting Al Qaeda to "come on in over the southern border" so party can "take your votes." *Media Matters* (April 13). https://www.media

matters.org/rush-limbaugh/limbaugh-claimed-democratic-party-inviting-al-qaeda-come-over-southern-border-so

Fisher, M. 2021. Disinformation for hire, a shadow industry, is quietly booming. *New York Times* (July 26). https://www.nytimes.com/2021/07/25/world/europe/disinformation-social-media.html

Fisher, M., Cox, J., and P. Hermann. 2016. Pizzagate: From rumor, to hashtag, to gunfire in DC. *Washington Post* (Dec. 6). https://www.washingtonpost.com/local/pizzagate-from-rumor-to-hashtag-to-gunfire-in-dc/2016/12/06/4c7def50-bbd4-11e6-94ac-3d324840106c_story.html

Fletcher, R., A. Cornia, L. Graves, and R. Nielsen. 2018. Measuring the reach of "fake news" and online disinformation in Europe. *Australasian Policing* 10(2):1–10.

Fleury, L., Monteiro, M. and Duarte, T., 2022. Brazil at COP26: political and scientific disputes under a post-truth government. *Engaging Science, Technology, and Society* 8(3):107–117.

Florida, R. 2004. *The Rise of the Creative Class.* Basic Books.

Florida, R. 2005. *Cities and the Creative Class.* Routledge.

Florida, R. and G. Gates. 2004. Technology and tolerance: The importance of diversity to high technology growth. In T. Clark (ed.) *The City as an Entertainment Machine.* pp. 199–219. JAI Press.

Florida, R., C. Mellander, and K. Stollarick. 2008. Inside the black box of regional development—human capital, the creative class and tolerance. *Journal of Economic Geography* 8(5):615–649.

Foege, A. 2009. *Right of the Dial: The Rise of Clear Channel and the Fall of Commercial Radio.* Farrar, Straus and Giroux.

Folkenfirk, D. 2009. Dobbs' focus on Obama birth draws fire to CNN. NPR.Org. https://www.npr.org/templates/story/story.php?storyId=111409944

Forgas, J. and R. Baumeister (eds.) 2019. *The Social Psychology of Gullibility: Conspiracy Theories, Fake News and Irrational Beliefs.* Routledge.

Foucault, M. 1965/1988. *Madness and Civilization: A History of Insanity in the Age of Reason.* Vintage Books.

Foucault, M. 1966/2002. *The Order of Things: An Archaeology of the Humans Sciences.* Routledge.

Foucault, M. 1969. *The Archaeology of Knowledge.* Tavistock.

Foucault, M. 1977. *Discipline and Punish: The Birth of the Prison.* Allen Lane.

Foucault, M. 1980. *Knowledge: Selected Interviews and Other Writings 1972–1977.* C. Gordon (ed.) Pantheon.

Foucault, M. 1997. *The Politics of Truth.* S. Lotringer and L. Hochroth (eds.) Semiotext.

Franken, A. 1996. *Rush Limbaugh is a Big, Fat Idiot and Other Observations.* Delacorte Press.

Frankfurt, H. 2005. *On Bullshit.* Princeton University Press.

Freeman, C. 2007. *The Closing of the Western Mind: The Rise of Faith and the Fall of Reason.* Vintage.

Fried, R. 1998. *The Russians are Coming! The Russians are Coming! Pageantry and Patriotism in Cold-War America.* Oxford University Press.

Friedrich. J. 1993. Primary error detection and minimization (PEDMIN) strategies in social cognition: a reinterpretation of confirmation bias phenomena. *Psychological Review* 100(2):298–319.

Fukuyama, F. 2016. The emergence of a post-fact world. *LiveMint* (Dec. 30). http://www.livemint.com/Opinion/93hZcSFMVKtz4y5cTylOxI/Francis-Fukuyama-The-emergence-of-a-postfact-world.html

Fuller, S. 2018. *Post-Truth: Knowledge as a Power Game.* Anthem Press.

Fuller, S. 2018. What can philosophy teach us about the post-truth condition. In *and Democracy: Mapping the Politics of Falsehood.* pp. 13–26. Routledge.

Gabler, N. 2016. Who's really to blame for fake news? Look in the mirror, America. Common Dreams (Nov. 30). https://www.commondreams.org/views/2016/11/30/whos-really-blame-fake-news-look-mirror-america

Galarza Molina, R. 2022. The pandemic in post-truth rimes: narratives about COVID-19 disinformation in the Mexican media. *Revista mexicana de opinión pública* (33):121–137.

Gauchat, G. 2012. Politicization of science in the public sphere: A study of public trust in the United States, 1974 to 2010. *American Sociological Review* 77(2):167–187.

Gaukroger, S. 2001. *Francis Bacon and the Transformation of Early-Modern Philosophy.* Cambridge University Press.

Gayozzo, P. 2022. Agustín Laje y el neo-conservadurismo Latinoamericano de derecha. *Revista Argentina de Ciencia Política* 1(29). https://publicaciones.sociales.uba.ar/index.php/re vistaargentinacienciapolitica/article/viewFile/8097/6780

Gelbspan, R. 2005. *Boiling Point: How Politicians, Big Oil and Coal, Journalists, and Activists Have Fueled a Climate Crisis – And What We Can Do to Avert Disaster.* Basic Books.

Gemes, K. 1992. Nietzsche's critique of truth. *Philosophy and Phenomenological Research* 52(1):47–65.

Giannakis, E. and A. Bruggeman. 2020. Regional disparities in economic resilience in the European Union across the urban–rural divide. *Regional Studies* 54(9):1200–1213.

Gibbs, N. 2022. Newspapers are disappearing where democracy needs them most. *Washington Post* (Dec. 27). https://www.washingtonpost.com/opinions/2022/12/27/newspapers-disappearing-de mocracy-media/

Gillett, E. 1998. Relativism and the social-constructivist paradigm. *Philosophy, Psychiatry, & Psychology* 5(1):37–48.

Gimpel, J., N. Lovin, B. Moy, and A. Reeves. 2020. The urban–rural gulf in American political behavior. *Political Behavior* 42(4):1343–1368.

Giroux, H. 2018. *The Terror of Neoliberalism: Authoritarianism and the Eclipse of Democracy.* Routledge.

Giusti, S. and E. Piras (eds.) 2020. *Democracy and Fake News: Information Manipulation and Post-Truth Politics.* Routledge.

Glaeser, E. 2000. Cities and ethics: an essay for Jane Jacobs. *Journal of Urban Affairs* 22(4):473–494.

Go, S.G. and M. Lee. 2020. Analysis of fake news in the 2017 Korean presidential election. *Asian Journal for Public Opinion Research* 8(2):105–125.

Goldenberg, S. 2015. Exxon knew of climate change in 1981, email says – but it funded deniers for 27 more years. *The Guardian* (July 8). https://www.theguardian.com/environment/2015/jul/08/exxon-climate-change-1981-climate-denier-funding

Goldin, C. and L. Katz. 2008. *The Race Between Education and Technology.* Belknap Press.

Gould, S. 2011. The late birth of a flat Earth. In *Dinosaur in a Haystack.* pp. 38–50. Harvard University Press.

Gregory D. 1994. *Geographical Imaginations.* Blackwell.

Gross, P. and N. Levitt. 1997. *Higher Superstition: The Academic Left and its Quarrels with Science.* Johns Hopkins University Press.

Grzesiak-Feldman, M. 2015. Are the high authoritarians more prone to adopt conspiracy theories? The role of right-wing authoritarianism in conspiratorial thinking. In M. Bilewicz, A. Cichocka, and W. Soral (eds.) *The Psychology of Conspiracy.* pp. 117–139. Routledge.

Guadagno, R. and K. Guttieri. 2021. Fake news and information warfare: An examination of the political and psychological processes from the digital sphere to the real world. In *Research*

Anthology on Fake News, Political Warfare, and Combatting the Spread of Misinformation. pp. 218–242. IGI Global.

Gudonis, M. and B. Jones (eds.) 2020. *History in a Post-truth World: Theory and Praxis.* Routledge.

Guelke, L. 2003. Nietzsche and postmodernism in geography: An idealist critique. *Philosophy & Geography* 6(1):97–116.

Guerra-Carrillo, B., K. Katovich, and S. Bunge. 2017. Does higher education hone cognitive functioning and learning efficacy? Findings from a large and diverse sample. *PloS One* 12(8): e0182276.

Gulyas, A. 2021. Local news deserts. In D. Harte and R. Mattews (eds.) *Reappraising Local and Community News in the UK.* pp. 16–28. Routledge.

Gunkel, D. 2019. The medium of truth: media studies in the post-truth era. *Review of Communication* 19(4):309–323.

Gunther, R., P. Beck, and E. Nisbet. 2019. Fake news" and the defection of 2012 Obama voters in the 2016 presidential election. *Electoral Studies* 61(102030):1–17.

Günzel, S. 2003. Nietzsche's geophilosophy. *Journal of Nietzsche Studies* 25(1):78–91.

Guo, L. 2020. China's "fake news" problem: Exploring the spread of online rumors in the government-controlled news media. *Digital Journalism* 8(8):992–1010.

Gurin, P., B. Nagda, and G. Lopez. 2004. The benefits of diversity in education for democratic citizenship. *Journal of Social Issues* 60(1):17–34.

Haack, S. 1976. The pragmatist theory of truth. *British Journal for the Philosophy of Science* 27(3):231–249.

Hagerty, P. 2004. Simulation and the decay of the real. In P. Hegarty (ed.) *Jean Baudrillard: Live Theory.* pp. 49–68. Continuum.

Hall, P. and D. Soskice. (eds.) 2001. *Varieties of Capitalism: The Institutional Foundations of Comparative Advantage.* Oxford University Press.

Hancké, B. (ed.) 2009. *Debating Varieties of Capitalism: A Reader.* Oxford University Press.

Hannah, M. 2021. A conspiracy of data: QAnon, social media, and information visualization. *Social Media+ Society* 7(3): p.20563051211036064.

Hansen, H., B. Asheim, and J. Vang. 2009. The European creative class and regional development: how relevant is Florida's theory for Europe? In L. Kong and J. O'Connor (eds.) *Creative Economies, Creative Cities: Asian-European Perspectives.* pp. 99–120. Springer.

Hanson, S. 1992. Geography and feminism: worlds in collision? *Annals of the Association of American Geographers* 82:569–586.

Hansson, S. 2006. Falsificationism falsified. *Foundations of Science* 11:275–286.

Hansson, S. 2008. Science and pseudo-science. *Stanford Encyclopedia of Philosophy.* https://plato.stanford.edu/entries/pseudo-science/?utm_source=instantmagazine&utm_medium=organic&utm_campaign=OImrt19

Hansson, S. 2017. Science denial as a form of pseudoscience. *Studies in History and Philosophy of Science Part A* 63:39–47.

Hansson, S. 2018. Dealing with climate science denialism: experiences from confrontations with other forms of pseudoscience. *Climate Policy* 18(9):1094–1102.

Hanushek, E. 2012. The economic value of education and cognitive skills. In G. Sykes, B. Schneider, and D. Plank (eds.) *Handbook of Education Policy Research.* pp.39–56. Routledge.

Haraway, D. 1988. Situated knowledges: The science question in feminism and the privilege of partial perspectives. *Feminist Studies* 14:575–599.

Haraway, D. 1991. *Simians, Cyborgs and Women: The Reinvention of Nature.* Routledge.

Harding, S. 1986. *The Science Question in Feminism.* Cornell University Press.

Harding, S. 1991. *Whose Science? Whose Knowledge? Thinking from Women's Lives.* Cornell University Press.

Hardy, J. 2022. The rural information penalty. In *International Conference on Information.* pp. 33–41. Springer.

Hardy, J. and L. McCann. 2017. Brexit one year on. *Competition & Change* 21(3):165–168.

Harmon, M. and C. White. 2001. How television news programs use video news releases. *Public Relations Review* 27(2):213–222.

Harris, Adam. 2018. America is divided by education. *The Atlantic* 7. theatlantic.com/education/archive/2018/11/education-gap-explains-american-politics/575113/

Harris, R. and M. Charlton. 2016. Voting out of the European Union: exploring the geography of Leave. *Environment and Planning A: Economy and Space* 48:2116–2128.

Harrison, P. 2006. Poststructuralist theories. In S. Aitken and G. Valentine (eds). *Approaches to Human Geography.* pp. 122–135. Sage.

Harsin, J. 2015. Regimes of posttruth, postpolitics, and attention economies. *Communication, Culture and Critique* 8(2):327–333.

Harsin, J. 2018. Post-truth populism: the French anti-gender theory movement and cross-cultural similarities. *Communication Culture & Critique* 11(1):35–52.

Harsin, J. 2018a. A critical guide to fake news: from comedy to tragedy. *Pouvoirs* 164(1):99–119.

Harsin, J. 2018b. Post-truth and critical communication studies. In J. Nussbaum (ed.) *Oxford Research Encyclopedia of Communication.* Oxford University Press. https://oxfordre.com/communication/view/10.1093/acrefore/9780190228613.001.0001/acrefore-9780190228613-e-757

Hart, S. and J. Hart. 2021. Magical realism is the language of the emergent post-truth world. *Orbis Litterarum* 76(4):158–168.

Hartsock, N. 1984. *Money, Sex, and Power: Toward a Feminist Historical Materialism.* Northeastern University Press.

Harvey, D. 1989. *The Condition of Postmodernity.* Blackwell.

Hassan, I., and J. Hitchen. 2019. Nigeria's 'propaganda secretaries'. *Mail & Guardian* (April 18). https://mg.co.za/article/2019-04-18-00- nigerias-propaganda-secretaries/

Hastie, B. 2007. Higher education and sociopolitical orientation: The role of social influence in the liberalisation of students. *European Journal of Psychology of Education* 22:259–274.

Hawkins, K. 2010. *Venezuela's Chavismo and Populism in Comparative Perspective.* Cambridge University Press.

Hayes, D. and J. Lawless. 2021. *News Hole: The Demise of Local Journalism and Political Engagement.* Cambridge University Press.

Heathcote, J., K. Storesletten, and G. Violante. 2010. The macroeconomic implications of rising wage inequality in the United States. *Journal of Political Economy* 118(4):681–722.

Heckler, N. and J. Ronquillo. 2019. Racist fake news in United States' history: lessons for public administration. *Public Integrity* 21(5):477–490.

Heckman, J. 1995. Lessons from *The Bell Curve. Journal of Political Economy* 103(5):1091–1120.

Hedges, C. 2016. The right-wing empire strikes back in Latin America. *Alternet* (Oct. 4). https://www.alternet.org/2016/10/right-wing-latin-america

Heft, A., E. Mayerhöffer, S. Reinhardt, and C. Knüpfer. 2020. Beyond Breitbart: Comparing right-wing digital news infrastructures in six Western democracies. *Policy & Internet* 12(1):20–45.

Heit, H. 2018. "There are no facts...": Nietzsche as predecessor of post-truth? *Studia Philosophica Estonica* 11(1):44–63.

Hekman, S. 1997. Truth and method: Feminist standpoint theory revisited. *Signs: Journal of Women in Culture and Society* 22(2):341–365.

Heller, A. 2019. Netanyahu channeling Trump in Israel's election campaign. AP News (Feb. 7). https://www.apnews.com/d8a444fcd7924c8e8e4561c7056d9319

Hem, M. 2017. *How to be a Dictator: An Irreverent Guide.* Simon and Schuster.

Henkel, I. 2021. Ideology and disinformation: How false news stories contributed to Brexit. In G. Lopez-Garcia, D. Palau-Sampio, B. Palomo, E. Campos-Dominguez, and P. Masip (eds.) *Politics of Disinformation.* pp. 79–90. Wiley.

Herman, E. and N. Chomsky. 1988. *Manufacturing Consent: The Political Economy of the Mass Media.* Pantheon.

Herrnstein, R. and C. Murray. 1994. *The Bell Curve: Intelligence and Class Structure in American Life.* Free Press.

Hick, J. 1990. *Classical and Contemporary Readings in the Philosophy of Religion* (third edition). Prentice Hall.

Higdon, N. 2020. What is fake news? A foundational question for developing effective critical news literacy education. *Democratic Communiqué* 29(1):1–18.

Higgins, A., M. McIntire, and G. Dance. 2016. Inside a fake news sausage factory: 'This is all about income'. *New York Times* (Nov. 25). https://www.nytimes.com/2016/11/25/world/europe/fake-news-donald-trump-hillary-clinton-georgia.html

Hintikka, J. 1962. Cogito, ergo sum: Inference or performance? *Philosophical Review* LXXI:3–32.

Hmielowski, J., E. Heffron, Y. Ma, and M. Munroe. 2021. You've lost that trusting feeling: diminishing trust in the news media in rural versus urban US communities. *Social Science Journal* 58:1–15.

Hodge Jr, S. 2021. Don't always believe what you see: shallowfake and deepfake media has altered the perception of reality. *Hofstra Law Review* 50:1–30.

Hofstadter, R. 1963/2012. *Anti-Intellectualism in American Life.* Vintage.

Hofstadter, R. 1965/2012. *The Paranoid Style in American Politics.* Vintage.

Hogarth, R. 2019. The myth of innate racial differences between White and Black people's bodies: Lessons from the 1793 yellow fever epidemic in Philadelphia, Pennsylvania. *American Journal of Public Health* 109(10):1339–41.

Holman, B. 2020. STS, Post-truth, and the rediscovery of bullshit. *Engaging Science, Technology, and Society* 6:370–390.

Horkheimer, M. and T. Adorno. 1944/2004. *Dialectic of Enlightenment: Philosophical Fragments.* E. Jephcott (trans.). Stanford University Press.

Horsthemke, K. 2017. '# FactsMustFall'?–education in a post-truth, post-truthful world. *Ethics and Education* 12(3):273–288.

Horsthemke, K. 2022. '# FactsMustFall'?—African philosophy in a post-truth world. In *African Philosophy in an Intercultural Perspective.* pp. 115–129. J.B. Metzler.

Hsu, T. 2021. Despite outbreaks among unvaccinated, Fox News hosts smear shots. *New York Times* (July 11). https://www.nytimes.com/2021/07/11/business/media/vaccines-fox-news-hosts.html

Huang, J., H. van den Brink, and W. Groot. 2011. College education and social trust: An evidence-based study on the causal mechanisms. *Social Indicators Research* 104:287–310.

Iannone, C. 2017. Postmodern truth? *Academic Questions* 30(2):129–133.

Inglis, D. and R. Robertson. 2006. Discovering the world: cosmopolitanism and globality in the 'Eurasian' renaissance. In G. Delanty (ed.) *Europe and Asia beyond East and West.* pp. 92–106. Routledge.

Ingraham, C. (2020). New research explores how conservative media misinformation may have intensified the severity of the pandemic. *Washington Post* (June 25). https://www.washington post.com/business/2020/06/25/fox-news-hannity-coronavirus-misinformation/?fbclid=IwAR3xH2QzZeAjPnlBw61aLpjrhk-5EmEWXBBNVg1zFKv-1RMpBg5tTR0nLHw

Ingraham, C. 2016. Why conservatives might be more likely to fall for fake news. *Washington Post* (Dec. 7). https://www.washingtonpost.com/news/wonk/wp/2016/12/07/why-conservatives-might-be-more-likely-to-fall-for-fake-news/

Iqbal, H., 2019. Partisan media under Modi: nationalism a driving force behind fake news in India. *Quarterly Journal of the Institute of Regional Studies, Islamabad* 37(2):3–40.

Isaac, M. and S. Shane. 2017. Facebook's Russia-linked ads came in many disguises. *New York Times* (Oct. 2). https://www.nytimes.com/2017/10/02/technology/facebook-russia-ads-.html

Ivaldi, G. and J. Gombin. 2015. The Front National and the new politics of the rural in France. In D. Strijker, G. Voerman and I. Terluin (eds.) *Rural Protest Groups and Populist Political Parties.* pp. 243–263. Wageningen Academic Publishers.

Iyengar, S. and D, Massey. 2019. Scientific communication in a post-truth society. *Proceedings of the National Academy of Sciences* 116(16):7656–7661.

Jacobs, J. 1961. *The Death and Life of Great American Cities.* Random House.

Jacobs, J. 2010. Sophisticated geographies. *ACME: An International E-Journal for Critical Geographies* 9(1):10–20.

Jacobs, N. and B. Munis. 2022. Place-based resentment in contemporary US elections: the individual sources of America's urban-rural divide. *Political Research Quarterly* p. 10659129221124864.

Jacobson, L. 2018. Donald Trump says Democrats want to give cars to undocumented immigrants. Nope. *Politifact* (Oct. 22). www.politifact.com/factchecks/2018/oct/22/donald-trump/donald-trump-says-democrats-want-give-cars-undocum/

Jacoby, S. 2008. *The Age of Unreason in a Culture of Lies.* Vintage.

Jahng, M. 2021. Is fake news the new social media crisis? Examining the public evaluation of crisis management for corporate organizations targeted in fake news. *International Journal of Strategic Communication* 15(1):18–36.

Jaiswal, J., C. LoSchiavo, and D. Perlman. 2020. Disinformation, misinformation and inequality-driven mistrust in the time of COVID-19: lessons unlearned from AIDS denialism. *AIDS and Behavior* 24(10):2776–2780.

Jalli, N., N. Jalli, and I. Idris. 2019. Fake news and elections in two Southeast Asian nations: A comparative study of Malaysia general election 2018 and Indonesia presidential election 2019. In *International Conference on Democratisation in Southeast Asia.* pp. 138–148. Atlantis Press.

James, W. 1907/1978. *Pragmatism and the Theory of Truth.* Harvard University Press.

Jameson, F. 1984. Postmodernism, or the cultural logic of late capitalism. *New Left Review* 146:53–92.

Jamieson, K. and J. Cappella. 2008. *Echo Chamber: Rush Limbaugh and the Conservative Media Establishment.* Oxford University Press.

Jensen, M. 2018. Russian trolls and fake news: information or identity logics? *Journal of International Affairs* 71:115–124.

Johnson, P. 2007. *The Renaissance: A Short History.* Modern Library.

Jones, M. 2013. Media-bodies and Photoshop. In F. Attwood, V. Campbell, I. Hunter, and S. Lockyer (eds.) *Controversial Images: Media Representations on the Edge.* pp. 19–35. Palgrave Macmillan.

Jongbloed, B. 2004. Tuition fees in Europe and Australasia: theory, trends and policies. In *Higher Education: Handbook of Theory and Research.* pp. 241–310. Springer.

Jordan, M. 2018. A century ago, progressives were the ones shouting 'fake news'. *The Conversation* (Feb. 1). https://theconversation.com/a-century-ago-progressives-were-the-ones-shouting-fake-news-90614

Jowett, G. and V. O'Donnell. 2014. *Propaganda & Persuasion*. Sage.

Juhász, A. and P. Szicherle. 2017. The political effects of migration-related fake news, disinformation and conspiracy theories in Europe. *Friedrich Ebert Stiftung*. Budapest. https://politicalcapital.hu/pc-admin/source/documents/FES_PC_FakeNewsMigrationStudy_EN_20170607.pdf

Kakutani, M. 2018. *The Death of Truth: Notes on Falsehood in the Age of Trump*. Crown Publishing.

Kanozia, R. and R. Arya. 2021. "Fake news", religion, and COVID-19 vaccine hesitancy in India, Pakistan, and Bangladesh. *Media Asia* 48(4):313–321.

Kavanagh, J. and M. Rich. 2018. *Truth Decay: An Initial Exploration of the Diminishing Role of Facts and Analysis in American Public Life*. Rand Corporation.

Keane, S. 2006. *Disaster Movies: The Cinema of Catastrophe*. Wallflower Press.

Keeton, G. 2018. Post-truth," "alternative facts" and "fakenomics". *South African Journal of Economics* 86(1):113–124.

Keevak, M. 2004. *The Pretended Asian: George Psalmanazar's Eighteenth-Century Formosan Hoax*. Wayne State University Press.

Kellner, D. 2007. Lying in politics: The case of George W. Bush and Iraq. *Cultural Studies, Critical Methodologies* 7(2):132–144.

Kempner, J. 2020. Post-truth and the production of ignorance. *Sociological Forum* 35(1):234–240.

Kendi, I. 2017. *Stamped from the Beginning: The Definitive History of Racist Ideas in America*. Bold Type Books.

Kenny, M. and D. Luca. 2021. The urban-rural polarisation of political disenchantment: an investigation of social and political attitudes in 30 European countries. *Cambridge Journal of Regions, Economy and Society* 14(3):565–582.

Kent, A. 2017. Trust me, I'm a cartographer: post-truth and the problem of a critical cartography. *Cartographic Journal* 54(3):193–195.

Kessler, G. 2015. Trump's outrageous claim that "thousands" of New Jersey Muslims celebrated the 9/11 attacks. *Washington Post* (Nov. 22). www.washingtonpost.com/news/fact-checker/wp/2015/11/22/donald-trumps-outrageous-claim-that-thousands-of-new-jersey-muslims-celebrated-the-911-attacks/

Kessler, G. 2017. Spicer earns four Pinocchios for false claims on inauguration crowd size. *Washington Post* (Jan. 22). www.washingtonpost.com/news/fact-checker/wp/2017/01/22/spicer-earns-four-pinocchios-for-a-series-of-false-claims-on-inauguration-crowd-size/

Kessler, G. 2018. Meet the Bottomless Pinocchio, a new rating for a false claim repeated over and over again. *Washington Post* (Dec. 10). www.washingtonpost.com/politics/2018/12/10/meet-bottomless-pinocchio-new-rating-false-claim-repeated-over-over-again/

Kessler, G., and M. Lee. 2017. Fact-checking President Trump's claims on the Paris climate change deal. *Washington Post* (June 1). www.washingtonpost.com/news/fact-checker/wp/2017/06/01/fact-checking-president-trumps-claims-on-the-paris-climate-change-deal/

Kessler, G., S. Rizzo, and M. Kelly. 2020. *Donald Trump and His Assault on Truth: The President's Falsehoods, Misleading Claims and Flat-Out Lies*. New York Scribner.

Keyes, R. 2004. *The Post-Truth Era: Dishonesty and Deception in Contemporary Life*. St. Martin's Press.

Khaled, F. 2019. Egypt begins legal crackdown on "fake news." *Washington Report on Middle East Affairs* 38(2):30–32.

Kiely, E. 2016. Yes, Trump said Bush "lied." *FactCheck.org*. (March 17). www.factcheck.org/2016/03/yes-trump-said-bush-lied/

Kincheloe, J., S. Steinberg, and A. Gresson III. 1997. *Measured Lies: The Bell Curve Examined*. St. Martin's Press.

Kitcher, P. 1980. A priori knowledge. *Philosophical Review* 89(1):3–23.

Klikauer, T. and N. Simms. 2021. The dark money and dirty politics of Brexit. *Counterpunch* (Feb. 5). https://www.counterpunch.org/2021/02/05/the-dark-money-and-dirty-politics-of-brexit/

Knight, P. (ed.) 2003. *Conspiracy Theories in American History: An Encyclopedia* (Vol. 1). Santa Barbara: ABC-CLIO.

Knuckey, J. and K. Hassan. 2022. Authoritarianism and support for Trump in the 2016 presidential election. *Social Science Journal* 59(1):47–60.

Koertge, N. (ed.) 1998. *A House Built on Sand: Exposing Postmodernist Myths about Science*. Oxford University Press.

Kofman, A. 2018. Bruno Latour, the post-truth philosopher, mounts a defense of science. *New York Times* (Oct. 25). https://www.nytimes.com/2018/10/25/magazine/bruno-latour-post-truth-philosopher-science.html

Kranish, M. and I. Stanley-Becker. 2023. Brazil's riot puts spotlight on close ties between Bolsonaro and Trump. *Washington Post* (Jan. 9). https://www.washingtonpost.com/politics/2023/01/09/bolsonaro-riots-us-election-deniers-trump-bannon/

Kratochwil, F. 2008. Constructivism: what it is (not) and how it matters. In D. della Porta and M. Keating (eds.) *Approaches and Methodologies in the Social Sciences: A Pluralist Perspective*. pp. 80–98. Cambridge University Press.

Kuhn, T. 1962/2012. *The Structure of Scientific Revolutions*. University of Chicago Press.

Kukla, A. 2013. *Social Constructivism and the Philosophy of Science*. Routledge.

Kux, D. 1985. Soviet active measures and disinformation: overview and assessment. *The US Army War College Quarterly: Parameters* 15(1):17.

Kwanda, F. and T. Lin. 2020. Fake news practices in Indonesian newsrooms during and after the Palu earthquake: a hierarchy-of-influences approach. *Information, Communication & Society* 23(6):849–866.

Kwong, J. 2018. "Truth isn't truth": Here are all the ways Trump's administration has claimed facts are no longer real. *Newsweek* (Aug. 20). www.newsweek.com/truth-isnt-truth-here-are-all-ways-trumps-administration-has-claimed-facts-1081618

Kyaw, N.N. 2019. *Facebooking in Myanmar: From Hate Speech to Fake News to Partisan Political Communication*. ISEAS – Yusof Ishak Institute.

Kyzyma, I. 2018. Rural-urban disparity in poverty persistence. *Focus* 34(3):13–19.

Ladyman, J. 2013. Toward a demarcation of science from pseudoscience. In M. Pigliucci and M. Boudry (eds.) *Philosophy of Pseudoscience*. pp. 45–59. University of Chicago Press.

LaFrance, A. 2017. How the fake news crisis of 1896 explains Trump. *The Atlantic*. https://www.theatlantic.com/technology/archive/2017/01/the-fakenews-crisis-120-years-ago/513710/

Lakatos I. 1970. Falsification and the methodology of scientific research programmes. In I. Lakatos and A. Musgrave (eds.) *Criticism and the Growth of Knowledge*. pp. 91–196. Cambridge University Press.

Lakatos, I. 1978. Science and pseudoscience. *Philosophical Papers* 1:1–7.

Laketa, S. 2019. "Even if it didn't happen, it's true": the fantasy of geopolitics in the "post-truth" era. *Emotion, Space and Society* 31:155–161.

Landler, M. 2021. As Fox News struggles at home, Murdoch brings its playbook to the U.K. *New York Times* (Feb. 16). https://www.nytimes.com/2021/02/16/world/europe/murdoch-uk-news-channel.html

Larison, D. 2019. Trump's invincible ignorance. *American Conservative* (Feb. 3). www.theamericanconservative.com/larison/trumps-invincible-ignorance/

Latour, B. 1993. *We have Never Been Modern*. Harvard University Press.

Latour, B. 2004. Why has critique run out of steam? From matters of fact to matters of concern. *Critical Inquiry* 30(2):225–248.

Latour, B. 2007. *Reassembling the Social: An Introduction to Actor-Network Theory*. Oxford University Press.

Lavender, P. 2016. Donald Trump totally accused George W. Bush of lying. *Huffington Post* (March 17). www.huffpost.com/entry/donald-trump-george-w-bush_n_56eb1707e4b03a640a6a0147

Lazer, D., M. Baum, Y. Benkler, A. Berinsky, K. Greenhill, F. Menczer, M. Metzger, B. Nyhan, G. Pennycook, D. Rothschild, and M. Schudson. 2018. The science of fake news. *Science* 359(6380):1094–1096.

Le Miere, J. 2018. Donald Trump says "my gut tells me more sometimes than anybody else's brain can ever tell me." *Newsweek* (Nov. 27). www.newsweek.com/donald-trump-gut-brain-climate-change-fed-1234540

Leber, A. and A. Abrahams. 2019. A storm of tweets: social media manipulation during the Gulf crisis. *Review of Middle East Studies* 53(2):1–18.

Lecklider, A. 2013. *Inventing the Egghead: The Battle over Brainpower in American Culture*. University of Pennsylvania Press.

Lee, E. 2019. *America for Americans: A History of Xenophobia in the United States*. Basic Books.

Lee, M. and B. Butler. 2019. How are information deserts created? A theory of local information landscapes. *Journal of the Association for Information Science and Technology* 70(2):101–116.

Lees, C. 2018. Fake news: The global silencer: The term has become a useful weapon in the dictator's toolkit against the media. Just look at the Philippines. *Index on Censorship* 47(1):88–91.

Lehrer, K. and T. Paxson Jr. 1969. Knowledge: undefeated justified true belief. *Journal of Philosophy* 66(8):225–237.

Leiferman, T.V. and Khrushcheva, N., 2019. Of Peñabots and Post Truth: The Use of Bots and Trolls in Online Disinformation Campaigns in Mexico During the Peña Nieto Administration (2012–2018).

Leonhardt, D. 2007. Truth, fiction and Lou Dobbs. *New York Times* (May 30). https://www.nytimes.com/2007/05/30/business/30leonhardt.html.

Leonhardt, D. and S. Thompson. 2017. Trump's lies. *New York Times* (Dec. 14). www.nytimes.com/interactive/2017/06/23/opinion/trumps-lies.html

Lepore, J. 2006. *New York Burning: Liberty, Slavery, and Conspiracy in Eighteenth-century Manhattan*. Vintage.

Lerer, L. 2021. How Republican vaccine opposition got to this point. *New York Times* (July 17). https://www.nytimes.com/2021/07/17/us/politics/coronavirus-vaccines-republicans.html

Levenson, M. 2021. A poll reveals another U.S. vaccine divide, this one by household. *New York Times* (June 30). https://www.nytimes.com/2021/06/30/us/vaccinated-households-poll-results.html

Levin, B. 2020. Fox: corona is a liberal 'scam' to hurt Trump. *Vanity Fair* (March 10). https://www.vanityfair.com/news/2020/03/fox-coronavirus-trish-regan

Levitin, D. 2017. *Weaponized Lies: How to Think Critically in the Post-Truth Era*. Dutton Press.

Levitsky, S. and D. Ziblatt. 2018. *How Democracies Die.* New York: Penguin House.

Lewandowski, S., W. Stritzke, K. Oberauer, and M. Morales. 2005. Memory for fact, fiction, and misinformation: The Iraq war 2003. *Psychological Science* 16(3):190 – 5.

Lewandowsky, S. 2021. Climate change disinformation and how to combat it. *Annual Review of Public Health* 42:1 – 21.

Lewandowsky, S. and K. Oberauer. 2016. Motivated rejection of science. *Current Directions in Psychological Science* 25:217 – 22.

Lewis, H. 2021. Fox News gets a British accent. *The Atlantic* (June 16). https://www.theatlantic.com/ideas/archive/2021/06/gb-news-fox-news-british/619210/

Lewis, N. 2017. President Trump's claim that a wall will "stop much of the drugs from pouring into this country." *Washington Post* (Sept. 11). www.washingtonpost.com/news/fact-checker/wp/2017/09/11/president-trumps-claim-that-a-wall-will-stop-much-of-the-drugs-from-pouring-into-this-country/

Licari, P. 2020. Sharp as a fox: are Fox news.com visitors less politically knowledgeable? *American Politics Research* 48(6):792 – 806.

Lim, E. 2008. *The Anti-Intellectual Presidency: The Decline of Presidential Rhetoric from George Washington to George W. Bush.* Oxford University Press.

Lockie, S., 2017. Post-truth politics and the social sciences. *Environmental Sociology* 3(1):1 – 5.

Lopez, A. and J. Share. 2020. Fake climate news: How denying climate change is the ultimate in fake news. *Education.* http://www.susted.com/wordpress/content/blog-post-fake-climate-news-how-de nying-climate-change-is-the-ultimate-in-fake-news_2020_04/

López, D. 2020. *Lukács: Praxis and the Absolute.* Brill.

Lucendo-Monedero, A., F. Ruiz-Rodríguez, and R. González-Relaño. 2019. Measuring the digital divide at regional level. A spatial analysis of the inequalities in digital development of households and individuals in Europe. *Telematics and Informatics* 41:197 – 217.

Lukito, J., J. Suk, Y. Zhang, L. Doroshenko, S. Kim, M. Su, Y. Xia, D. Freelon, and C. Wells 2020. The wolves in sheep's clothing: How Russia's internet research agency tweets appeared in US News as vox populi. *International Journal of Press/Politics* 25(2):196 – 216.

Lyon, T. and J. Maxwell. 2004. Astroturf: Interest group lobbying and corporate strategy. *Journal of Economics & Management Strategy* 13(4):561 – 597.

Lyotard, J.-F. 1984. *The Postmodern Condition: A Report on Knowledge.* B. Massumi (trans.). University of Minnesota Press.

MacKenzie, A. and I. Bhatt. 2020. Opposing the power of lies, bullshit and fake news: The value of truth. *Postdigital Science and Education* 2(1):217 – 232.

Mamonova, N. and J. Franquesa. 2020. Populism, neoliberalism and agrarian movements in Europe. Understanding rural support for right-wing politics and looking for progressive solutions. *Sociologia Ruralis* 60(4):710 – 731.

Mandelbrot, B. 1967. How long is the coast of Britain? Statistical self-similarity and fractional dimension. *Science* 156(3775):636 – 638.

Manjoo, F. 2004. A picture is no longer worth a thousand words. *Salon* (April 22). https://www.salon.com/2004/04/22/doctored_photos/

Manjoo, F. 2008. *True Enough: Learning to Live in a Post-Fact Society.* Wiley.

Mann, M. 1986. *The Sources of Social Power,* volume I. Cambridge University Press.

Marche, S. 2017. The left has a post-truth problem too: it's called comedy. *Los Angeles Times* (Jan. 6). https://www.latimes.com/opinion/op-ed/la-oe-marche-left-fake-news-problem-comedy-20170106-story.html

Marcinkiewicz, K. 2018. The economy or an urban–rural divide? Explaining spatial patterns of voting behaviour in Poland. *East European Politics and Societies* 32(4):693–719.

Marcus, G., J. Sullivan, E. Theiss-Morse, and S. Wood. 1995. *With Malice Toward Some: How People Make Civil Liberties Judgments.* Cambridge University Press.

Marcus, R. 2021. Giuliani disgraced his profession – and his country – by defending the indefensible. *Washington Post* (June 24). https://www.washingtonpost.com/opinions/2021/06/24/giuliani-disgraced-his-profession-his-country-by-defending-indefensible

Mare, A., H. Mabweazara, and D. Moyo. 2019. "Fake news" and cyber-propaganda in Sub-Saharan Africa: recentering the research agenda. *African Journalism Studies* 40(4):1–12.

Mare, Admire, and Trust Matsilele. 2020. Digital media and the July 2018 elections in 'post-Mugabe' Zimbabwe. In M. Ndlela, and W. Mano (eds.) *Social Media and Elections in Africa: Theoretical and Methodological Perspectives.* Palgrave and MacMillan.

Markel, H. 2000. 'The eyes have it': Trachoma, the perception of disease, the United States Public Health Service, and the American Jewish immigration experience, 1897–1924. *Bulletin of the History of Medicine* 74(3):525–60.

Marr, J. 2003. Empiricism. In K. Lattal and P. Chase (eds.) *Behavior Theory and Philosophy.* pp. 63–81. Springer.

Marré, A. 2017. Rural Education at a Glance. U.S. Dept. of Agriculture. No. 1476–2017–3899.

Marshall, H. and Drieschova, A. 2018. Post-truth politics in the UK's Brexit referendum. *New Perspectives* 26(3):89–105.

Martin, M. 2021. Computer and Internet Use in the United States: 2018. U.S. Census American Community Survey Reports. https://www.census.gov/content/dam/Census/library/publications/2021/acs/acs-49.pdf

Marx, K. and F. Engels. 1976. The ruling class and the ruling ideas. In *Karl Marx, Friedrich Engels: Collected Works*, volume 5. pp. 59–62. R. Dixon (trans.) International Publishers.

Masharqa, S. 2020. Fake news in Palestine: exploratory research into the content, channels, and responses. https://fada.birzeit.edu/bitstream/20.500.11889/7194/1/Fake%20News%20Research.pdf

Mathews, N. and C. Ali. 2022. Desert work: life and labor in a news and broadband desert. *Mass Communication and Society* 25:1–21.

Mavelli, L. 2020. Neoliberalism as religion: sacralization of the market and post-truth politics. *International Political Sociology* 14(1):57–76.

Maweu, J. 2019. "Fake elections"? Cyber propaganda, disinformation and the 2017 general elections in Kenya. *African Journalism Studies* 40(4):62–76.

Maxwell, R. 2019. Cosmopolitan immigration attitudes in large European cities: contextual or compositional effects? *American Political Science Review* 113(2):456–474.

Maxwell, R. 2019. Why are urban and rural areas so politically divided? *Washington Post* (March 5). https://www.washingtonpost.com/politics/2019/03/05/why-are-urban-rural-areas-so-politically-divided/

Mayer, W. 2004. Why talk radio is conservative. *The Public Interest* (Summer):86–103.

McAdams, J. 2011. *JFK Assassination Logic: How to Think about Claims of Conspiracy.* Potomac Books.

McDonald, K. 2021. Unreliable news sites more than doubled their share of social media engagement in 2020. *NewsGuard.* https://www.newsguardtech.com/special-report-2020-engagement-analysis/

McIntyre, L. 2018. *Post-Truth.* MIT Press.

McKee, S. 2008. Rural voters and the polarization of American presidential elections. *PS: Political Science & Politics* 41(1):101–108.

McKernan, E. 1925. Fake news and the public: How the press combats rumour, the market rigger, and the propagandist. *Harper's* (October).

McKnight, D. 2010. Rupert Murdoch's News Corporation: A media institution with a mission. *Historical Journal of Film, Radio & Television* 30(3):303–16.

McLintic, A. 2019. The motivations behind science denial. *New Zealand Medical Journal* 132(1504):88–94.

McQueen, S. 2018. From yellow journalism to tabloids to clickbait: The origins of fake news in the United States. In D. Agosto (ed.) *Information Literacy and Libraries in the Age of Fake News.* Libraries Unlimited.

Meagher, R. 2012. The "vast right-wing conspiracy": Media and conservative networks. *New Political Science* 34(4):469–484.

Mehra, B. 2019. Information ACTism in "Trumping" the contemporary fake news phenomenon in rural libraries. *Open Information Science* 3(1):181–196.

Meixler, E. 2018. President Trump suggested Spain build its own border wall across the Sahara. *Time* (Sept. 20). https://time.com/5401489/donald-trump-spain-sahara-border-wall/

Mejia, R., K. Beckermann, and C. Sullivan. 2018. White lies: A racial history of the (post) truth. *Communication and Critical/Cultural Studies* 15(2):109–126.

Mellander, C., R. Florida, B. Asheim, and M. Gertler(eds.) 2013. *The Creative Class Goes Global.* Routledge.

Menand, L. 2020. Joseph McCarthy and the force of political falsehoods. *The New Yorker* (July 27). https://www.newyorker.com/magazine/2020/08/03/joseph-mccarthy-and-the-force-of-political-falsehoods

Merchant, C. 1990. *The Death of Nature.* Harper.

Mercier, H. 2020. *Not Born Yesterday: The Science of Who We Trust and What We Believe.* Princeton University Press.

Merkley, E. 2020. Anti-intellectualism, populism, and motivated resistance to expert consensus. *Public Opinion Quarterly* 84(1):24–48.

Michaels, J. 2017. *McCarthyism: The Realities, Delusions and Politics Behind the 1950s Red Scare.* Routledge.

Milburn, M. and S. Conrad. 1998. *The Politics of Denial.* MIT Press.

Miller, J. 2018. News deserts: No news is bad news. In *Urban Policy.* pp. 59–76. Manhattan Institute.

Miller-Idriss, C. 2019. The global dimensions of populist nationalism. *The International Spectator* 54(2):17–34.

Milligan, E. and A. Tartar. 2023. Pro-Brexit areas fall even further behind three years after leaving EU. *Bloomberg* (Jan. 30). https://www.bloomberg.com/graphics/uk-levelling-up/brexit-three-years-after.html

Mindich, D. 2020. Trump's campaign against Fauci ignores the proven path for defeating pandemics. *Washington Post* (July 22). https://www.washingtonpost.com/outlook/2020/07/22/trumps-campaign-against-fauci-ignores-proven-path-defeating-pandemics/

Mishra, P. 2018. Gandhi for the post-truth age. *New Yorker* (Oct. 15). https://www.newyorker.com/magazine/2018/10/22/gandhi-for-the-post-truth-age

Moghadam, V. 2020. *Globalization and Social Movements: The Populist Challenge and Democratic Alternatives.* Rowman & Littlefield.

Monmonier, M. 1996. *How to Lie with Maps.* University of Chicago Press.

Mooney, C. 2006. *The Republican War on Science.* Basic Books.

Mooney, C. 2012. *The Republican Brain: The Science of Why They Deny Science—and Reality.* John Wiley.

Moore, L. and S. Ovadia. 2006. Accounting for spatial variation in tolerance: the effects of education and religion. *Social Forces* 84(4):2205–22.

Moore, N. 2020. Study finds more COVID-19 cases among viewers of Fox News host who downplayed pandemic. NPR (May 4). https://www.npr.org/local/309/2020/05/04/849109486/study-finds-more-c-o-v-i-d-19-cases-among-viewers-of-fox-news-host-who-downplayed-pandemic

Moretti, E. 2012. *The New Geography of Jobs.* Houghton Mifflin Harcourt.

Motta, M. 2018. The dynamics and political implications of anti-intellectualism in the United States. *American Politics Research* 46(3):465–498.

Mudde, C. 2016. Europe's populist surge: A long time in the making. *Foreign Affairs* 95:25–30.

Muir, D. 2008. A land without a people for a people without a land. *Middle East Quarterly* Spring: 55–62.

Müller-Merbach, H. 2007. Kant's two paths of knowledge creation: a priori vs a posteriori. *Knowledge Management Research & Practice* 5(1):64–65.

Murdoch, J. 2005. *Poststructuralist Geography: A Guide to Relational Space.* Sage.

Musgrave, S. and M. Nussbaum. 2018. How Trump thrives in 'news deserts'. Politico (April 9). https://www.politico.eu/blogs/on-media/2018/04/trump-media-news-desert-how-thrives/amp/

Mutz, D. 2002. The consequences of cross-cutting networks for political participation. *American Journal of Political Science* 46(4):838–55.

Muzykant, V., M. Muqsith, R. Pratomo, and V. Barabash. 2021. Fake news on COVID-19 in Indonesia. In D. Berube (ed.) *Pandemic Communication and Resilience.* pp. 363–378. Springer.

Naim, M. 2015. The summit of lies. *The Atlantic* (April 9). https://www.theatlantic.com/international/archive/2015/04/summit-of-the-americas-lies-venezuela/390084/

Nakamura, D. 2019. Amid warnings of dangerous immigrants, Trump paints an incomplete and misleading picture. *Washington Post* (Jan. 8). www.washingtonpost.com/politics/amid-warnings-of-dangerous-immigrants-trump-paints-an-incomplete-and-misleading-picture/2019/01/08/2ecb909a-13b9-11e9-b6ad-9cfd62dbb0a8_story.html

Nalvarte, P. 2016. Consumption of news via social media grows in Venezuela in the midst of restrictions to traditional media. Journalism in the Americas. The Knight Center for Journalism at the University of Texas at Austin. https://latamjournalismreview.org/articles/consumption-of-news-via-social-media-grows-in-venezuela-in-the-midst-of-restrictions-to-traditional-media/

Narayanan, V., P. Howard, B. Kollanyi, and M. Elswah. 2017. Russian involvement and junk news during Brexit. The computational propaganda project. Algorithms, automation and digital politics. https://blogs.oii.ox.ac.uk/wp-content/uploads/sites/93/2017/12/Russia-and-Brexit-v27.pdf

Navin, M. 2013. Competing epistemic spaces: how social epistemology helps explain and evaluate vaccine denialism. *Social Theory and Practice* 39(2):241–264.

Ncube, L. 2019. Digital media, fake news and pro-Movement for Democratic Change (MDC) alliance cyber-propaganda during the 2018 Zimbabwe election. *African Journalism Studies* 40(4):44–61.

Negi, S., M. Jayachandran, and S. Upadhyay. 2021. Deep fake: an understanding of fake images and videos. *International Journal of Scientific Research in Computer Science, Engineering and Information Technology* 7(3):183–189.

Neimark, B., J. Childs, A. Nightingale, C. Cavanagh, S. Sullivan, T. Benjaminsen, S. Batterbury, S. Koot, and W. Harcourt. 2019. Speaking power to "post-truth": critical political ecology and the new authoritarianism. *Annals of the American Association of Geographers* 109(2):613–623.

Neo, R. 2022. When would a state crack down on fake news? Explaining variation in the governance of fake news in Asia-Pacific. *Political Studies Review* 20(3):390–409.

New York Times Editorial Board. 2018. Presidential lying is contagious. *New York Times* (Sept. 23). www.nytimes.com/2018/09/23/opinion/trump-lies-white-house-dishonesty.html

Nicas, J., F. Milhorance, and A. Ionova. 2022. How Bolsonaro built the myth of stolen elections in Brazil. *New York Times* (Oct. 25). https://www.nytimes.com/interactive/2022/10/25/world/amer icas/brazil-bolsonaro-misinformation.html

Nichols, T. 2017. *The Death of Expertise: The Campaign against Established Knowledge and Why it Matters.* Oxford University Press.

Nicholson, K. 2019. On the space/time of information literacy, higher education, and the global knowledge economy. *Journal of Critical Library and Information Studies* 2(1).

Nickerson, R. 1998. Confirmation bias: a ubiquitous phenomenon in many guises. *Review of General Psychology* 2(2):175–220.

Niebuhr, A. 2010. Migration and innovation: does cultural diversity matter for regional R & D activity? *Papers in Regional Science* 89(3):563–585.

Nielsen, K. 1997. Habermas and Foucault: How to carry out the Enlightenment project. *Journal of Value Inquiry* 31(1):5–21.

Nietzsche, F. 1888/1997. *Daybreak: Thoughts on the Prejudices of Morality* (second edition). M. Clark and B. Leiter (eds.) Cambridge University Press.

Norris, P. and R. Inglehart. 2019. *Cultural Backlash: Trump, Brexit, and Authoritarian Populism.* Cambridge University Press.

Nortey, J. 2020. Republicans more open to in-person worship, but most oppose religious exemptions from COVID restrictions. Pew Research Center (Aug. 11). https://www.pewresearch.org/fact-tank/ 2020/08/11/republicans-more-open-to-in-person-worship-but-most-oppose-religious-exemptions- from-covid-restrictions/

Nortio, E., M. Niska, T. Renvik, and I. Jasinskaja-Lahti. 2021. 'The nightmare of multiculturalism': interpreting and deploying anti-immigration rhetoric in social media. *New Media & Society* 23(3):438–456.

Nounkeu, C. 2020. Facebook and fake news in the "Anglophone crisis" in Cameroon. *African Journalism Studies* 41(3):20–35.

Nussbaum, M. 2017. Justice Department: no evidence Obama wiretapped Trump Tower. *Politico* (Sept. 2). www.politico.com/story/2017/09/02/obama-trump-tower-wiretap-no-evidence-242284

Nygren, G., S. Leckner, and C. Tenor. 2018. Hyperlocals and legacy media: media ecologies in transition. *Nordicom Review* 39(1):33–49.

Ó Tuathail, G. 1996. *Critical Geopolitics.* University of Minnesota Press.

O'Brien, T. 2017. My lawyers got Trump to admit 30 lies under oath. *Bloomberg Opinion* (June 12). www.bloomberg.com/opinion/articles/2017-06-12/trump-s-history-of-lies-according-to-biographer- timothy-o-brien

O'Connor, C. and J. Weatherall. 2019. Why we trust lies. *Scientific American* 321(3):54–61.

Odell, J. 2020. *How to do Nothing: Resisting the Attention Economy.* Melville House.

Ogasawara, M. 2019. The daily us (vs. them) from online to offline: Japan's media manipulation and cultural transcoding of collective memories. *Journal of Contemporary Eastern Asia* 18(2):49–67.

Ogola, G. 2017. Africa has a long history of fake news after years of living with non-truth. *The Conversation* (Feb. 27). https://theconversation.com/africa-has-a-long-history-of-fake-news-after- years-of-living-with-non-truth-73332

Oh, Y.J., J.Y. Ryu, and H.S. Park. 2020. Talking with the 'hermit regime': What's going on in the Korean Peninsula? A study on perception and influence of South and North Korea-related fake news. *International Journal of Communication* 14:1463–1479.

Okoro, N. and N. Emmanuel. 2018. Beyond misinformation: Survival alternatives for Nigerian media in the "post-truth" era. *African Journalism Studies* 39(4):67–90.

Oreskes, N. and E. Conway. 2011. *Merchants of Doubt: How a Handful of Scientists Obscured the Truth on Issues from Tobacco Smoke to Climate Change.* Bloomsbury.

Orwell, G. 1948/2014. *1984.* Harper.

Pang, H., J. Liu, and J. Lu. 2022. Tackling fake news in socially mediated public spheres: a comparison of Weibo and WeChat. *Technology in Society* p. 102004.

Parekh, B. 2015. *Marx's Theory of Ideology.* Routledge.

Pariser, E. 2011. *The Filter Bubble: What the Internet is Hiding from You.* Penguin.

Pecheny, M. 2019. Conservative restorations in Argentina and Brazil: the intimate and the public under attack. *Interface-Comunicação, Saúde, Educação* 23. https://www.scielo.br/j/icse/a/VxkRtqdTV4gcccWNK4Typpf/?lang=en

Peirce, C. 1931. *Collected Papers of Charles Sanders Peirce, volume 1: Principles of Philosophy.* C. Hartshorne and P. Weiss. (eds.) Harvard University Press.

Perini-Santos, E. 2020. What is post-truth? A tentative answer with Brazil as a case study. In B. Bianchi, J. Chaloub, and P. Rangel (eds.) *Democracy and Brazil: Collapse and Regression.* pp. 226–249. Routledge.

Perrin, A. 2017. Stop blaming postmodernism for post-truth politics. *Chronicle of Higher Education* (Aug. 4). https://www.chronicle.com/article/stop-blaming-postmodernism-for-post-truth-politics/

Peters, C. 2010. No-spin zones: The rise of the American cable news magazine and Bill O'Reilly. *Journalism Studies* 11(6):832–851.

Peters, J. and A. Feuer. 2020. How Richard Jewell's lawyer became a pro-Trump conspiracy theorist. *New York Times* (Dec. 29). https://www.nytimes.com/2020/12/29/us/politics/lin-wood-georgia-trump.html

Peters, M. 2017. Education in a post-truth world. *Educational Philosophy and Theory* 49(6):563–566.

Phillip, A. and M. DeBonis. 2017. Without evidence, Trump tells lawmakers 3 million to 5 million illegal ballots cost him the popular vote. *Washington Post* (Jan. 23). www.washingtonpost.com/news/post-politics/wp/2017/01/23/at-white-house-trump-tells-congressional-leaders-3-5-million-illegal-ballots-cost-him-the-popular-vote/

Pickard, V. 2019. *Democracy without Journalism? Confronting the Misinformation Society.* Oxford University Press.

Pierre-Louis, K. 2018. Trump's misleading claims about California's fire "mismanagement." *New York Times* (Nov. 12). www.nytimes.com/2018/11/12/us/politics/fact-check-trump-california-fire-tweet.html

Pigliucci, M. 2002. *Denying Evolution: Creationism, Scientism, and the Nature of Science.* Sinauer Associates.

Pines, C. 1993. *Ideology and False Consciousness: Marx and his Historical Progenitors.* State University of New York Press.

Pinna, M., L. Picard, and C. Goessmann. 2022. Cable news and COVID-19 vaccine uptake. *Scientific Reports* 12(1):1–7.

Pitofsky, M. 2020. Doctor retweeted by Trump has warned of alien DNA, sex with demons. *MSN News* (July 28). https://www.msn.com/en-us/news/us/doctor-retweeted-by-trump-has-warned-of-alien-dna-sex-with-demons/ar-BB17iaN4

Pocock, J. 2008. Historiography and enlightenment: a view of their history. *Modern Intellectual History* 5(1):83–96.

Poe, E. 1835. The Unparalleled Adventure of One Hans Pfaall. http://xroads.virginia.edu/~Hyper/POE/phall.html

Policy Times. 2018 (Dec. 27). Trump worst perpetrator of fake news: David Kaye. https://thepolicytimes.com/trump-worst-perpetrator-of-fake-news-david-kaye/

Pompa, L. 1984. The incoherence of the Cartesian cogito. *Inquiry* 27(1–4):3–21.

Poovey, M. 1998. *A History of the Modern Fact. Problems of Knowledge in the Sciences of Wealth and Society.* University of Chicago Press.

Popper, K. 1963. Science as falsification. *Conjectures and Refutations* 1:33–39.

Porter, R. 1990. *The Enlightenment.* Macmillan International Higher Education.

Porter, R. 2001. *The Creation of the Modern World: The Untold Story of the British Enlightenment.* W.W. Norton.

Posetti, J. and A. Matthews. 2018. A short guide to the history of 'fake news' and disinformation. *International Center for Journalists* 7:1–19.

Postman, N. 1985. *Amusing Ourselves to Death: Public Discourse in the Age of Show Business.* Viking.

Potter, E. 2006. Feminist epistemology and philosophy of science. In E. Kitay and L. Alcoff (eds.) *The Blackwell Guide to Feminist Philosophy.* pp. 235–253. Blackwell.

Powell, R. 2007. Geographies of science: histories, localities, practices, futures. *Progress in Human Geography* 31(3):309–329.

Prado, C. (ed.) 2018. *America's Post-Truth Phenomenon: When Feelings and Opinions Trump Facts and Evidence.* Praeger.

Prier, J. 2017. Commanding the trend: social media as information warfare. *Strategic Studies Quarterly* 11(4):50–85.

Prinanda, D. 2019. The dynamics of the post-truth era in Africa: history and critical thinking. *Proceedings of the 4th International Conference on Contemporary Social and Political Affairs.* pp 332–338. https://pdfs.semanticscholar.org/b2e3/2024cc39fea72739d1883a6c0a1395cc311a.pdf?_ga=2.102089029.576024297.1674327356-271735847.1649798550

Proctor, R. and L. Schiebinger. 2008. *Agnotology: The Making and Unmaking of Ignorance.* Stanford University Press.

PublicMind. 2011. Some News Leaves People Knowing Less. Fairleigh Dickinson University. http://publicmind.fdu.edu/2011/knowless/

Qiu, L. 2020. Trump's inaccurate claims on hydroxychloroquine. *New York Times* (May 21). https://www.nytimes.com/2020/05/21/us/politics/trump-fact-check-hydroxychloroquine-coronavirus-.html

Rabin-Havt, A. and Media Matters. 2016. *Lies, Incorporated: The World of Post-Truth Politics.* Anchor Books.

Rahmanian, E. 2021. Typology of fake social media news in the context of Iran: an ethnographic approach. *Journal of Business Management* 13(3):814–844.

Ranganathan, M. 2022. Re-scripting the nation in 'post truth' era: the Indian story. *Asian Ethnicity* 23(1):1–15.

Rantanen, T. 1997. The globalization of electronic news in the 19th century. *Media, Culture & Society* 19:605–620.

Reich, J. 2016. *Calling the Shots: Why Parents Reject Vaccines.* New York University Press.

Reich, R. 2010. *The Work of Nations: Preparing Ourselves for 21st Century Capitalism.* Vintage.

Reichman, H. 2021. "Professors are the enemy": Right-wing attacks on academic freedom have real repercussions. *Chronicle of Higher Education* (Dec. 14). https://www.chronicle.com/article/the-professors-are-the-enemy?cid2=gen_login_refresh&cid=gen_sign_in

Remhof, J. 2015. Nietzsche's conception of truth: Correspondence, coherence, or pragmatist? *Journal of Nietzsche Studies* 46(2):229 – 238.

Renaldo, J. 1976. Bacon's empiricism, Boyle's science, and the Jesuit response in Italy. *Journal of the History of Ideas* 37(4):689 – 695.

Reuters. 2021. 53 % of Republicans view Trump as true U.S. president. (May 24). https://www.reuters.com/world/us/53-republicans-view-trump-true-us-president-reutersipsos-2021-05-24/

Reuters. 2021. 53 % of Republicans view Trump as true U.S. president. (May 24). https://www.reuters.com/world/us/53-republicans-view-trump-true-us-president-reutersipsos-2021-05-24/

Reyes, A. 2020. I, Trump: The cult of personality, anti-intellectualism and the post-truth era. *Journal of Language and Politics* 19(6):869 – 892.

Ricard, J. and J. Medeiros. 2020. Using misinformation as a political weapon: COVID-19 and Bolsonaro in Brazil. *Harvard Kennedy School Misinformation Review* 1(3):1 – 8. https://misinforeview.hks.harvard.edu/wp-content/uploads/2020/04/ricard_misinformation_weapon_brazil_20200417.pdf

Riddlesden, D. and A. Singleton. 2014. Broadband speed equity: A new digital divide? *Applied Geography* 52:25 – 33.

Rigney, D. 1991. Three kinds of anti-intellectualism: rethinking Hofstadter. *Sociological Inquiry* 61(4):434 – 451.

Riotta, C. 2017. Majority of Republicans say colleges are bad for America (yes, really). *Newsweek* (July 10). https://www.newsweek.com/republicans-believe-college-education-bad-america-donald-trump-media-fake-news-634474

Riskin, J. 2002. *Science in the Age of Sensibility: The Sentimental Empiricists of the French Enlightenment.* University of Chicago Press.

Rizzo, S., G. Kessler, and M. Kelly. 2019. Your fact-checking cheat sheet for Trump's immigration address. *Washington Post* (Jan. 8). www.washingtonpost.com/politics/2019/01/08/your-fact-checking-cheat-sheet-trumps-immigration-address/

Roccas, S. and A. Amit. 2011. Group heterogeneity and tolerance: The moderating role of conservation values. *Journal of Experimental Social Psychology* 47(5):898 – 907.

Rodden, J. 2019. *Why Cities Lose: The Deep Roots of the Urban-Rural Political Divide.* Basic Books.

Rogers, K., C. Hauser, A. Yuhas, and M. Haberman. 2020. Trump's suggestion that disinfectants could be used to treat coronavirus prompts aggressive pushback. *New York Times* (April 24). https://www.nytimes.com/2020/04/24/us/politics/trump-inject-disinfectant-bleach-coronavirus.html

Romer, D. and K. Jamieson. 2020. Conspiracy theories as barriers to controlling the spread of COVID-19 in the US. *Social Science & Medicine* 263:113356.

Rorty, R. 1987. *Philosophy and the Mirror of Nature.* Princeton University Press.

Roscigno, V., D. Tomaskovic-Devey, and M. Crowley. 2006. Education and the inequalities of place. *Social Forces* 84(4):2121 – 2145.

Rose, G. 1993. *Feminism and Geography: The Limits of Geographical Knowledge.* University of Minnesota Press.

Rose, G. 1995. Distance, surface, elsewhere: A feminist critique of the space of phallocentric self/knowledge. *Environment and Planning D: Society and Space* 13(6):761 – 781.

Rose, G. 1997. Situating knowledges: positionality, reflexivities and other tactics. *Progress in Human Geography* 21(3):305 – 320.

Rose, H. 1994. *Love, Power, and Knowledge: Towards a Feminist Transformation of the Sciences.* Indiana University Press.

Rose, J. 2017. Brexit, Trump, and post-truth politics. *Public Integrity* 19(6):555–558.

Rosenau, J. 2012. Science denial: a guide for scientists. *Trends in Microbiology* 20(12):567–569.

Rosenberg, E. 2018. Trump admitted he attacks press to shield himself from negative coverage, Lesley Stahl says. *Washington Post* (May 22). https://www.washingtonpost.com/news/the-fix/wp/2018/05/22/trump-admitted-he-attacks-press-to-shield-himself-from-negative-coverage-60-minutes-reporter-says/

Rossi, U. 2018. The populist eruption and the urban question. *Urban Geography* 39(9):1425–1430.

Roth, M. 2014. *Beyond the University: Why Liberal Education Matters.* Yale University Press.

Rothschild, M. 2021. *The Storm is upon Us: How QAnon became a Movement, Cult, and Conspiracy Theory of Everything.* Melville House.

Rubin, J. 2018. Trump shows the rank dishonesty of climate-change deniers. *Washington Post* (Oct. 15). www.washingtonpost.com/news/opinions/wp/2018/10/15/trump-shows-the-rank-dishonesty-of-climate-change-deniers

Rucker, P. and A. Parker. 2020. Seven days as a 'wartime president': Trump's up-and-down command of a pandemic. *Washington Post* (March 20). https://www.washingtonpost.com/politics/seven-days-as-a-wartime-president-trumps-up-and-down-command-of-a-pandemic/2020/03/20/0dac3610-6ad6-11ea-9923-57073adce27c_story.html

Russell, B. 1912/1971. *Problems of Philosophy.* Oxford University Press.

Rutenberg, J., J. Becker, E. Lipton, M. Haberman, J. Martin, M. Rosenberg, and M. Schmidt. 2021. 77 days: Trump's campaign to subvert the election. *New York Times* (Feb. 1). https://www.nytimes.com/2021/01/31/us/trump-election-lie.html?action=click&module=Spotlight&pgtype=Homepage

Safieddine, F. 2020. History of fake news. *Fake News in an Era of Social Media: Tracking Viral Contagion.* pp. 1–26. Rowman and Littlefield.

Saka, E. 2018. Social media in Turkey as a space for political battles: AKTrolls and other politically motivated trolling. *Middle East Critique* 27(2):161–177.

Sambuli, N. 2017. How Kenya became the latest victim of 'fake news'. *AlJazeera* (Aug. 17). https://www.aljazeera.com/opinions/2017/8/17/how-kenya-became-the-latest-victim-of-fake-news/

Samenow, J. 2018. Trump's claim about climate scientists is "misleading and very damaging," weather group says. *Washington Post* (Oct. 17). www.washingtonpost.com/weather/2018/10/17/trumps-claim-about-climate-scientists-is-misleading-very-dangerous-leading-weather-group-says/

Saul, H. 2015. Trump claims Mexicans bring 'infectious disease' across border. *The Independent* (July 7). https://www.independent.co.uk/news/people/donald-trump-claims-mexican-immigrants-bring-tremendous-infectious-disease-across-border-10371739.html

Sayer, D. 2017. White riot—Brexit, Trump, and post-factual politics. *Journal of Historical Sociology* 30(1):92–106.

Scala, D. and K. Johnson. 2017. Political polarization along the rural-urban continuum? The geography of the presidential vote, 2000–2016. *Annals of the American Academy of Political and Social Science* 672(1):162–184.

Schaer, C. 2021. The Middle East's dangerous 'electronic armies'. *DW.* https://www.dw.com/en/the-middle-easts-electronic-armies-most-dangerous/a-57782768#:~:text=The%20term%20%22electronic%20armies%22%20is%20commonly%20used%20in,send%20%E2%80%94%20or%20suppress%20%E2%80%94%20a%20specific%20message.%22

Schaffner, B., M. MacWilliams, and T. Nteta. 2017. Hostile sexism, racism denial, and the historic education gap in support for Trump. In A. Cavari, R. Powell, and K. Mayer (eds.) *The 2016 Presidential Election: The Causes and Consequences of a Political Earthquake.* pp. 99–116. Lexington Books.

Scharp, K. 2013. *Replacing Truth.* Oxford University Press.

Schmid, P. and C. Betsch. 2019. Effective strategies for rebutting science denialism in public discussions. *Nature Human Behaviour* 3(9):931–939.

Schmidt, T., A. Cloete, A. Davids, L. Makola, N. Zondi, and M. Jantjies. 2020. Myths, misconceptions, othering and stigmatizing responses to Covid-19 in South Africa: a rapid qualitative assessment. *PloS One* 15(12):e0244420.

Schram, J. 2003. How popular perceptions of risk from SARS are fermenting discrimination. *BMJ: British Medical Journal* 326(7395):939.

Schrecker, E. 1999. *Many are the Crimes: McCarthyism in America.* Princeton University Press.

Schudson, M. 1981. *Discovering the News: A Social History of American Newspapers.* Basic Books.

Schwartz, T. 2017. I wrote *The Art of the Deal* with Donald Trump. In B. Lee (ed.) *The Dangerous Case of Donald Trump.* pp. 69–74. St. Martin's Press.

Schwirtz, M., M. Varenikova, and R. Gladstone. 2022. Putin calls Ukrainian statehood a fiction. History suggests otherwise. *New York Times* (Feb. 21). https://www.nytimes.com/2022/02/21/world/europe/putin-ukraine.html#:~:text=With%20a%20conviction%20of%20an%20authoritarian%20unburdened%20by,it%20autonomy%20within%20the%20newly%20created%20Soviet%20state.

Scott, A. 2007. Capitalism and urbanization in a new key? The cognitive-cultural dimension. *Social Forces* 85(4):1465–1482.

Scott, A. 2008. *Social Economy of the Metropolis: Cognitive-Cultural Capitalism and the Global Resurgence of Cities.* Oxford University Press.

Scott, A. 2011. A world in emergence: Notes toward a resynthesis of urban-economic geography for the 21st century. *Urban Geography* 32(6):845–870.

Scott, A. 2012. *A World in Emergence: Cities and Regions in the 21st Century.* Edward Elgar.

Scott, A. 2014. Beyond the creative city: cognitive–cultural capitalism and the new urbanism. *Regional Studies* 48(4):565–578.

Scott, A. 2019. City-regions reconsidered. *Environment and Planning A: Economy and Space* 51(3):554–580.

Scruton, R. 2017. Post-truth? It's pure nonsense. *The Spectator* (June 10). https://www.spectator.co.uk/2017/06/post-truth-its-pure-nonsense/

Seabra, M. and L. Vasconcellos de Verçoza. 2019. Sociology and philosophy are just the first victims in Bolsonaro's culture war. *The Conversation* (July 16). https://theconversation.com/sociology-and-philosophy-are-just-the-first-victims-in-bolsonaros-culture-war-120052

Seldes, G. 1938. *Lords of the Press.* J. Messner.

Serhan, Y. 2017. The year in Brexit, as seen through British tabloids. *The Atlantic* (Dec. 18). https://www.theatlantic.com/international/archive/2017/12/the-year-in-brexit/548141/

Shafick, H. 2021. From deception to inception: social media and the changing function of fake news (lessons from Egypt 2013). *CyberOrient* 15(2):43–77.

Shapiro, B. 2000. *A Culture of Fact: England, 1550–1720.* Cornell University Press.

Sharma, A. 2023. Ordinary conspiracy theories and everyday communalism: Hindutva on the Indian cyberspace. In I. Roy (ed.) *Passionate Politics: Democracy, Development and India's 2019 General Election.* Manchester University Press.

Sherman, G. 2014. *The Loudest Voice in the Room: How the Brilliant, Bombastic Roger Ailes Built Fox News – and Divided a Country.* Random House.

Siddiquee, M. 2020. The portrayal of the Rohingya genocide and refugee crisis in the age of post-truth politics. *Asian Journal of Comparative Politics* 5(2):89–103.

Sidky, H. 2018. The war on science, anti-intellectualism, and alternative ways of knowing in 21st century America. *Skeptical Inquirer* 42(2):38 – 43.

Siles, I., L. Tristán, and C. Carazo. 2021. Populism, media, and misinformation in Latin America. In H. Tumber and S. Waisbord (eds.) *The Routledge Companion to Media Disinformation and Populism.* pp. 356 – 365. Routledge.

Silverman, C. and L. Alexander. 2016. How teens in the Balkans are duping Trump supporters with fake news. *BuzzFeed* (Nov. 3). https://www.buzzfeednews.com/article/craigsilverman/how-mace donia-became-a-global-hub-for-pro-trump-misinfo#.dj5Pk1DAm

Simon, G. 2022. Disingenuous natures and post-truth politics: Five knowledge modalities of concern in environmental governance. *Geoforum* 132:162 – 170.

Smith, D. and E. Hanley. 2018. The anger games: who voted for Donald Trump in the 2016 election, and why? *Critical Sociology* 44(2):195 – 212.

Smith, J. 2010. *Pseudoscience and Extraordinary Claims of the Paranormal.* Wiley-Blackwell.

Smith, J. 2016. Truth after Trump. *Chronicle of Higher Education* (Oct. 30). www.chronicle.com/article/ Truth-After-Trump/238174

Snow, N. and P. Taylor. 2006. The revival of the propaganda state: US propaganda at home and abroad since 9/11. *International Communication Gazette* 68(5 – 6):389 – 407.

Snyder, A. 1997. *Warriors of Disinformation: American Propaganda, Soviet Lies, and the Winning of the Cold War: An Insider's Account.* Arcade Publishing.

Snyder, T. 2017. *On Tyranny: Twenty Lessons from the Twentieth Century.* Tim Duggan Books.

Soave, R. 2019. Survey: 59 % of Republicans now think college is bad for America. *Reason* (Aug. 19). https://reason.com/2019/08/19/pew-survey-republicans-college-campus-safe-spaces/

Sober, E. 2008. Empiricism. In M. Curd and S. Psillos (eds.) *The Routledge Companion to Philosophy of Science.* pp. 157 – 166. Routledge.

Soja, E. 1989. *Postmodern Geographies: The Reassertion of Space in Critical Social Theory.* Verso.

Soja, E. 1993. Postmodern geographies and the critique of historicism. In J. Jones, W. Natter, and T. Schatzki (eds.) *Postmodern Contentions.* Guilford.

Sokal, A. 1996. Transgressing the boundaries: Toward a transformative hermeneutics of quantum gravity. *Social Text* 46/47:217 – 252.

Sokal, A. 2008. *Beyond the Hoax: Science, Philosophy and Culture.* Oxford University Press.

Sokal, A. and J. Bricmont. 1998. *Fashionable Nonsense: Postmodern Intellectuals' Abuse of Science.* Picador.

Sokolowski, R. 2000. *Introduction to Phenomenology.* Cambridge University Press.

Soll, J. 2016. The long and brutal history of fake news. *Politico* (December 18). www.politico.com/mag azine/story/2016/12/fake-news-history-long-violent-214535

Song, Y. 2009. Training, technological changes, and displacement. *Journal of Labor Research* 30(3):201 – 218.

Sontag, S. 1977. *On Photography.* Farrar, Straus, and Giroux.

Sorell, T. 1994. *Scientism: Philosophy and the Infatuation with Science.* Routledge.

Soukup, C. 2008. 9/11 conspiracy theories on the World Wide Web: digital rhetoric and alternative epistemology. *Journal of Literacy and Technology* 9(3):2 – 25.

Specter, M. 2007. The denialists: the dangerous attacks on the consensus about H.I.V. and AIDS. *The New Yorker* (March 12). https://www.newyorker.com/magazine/2007/03/12/the-denialists

Specter, M. 2009. *Denialism. How Irrational Thinking Hinders Scientific Progress, Harms the Planet, and Threatens our Lives.* Penguin.

Spencer, D. and J. Spencer. 2007. *The Yellow Journalism: The Press and America's Emergence as a World Power*. Northwestern University Press.

Spohr, D. 2017. Fake news and ideological polarization: filter bubbles and selective exposure on social media. *Business Information Review 34*(3):150–160.

Sprague, J. and D. Kobrynowicz. 1999. A feminist epistemology. In J. Chafetz (ed.). *Handbook of the Sociology of Gender*. pp. 25–43. Kluwer.

Stecula, D. and M. Pickup. 2021. How populism and conservative media fuel conspiracy beliefs about COVID-19 and what it means for COVID-19 behaviors. *Research & Politics* 8(1): 2053168021993979.

Stein, R. 2021. "Hoax!" Palestinian cameras, Israeli state violence, and the "fake news" fantasy. In D. Della Ratta, G. Lovink, T. Numerico, and P. Sarram (eds.) *The Aesthetics and Politics of the Online Self: A Savage Journey into the Heart of Digital Cultures*. pp. 115–128. Palgrave Macmillan.

Stelter, B. 2020. *Hoax: Donald Trump, Fox News, and the Dangerous Distortion of Truth*. Atria/One Signal Publishers.

Stempel, C., T. Hargrove, and G. Stempel III. 2007. Media use, social structure, and belief in 9/11 conspiracy theories. *Journalism & Mass Communication Quarterly* 84(2):353–372.

Stephens, B. 2019. What "Chernobyl" teaches about Trump. *New York Times* (June 20). www.nytimes.com/2019/06/20/opinion/chernobyl-hbo-lies-trump.html

Stove, D. 2001. *Scientific Irrationalism: Origins of a Postmodern Cult*. Transaction Publishers.

Strassheim, J. 2022. Neoliberalism and post-truth: expertise and the market model. *Theory, Culture & Society* p. 02632764221119726.

Strauss, V. 2016. Why in the world would rapper B.o.B think the Earth is flat? A quick science lesson. *Washington Post* (Feb. 2). https://www.washingtonpost.com/news/answer-sheet/wp/2016/02/02/why-in-the-world-would-rapper-b-o-b-think-the-earth-is-flat-a-quick-science-lesson/

Strong, S. 2016. Alternative facts and the post-truth society: Meeting the challenge. *University of Pennsylvania Law Review* 165:137–146.

Subramanian, S. 2017. Inside the Macedonian fake news complex. *Wired* (Feb. 15). https://www.wired.com/2017/02/veles-macedonia-fake-news/

Sukhankin, S. 2019. The Western Alliance in the Face of the Russian (Dis)information Machine: Where does Canada Stand? University of Calgary School of Public Policy Publications, 12(26). https://www.policyschool.ca/wp-content/uploads/2019/09/Final-Version_Western-Alliance-Sukhankin.pdf

Sullivan, M. 2020. The data is in: Fox News may have kept millions from taking the coronavirus threat seriously. *Washington Post* (June 28). https://www.washingtonpost.com/lifestyle/media/the-data-is-in-fox-news-may-have-kept-millions-from-taking-the-coronavirus-threat-seriously/2020/06/26/60d88aa2-b7c3-11ea-a8da-693df3d7674a_story.html

Suskind, R. 2004. Faith, certainty and the presidency of George W. Bush. *New York Times Magazine* (Oct. 17). www.nytimes.com/2004/10/17/magazine/faith-certainty-and-the-presidency-of-george-w-bush.html

Swenson, A. 2020. Family of Hugo Chavez does not own Dominion Voting Systems. Associated Press (Dec. 1). https://apnews.com/article/fact-checking-afs:Content:9809670730

Tally, R., Jr. 2018. In the deserts of cartography: building, dwelling, mapping. In M. Houellebecq and G. Bowd (eds.) *The Map and the Territory*. pp. 599–608. Springer.

Tandoc, E., Jr., W.L. Zheng, and R. Ling. 2018. Defining "fake news." A typology of scholarly definitions. *Digital Journalism* 6(2):137–153.

Tang, S., L. Willnat, and H. Zhang. 2021. Fake news, information overload, and the third-person effect in China. *Global Media and China* 6(4):492–507.

Taranto, J. 2016. "I love the poorly educated!" *Wall Street Journal* (Feb. 24). www.wsj.com/articles/i-love-the-poorly-educated-1456337093

Taş, H. 2018. The 15 July abortive coup and post-truth politics in Turkey. *Southeast European and Black Sea Studies* 18(1):1–19.

Taylor, P. 1995. *Munitions of the Mind: A History of Propaganda from the Ancient World to the Present Era.* Manchester University Press.

Tchen, J. and Yeats, D. (eds.) 2014. *Yellow Peril! An Archive of Anti-Asian Fear.* Verso.

Tesich, S. 1992. Government of lies. *The Nation* (January), pp. 12–14. https://archive.org/details/steve-tesich-government-of-lies-article/mode/2up

Thompson, J. 2020. Mediated interaction in the digital age. *Theory, Culture & Society* 37(1):3–28.

Thompson, M. 1981. On a priori truth. *Journal of Philosophy* 78(8):458–482.

Thorson, K. 2019. Time to get mad about information inequality (again). NiemanLab. https://www.niemanlab.org/2019/01/time-to-get-madabout-information-inequality-again/

Thrift, N. 1985. Flies and germs: a geography of knowledge. In *Social Relations and Spatial Structures.* pp. 366–403. Palgrave.

Thrift, N. 1995. The geography of truth. *Environment and Planning D: Society and Space* 13(1):1–4.

Thussu, D. 2007. The Murdochization of news? The case of Star TV in India. *Media, Culture & Society* 29(4):593–611.

Tobias, M. 2018. No, U.S. Steel is not opening six new mills as Donald Trump said. *Politifact* (Aug. 2). www.politifact.com/factchecks/2018/aug/02/donald-trump/us-steel-not-opening-six-new-mills-donald-trump/

Todisco, E. 2020. President Trump claims coronavirus will 'fade away' even without vaccine as cases rise in U.S. *New York Times* (June 18). https://people.com/politics/donald-trump-says-coronavirus-fade-away-without-vaccine/

Tomczyk, Ł., M. Eliseo, V. Costas, G. Sánchez, I. Silveira, M. Barros, H. Amado-Salvatierra, and S. Oyelere. 2019. Digital divide in Latin America and Europe: main characteristics in selected countries. In *2019 14th Iberian Conference on Information Systems and Technologies.* pp. 1–6. IEEE.

Torrance, J. 1995. *Karl Marx's Theory of Ideas.* Cambridge University Press.

Toulmin, S. 1958. *The Uses of Argument.* Cambridge University Press.

Traub, J. 2016. The party that wants to make Poland great again. *New York Times* (Nov. 2). https://www.nytimes.com/2016/11/06/magazine/the-party-that-wants-to-make-poland-great-again.html

Troianovski, A. 2022. Why Vladimir Putin invokes Nazis to justify his invasion of Ukraine. *New York Times* (March 17). https://www.nytimes.com/2022/03/17/world/europe/ukraine-putin-nazis.html

Trotter, P. and R. Maconachie. 2018. Populism, post-truth politics and the failure to deceive the public in Uganda's energy debate. *Energy Research & Social Science* 43:61–76.

Trujillo, K. and Z. Crowley. 2022. Symbolic versus material concerns of rural consciousness in the United States. *Political Geography* 96:102658.

Truscott, L. 2020. We need to quarantine Donald Trump: He's confused, ignorant and afraid. (March 14). https://www.salon.com/2020/03/14/we-need-to-quarantine-donald-trump-hes-confused-ignorant-and-afraid/

Tsu, T. and S. Thompson. 2023. Disinformation researchers raise alarms about A.I. chatbots. *New York Times* (Feb. 8). https://www.nytimes.com/2023/02/08/technology/ai-chatbots-disinformation.html

Tumber, H. and S. Waisbord (eds.) 2021. *The Routledge Companion to Media Disinformation and Populism.* Routledge.

Tuters, M., E. Jokubauskaitė, and D. Bach. 2018. Post-truth protest: How 4chan cooked up the Pizzagate bullshit. *M/c Journal 21*(3). https://journal.media-culture.org.au/index.php/mcjournal/article/view/1422

Tversky, A. and D. Kahneman. 1973. Availability: a heuristic for judging frequency and probability. *Cognitive Psychology* 5(2):207 – 232.

Tyler, A. 1992. *Nativism and Slavery: The Northern Know Nothings and the Politics of the 1850s.* Oxford University Press

U.S. Department of State. 2022. Russia's Five Top Disinformation Narratives. https://www.state.gov/russias-top-five-persistent-disinformation-narratives/

Uberti, D. 2016. The real history of fake news. *Columbia Journalism Review 15.* https://www.cjr.org/special_report/fake_news_history.php

Valentine, G. 2008. Living with difference: Reflections on geographies of encounter. *Progress in Human Geography* 32(3):323 – 337.

Valverde, M. 2018. Donald Trump falsely says Democrats invite migrant caravans. *Politifact* (Nov. 1). www.politifact.com/factchecks/2018/nov/01/donald-trump/donald-trump-falsely-says-democrats-invite-migrant/

van den Heuvel, K. 2007. Lou Dobbs and leprosy. *The Nation* (June 5). https://www.thenation.com/article/archive/lou-dobbs-and-leprosy/

Van Dijk, T. 2017. How Globo media manipulated the impeachment of Brazilian president Dilma Rousseff. *Discourse & Communication* 11(2):199 – 229.

Van Dyk, S. 2022. Post-truth, the future of democracy and the public sphere. *Theory, Culture & Society* 39(4):37 – 50.

van Prooijen, J., T. Cohen Rodrigues, C. Bunzel, O. Georgescu, D. Komáromy, and A. Krouwel. 2022. Populist gullibility: Conspiracy theories, news credibility, bullshit receptivity, and paranormal belief. *Political Psychology* 43(6):1061 – 1079.

Vannini, S. and I. Rega. 2020. Mobile information literacy and public access in the era of post-truth: reflections from community curricular experiences in Latin America. In *Critical Mobile Pedagogy.* pp. 110 – 122. Routledge.

Ventre, D. (ed.) 2012. *Cyberwar and Information Warfare.* John Wiley.

Wade, P. 2020. Trump's son pushes dimwitted rigged election conspiracy: Virus 'will magically go away' after November 3rd. *Rolling Stone* (May 17). https://www.rollingstone.com/politics/politics-news/eric-trump-pushes-conspiracy-virus-will-magically-go-away-1001155/

Wagner, J. 2018. "When I can, I tell the truth": Trump pushes back against his peddling of falsehoods. *Washington Post* (Nov. 1). www.washingtonpost.com/politics/when-i-can-i-tell-the-truth-trump-pushes-back-against-his-peddling-of-falsehoods/2018/11/01/e8278d68-ddbe-11e8-85df-7a6b4d25cfbb_story.html

Waisbord, S. 2018a. The elective affinity between post-truth communication and populist politics. *Communication Research and Practice* 4(1):17 – 34.

Waisbord, S. 2018b. Truth is what happens to news: on journalism, fake news, and post-truth. *Journalism Studies* 19(13):1866 – 1878.

Waisbord, S. and A. Amado. 2017. Populist communication by digital means: presidential Twitter in Latin America. *Information, Communication & Society* 20(9):1330 – 1346.

Wakefield, A., S. Murch, A. Anthony, J. Linnell, D. Casson, M. Malik, M. Berelowitz, A. Dhillon, M. Thomson, P. Harvey, A. Valentine, S. Davies, and J. Walker-Smith. 1998. Ileal-lymphoid-nodular hyperplasia, non-specific colitis, and pervasive developmental disorder in children. *Lancet* 351:637–641.

Waldman, P. 2019a. Trump's corruption keeps getting more obvious. *Washington Post* (Jan. 21). www.washingtonpost.com/opinions/2019/01/21/trumps-corruption-keeps-getting-more-obvious/

Waldman, P. 2019b. Trump may have degraded U.S. politics for a generation to come. *Washington Post* (April 29). www.washingtonpost.com/opinions/2019/04/29/trump-may-have-degraded-us-politics-generation-come/

Walker, R. 1985. Spinoza and the coherence theory of truth. *Mind* 94(373):1–18.

Walker, R. 1989. The coherence theory of truth. In M. Glanzberg (ed.) *The Oxford Handbook of Truth*. Oxford University Press.

Wallerstein, I. 1980. *The Modern World-System II: Mercantilism and the Consolidation of the European World-Economy, 1600–1750*. Academic Press.

Ward, M. 2014. 9 Things You'd Believe about World Geography if You Only Listened to Fox News. https://www.mic.com/articles/89381/9-things-you-d-believe-about-world-geography-if-you-only-listened-to-fox-news

Warf, B. and S. Arias (eds.) 2008. *The Spatial Turn: Interdisciplinary Perspectives*. Routledge.

Wason, P. 1960. On the failure to eliminate hypotheses in a conceptual task. *Quarterly Journal of Experimental Psychology* 12(3):129–140.

Wasserman, H. 2020. Fake news from Africa: panics, politics and paradigms. *Journalism* 21(1):3–16.

Wasserman, H., and D. Madrid-Morales. 2019. An exploratory study of "fake news" and media trust in Kenya, Nigeria and South Africa. *African Journalism Studies* 40(1):107–123.

Watson, C. 2018. Information literacy in a fake/false news world: An overview of the characteristics of fake news and its historical development. *International Journal of Legal Information* 46(2):93–96.

Watzlawick, P. 1984. *Invented Reality: How Do We Know What We Believe We Know?* W.W. Norton.

Waxman, O. 2016. Donald Trump says Central Park Five "admitted they were guilty." Here's what to know about the case. *Time* (Oct. 7). https://time.com/4523257/donald-trump-central-park-five/

Webb, H. and M. Emam. 2021. Social media and fake news impact on social movements: examples from Tunisia and Egypt. In S. Aririguzoh (ed.) *Global Perspectives on the Impact of Mass Media on Electoral Processes*. pp. 40–56. IGI Global.

Wehner, P. 2019. Trump's sinister assault on truth. *The Atlantic* (June 18). www.theatlantic.com/ideas/archive/2019/06/donald-trumps-sinister-assault-truth/591925/

Weiner, R. 2021. Rudy Giuliani suspended from practicing law in D.C. court. *Washington Post* (July 7). https://www.washingtonpost.com/local/legal-issues/giuliani-washington-court/2021/07/07/9f7a7f5c-df6a-11eb-9f54-7eee10b5fcd2_story.html

Weisman, J. and S. Stolberg. 2021. As virus resurges, G.O.P. lawmakers allow vaccine skepticism to flourish. *New York Times* (July 20). https://www.nytimes.com/2021/07/20/us/politics/republicans-coronavirus.html

Wells, C., A. Lewis, A. Friedland, C. Hughes, D. Shah, J. Suk, and M. Wagner. 2021. News media use, talk networks, and anti-elitism across geographic location: evidence from Wisconsin. *International Journal of Press/Politics* 26(2):438–463.

Wemple, E. 2016. CNN commentator Scottie Nell Hughes: Facts no longer exist. *Washington Post* (Dec. 1). https://www.washingtonpost.com/blogs/erik-wemple/wp/2016/12/01/cnn-commentator-scottie-nell-hughes-facts-no-longer-exist/

Westlund, H. and Calidoni, F. 2010, July. The creative class, social capital and regional development in Japan. *Review of Urban & Regional Development Studies* 22(2-3):89–108.

Weyland, K. 2001. Clarifying a contested concept: populism in the study of Latin American politics. *Comparative Politics* 34(1):1–22.

Weyland, K. 2003. Neopopulism and neoliberalism in Latin America: How much affinity? *Third World Quarterly* 24(6):1095–1115.

Wheeler, K. and H. Hussein. 2021. Water research and nationalism in the post-truth era. *Water International* 46(7–8):1216–1223.

Whine, M. 2008. Expanding holocaust denial and legislation against it. *Jewish Political Studies Review* 20(1):57–77.

Wilber, K. 2017. *Trump and a Post-Truth World.* Shambhala Publications.

Will, I. 2013. The Shroud of Turin: Tell me what you want to believe and I will tell you what you will believe. In E. Steers and J. Nickell (eds.) *Hoax: Hitler's Diaries, Lincoln's Assassins, and Other Famous Frauds.* University Press of Kentucky.

Williams, J. 2005. *Understanding Poststructuralism.* Routledge.

Wimmer, A. 1997. Explaining xenophobia and racism: A critical review of current research approaches. *Ethnic and Racial Studies* 20(1):17–41.

Winters, J. 2020. What You Make Depends on Where You Live: College Earnings Across States and Metropolitan Areas. Fordham Institute. https://fordhaminstitute.org/national/research/what-you-make-depends-on-where-you-live

Wistrich, R. 2012. *Holocaust Denial: The Politics of Perfidy.* de Gruyter.

Withers, C. 2007. *Placing the Enlightenment: Thinking Geographically about the Age of Reason.* University of Chicago Press.

Wolff, M. 2002. One nation under Fox. *New York* (Dec. 9). https://nymag.com/nymetro/news/media/columns/medialife/n_8080/

Wood, E. 2002. *The Origin of Capitalism: A Longer View.* Verso.

Woodward, K., D. Dixon, and J.P. Jones III. 2009. Poststructuralism/poststructuralist geographies. In R. Kitchin and N. Thrift (eds.) *International Encyclopedia of Human Geography* vol. 8. pp. 396–407. Amsterdam: Elsevier.

Wren-Lewis, S. 2018. *The Lies We were Told: Politics, Economics, Austerity and Brexit.* Bristol University Press.

Wright, C. and H. Duong. 2021. COVID-19 fake news and attitudes toward Asian Americans. *Journal of Media Research* 14(1).

Yablokov, I. 2015. Conspiracy theories as a Russian public diplomacy tool: The case of Russia Today. *Politics* 35(3–4):301–315.

Yee, A. 2017. Post-truth politics & fake news in Asia. *Global Asia* 12(2):66–71.

Yerlikaya, T. 2020. Social media and fake news in the post-truth era. *Insight Turkey* 22(2):177–196. https://www.insightturkey.com/articles/social-media-and-fake-news-in-the-post-truth-era-the-manipulation-of-politics-in-the-election-process

Young, J. 2018. The coherence theory of truth. In E. Zalta (ed.) *Stanford Encyclopedia of Philosophy* https://plato.stanford.edu/entries/truth-coherence/

Zappetteni, F. 2019. Tabloid populism and the legitimation of Brexit in the British press. NewEuropeans.net (Jan. 10). https://neweuropeans.net/article/2583/tabloid-populism-and-legitimation-brexit-british-press

Zgheib, P. 2017. Advertising deceit: manipulation of information, false advertising, and promotion. In *Advertising and Branding: Concepts, Methodologies, Tools, and Applications.* pp. 1482–1494. IGI Global.

Zhang, S., B. Zhao, Y. Tian, and S. Chen. 2021. Stand with #StandingRock: Envisioning an epistemological shift in understanding geospatial big data in the "post-truth" era. *Annals of the American Association of Geographers* 111(4):1025–1045.

Zielinski, S. 2015. The great moon hoax was simply a sign of its time. *Smithsonian Magazine* (July 2). www.smithsonianmag.com/smithsonian-institution/great-moon-hoax-was-simply-sign-its-time-180955761/

Zitser, J. 2020. Brazil's Jair Bolsonaro bizarrely suggests COVID-19 vaccines could turn people into crocodiles or bearded ladies. *Business Insider* (Dec. 19). https://www.businessinsider.com/bolsonaro-claims-covid-19-vaccines-could-turn-people-into-crocodiles-2020-12

Zuckerman, E. 2019. QAnon and the emergence of the unreal. *Journal of Design and Science* (6). https://jods.mitpress.mit.edu/pub/tliexqdu/release/1

Index

5G conspiracy theory   11, 110, 176
9/11 terrorist attacks   78

Africa   13, 76, 106, 147, 151, 165, 169-171
African-Americans   28, 60, 70, 119, 136, 155
algorithms   8, 9, 50, 52, 79, 81, 86, 88, 139, 154, 161, 175
alternative facts   5, 11, 116, 123
anti-intellectualism   5, 10, 45, 89-93, 95, 103, 106, 122, 124, 130, 131, 176, 177
Arendt, Hannah   65-66, 147
Argentina   161, 164-165
attention economy   149-150
availability bias   51

Baudrillard, Jean   44-45, 77, 150
Bolsonaro, Jair   11, 13, 147, 149, 162-163, 172, 178
Borges, Jorge Luis   45, 160
bots   13, 69, 71, 79, 86, 88, 106, 126, 130, 153, 154, 156, 164, 165, 170
Brazil   11, 35, 106, 147, 149, 162-163, 172, 176-177, 178
Brexit   2, 12, 13, 86, 90, 127-132, 145, 149, 152, 156, 172, 173, 177
Breitbart News   11, 106-107, 152, 156, 176,
bullshit   1, 11, 27, 49, 54, 124
Bush, George W.   68, 78, 83, 91, 103, 117

Carlson, Tucker   11, 104, 107, 119, 127, 155
cartography   6, 22, 24, 106
China   13, 106, 122, 124, 125, 157, 158-159, 160, 171
class war   7, 9, 15, 131
clickbait   61, 86, 150
climate change denialism   2, 8, 10, 28, 54, 81, 82, 83, 84, 89, 90, 92, 94, 97-101, 105, 107, 108, 122, 131, 162, 171, 173, 176, 177
CNews   106, 152
cognitive-cultural capitalism   8, 12, 133, 134-135, 141, 145, 152, 175, 177
coherence theory of truth   18, 40, 66
college wage premium   141-142

confirmation bias   9, 50, 51, 53, 88, 131, 137, 144, 161, 175, 177
consensus theory of truth   20
corporate fake news   84
correspondence theory of truth
covid denialism   90, 124-127
creative class   12, 134-135, 144-145, 157, 177

deepfake videos   2, 69, 87, 173
democracy   3, 13, 48, 51, 68, 84, 89, 131, 147, 151, 162, 163, 165, 167, 174, 177, 178
Descartes, Rene   17, 23, 24
discourse   9, 15, 20, 30, 35, 36-37, 39, 41, 43, 47, 52, 54, 55, 70, 110, 120, 135, 136, 158, 169
distrust of expertise   5, 52
Dobbs, Lou   71, 104, 105, 113
Dunning-Kruger effect   51

earthquakes   60, 147, 157, 167, 172
Ecuador   161
Egypt   58, 106, 166-167, 178
election denialism   113, 147, 160, 163, 173, 176, 178
elites   5, 7, 12, 13, 88, 91, 92, 99, 132, 133, 143, 146, 149, 150, 171, 174, 178
emotions   5, 23, 48, 54, 65, 66, 69, 86, 89, 95, 100, 128, 148, 153, 159, 160, 162, 175, 176
empiricism   9, 16, 17, 19, 22-23, 25, 33, 42, 173
Enlightenment   5, 9, 10, 15, 18, 20, 21-22, 24, 26, 29, 38, 40, 41, 42, 46, 50, 54, 58, 75, 90, 173, 174, 175, 178
Erdogan, Tayyip   13, 149, 167, 172, 178
evolution denial   10, 90, 92, 94-95, 176

Facebook   2, 69, 71, 86, 88, 100, 106, 111, 130, 150, 154, 155, 156, 157, 158, 159, 161, 169
facts, social construction of   4, 17, 25, 31, 43
fake news   2, 5, 7, 8, 9, 10, 11, 12, 13, 14, 29, 52, 53, 54, 55, 56-62, 64-71, 72, 73, 75, 77, 78, 79-81, 84, 86-89, 90, 93, 106, 107, 108-109, 110-111, 113, 119, 123, 124, 127, 128, 130, 131, 132, 133, 127, 139, 141, 144, 146, 147, 150,

https://doi.org/10.1515/9783110749847-010

151, 153, 154, 156, 158-160, 162, 165, 166-167, 168, 169, 170, 171, 173-177, 178
false advertising   10, 56, 79-80, 81, 89
feminist theories of truth   9, 15, 23, 38-40, 43, 54, 55
fictional geographies   7
filter bubbles   52, 88, 150, 175, 176
flat Earth theory   26, 96
Foucault, Michel   5, 9 15, 32, 35-38, 40, 41, 42, 46, 47, 54, 55, 149, 174
Fox News   2, 11, 71, 73, 85, 88, 90, 102, 103-106, 107, 113, 119, 123, 124, 125, 126, 127, 131, 155, 159, 171, 176
Frankfurt School   26, 29, 30
Franklin, Benjamin   21, 60, 72

Gateway Pundit   106, 111, 156
geopolitics   2, 6, 8, 12, 13, 89, 90, 127, 132, 165, 167
George C. Marshall Institute   81, 82, 98
Giuliani, Rudy   110, 112
Google   2, 95, 100, 111, 150
Great Moon Hoax   60, 61
Gulf of Tonkin incident   10, 67, 77
gullibility   5, 12, 50, 108, 133, 140-144, 146

Hannity, Sean   11, 104, 105, 119, 124, 125
Haraway, Donna   23. 24, 39, 41
Harding, Sandra   39, 43
Hearst, William Randolph   10, 62-64, 67, 70, 84, 89
Heritage Foundation   81, 98, 101
hermeneutics   34, 41
hindutva   13, 147, 157-158, 172, 178
HIV/AIDS   170
Hofstadter, Richard   67, 78, 91
Hollywood   28, 73, 75, 76, 77, 109
Holocaust denial   10, 75-76, 153
Holy Grail   58
humanism   20, 21

immigrants   2, 7, 10, 11, 12, 29, 62, 66, 69, 70-71, 73, 80, 89, 101, 102, 105, 106, 107, 108, 118, 120, 121, 122, 123, 128, 135, 137, 141, 147, 148, 152, 159, 170, 171, 174, 176, 177, 178
information warfare   10, 56, 69, 72, 78, 81, 82, 84, 87, 94, 153

InfoWars   11, 102, 106, 109, 156
internet   2, 5, 8, 10, 11, 49, 50, 53, 55, 56, 58, 68, 69, 76, 77, 78, 79, 84, 86, 87, 88, 89, 109, 110, 138, 139, 150, 154, 157, 158, 160, 161, 169, 172, 175, 176, 177
Internet Research Agency 13, 108, 155-156, 172
Iraq   10, 12, 68, 77, 78, 83, 105, 106, 108, 116, 117, 165, 167
Israel   158, 166, 168

January 6, 2021 Capitol attack   11, 105, 113-114, 163, 176
Japan   75. 106, 109, 157, 159, 160
JFK assassination   67, 78
Jones, Alex   11, 106, 109, 119, 155, 156

Kant, Immanuel   16, 18, 21, 124
Khashoggi, Jamal   13, 147, 166, 172
Kim Jong Un   13, 147, 159
Know Nothing Party   70
Koch Brothers   83, 98, 131
Korea   13, 76, 129, 147, 157, 159, 160
Kuhn, Thomas   9, 15, 32-34, 35, 54

Latour, Bruno   25, 44, 46, 48
lies, lying   3, 4, 27, 49, 52, 55, 59, 65, 66, 75, 78, 87, 114-124,
Likud   168
Limbaugh, Rush   11, 90, 104, 107-108, 125, 176
Lyotard, Francois   40, 42, 46

Macedonia   110, 128, 173
Marquez, Gabriel Garcia   161
Marx, Chico   87
Marxism   9, 15, 29-30, 38, 40, 42, 47, 54, 55
McCarthy, Joseph   77, 91, 116
media fragmentation   51
Mexico   11, 71, 101, 111, 116, 120, 121, 164, 173
Modi, Narendra   13, 157-158, 178
Murdoch, Rupert   85, 99, 103, 129, 151-152
Muslims   11, 69, 71, 102, 104, 105, 107, 121, 122, 136, 155-156, 158, 159, 165, 166

Nazis   10, 59, 75, 77, 156, 174
neoliberalism   2, 7, 8, 10, 12, 13, 22, 51, 102, 131, 132, 134, 138, 142, 143, 146, 147, 148-151, 160, 167, 168, 171, 174, 175, 177, 178

news deserts 8, 12, 133, 138-140, 145, 146, 177
newspapers 8, 10, 21, 49, 57, 58, 60, 61, 62-64, 65, 66, 67, 68, 70, 72, 73, 82, 83, 111, 129, 138-140, 150, 162, 164, 170, 176
Newton, Isaac 21, 24, 25, 43
Nietzsche, Frederick 9, 15, 30, 31-32, 34, 40, 54, 55, 116, 173

O'Reilly, Bill 105-106
Obama, Barack 106, 107, 111, 116, 119, 125, 156
– Birther conspiracy 69, 105, 108, 111, 116, 122
One America News Network 102, 107, 127
Orban, Viktor 13, 149, 151, 152, 178
Orwell, George 65, 123, 131, 140

Palestinians 168
perjury 3
petroleum companies 83, 97, 98, 131
phenomenology 9, 15, 34, 47, 55
Philippines 62, 63, 178
Pizzagate 107, 108-109
Plato 16, 24
Platonic realm of ideas 14, 19, 41, 54, 174
Poe, Edgar Allan 60
polarization (political) 52, 88, 89, 95, 103, 142, 174
Pope 11, 59, 69, 70, 73, 108, 111
populism 7, 10, 52, 92, 93, 132, 140, 141, 143, 144, 145, 149, 151, 152, 161, 163, 171
positivism 9, 17, 20, 23, 24, 25, 29, 33, 35, 39, 40, 55, 173, 175
post-modernism 9, 15, 40-46, 47, 50, 53, 54, 158
post-structuralism 15, 42, 46-48, 53, 54, 158
post-truth
– climate change and 97-102
– conspiracy theories and 6, 11, 57
– definition 5, 6
– democracy and 8
– emotion and affect and 5, 48, 65, 162, 175
– epistemology 48-50, 54-55
– fake news and 58
– geography and 2, 6-7, 13, 96, 105-106, 113, 127-131, 133, 135, 140, 143, 146, 147-171, 152, 157, 171, 177, 178
– internet and 5, 8, 50
– neoliberalism and 148, 150-151, 158, 174
– origins 5
– politics and 65-70, 89, 132, 152-153, 165, 167, 169
– populism and 149
– post-truth society/world 1, 2, 5, 6, 14, 15, 47, 48, 51-52, 90, 131, 140, 148, 173, 177
– racism and 60
pragmatist theory of truth 4, 9, 16, 18-19, 32, 120, 173
Pravda 73, 104
propaganda 6, 9, 10, 11, 13, 56, 57, 71-79, 83, 101, 104, 105, 153-154, 158, 165, 166, 167, 168, 169, 170, 174, 175, 176
pseudo-science 9, 15, 26-29, 70, 81, 93, 99
pundits 82, 104, 105, 131
Putin, Vladmir 153, 154, 156

QAnon conspiracy theory 11, 105, 109, 1160, 131, 153, 176

racism 22, 28, 37, 60, 62, 70, 109, 132, 136, 137, 170, 174, 177
radio 11, 64, 72, 73, 75, 76, 102, 104, 106, 107, 108, 110, 1251, 131, 160, 161, 163, 176
Reagan, Ronald 48, 67, 82, 97
Renaissance 10, 16, 19, 20-21, 22, 24, 25, 58, 59, 72
Republican Party 11, 66, 90, 92, 101, 104, 119, 121, 122, 141, 176
resentment 5, 7, 69, 91, 143, 146, 148, 176
Rohingya 13, 147, 159, 172
rumor bombs 2, 69, 173
rural areas 8, 12, 13, 93, 128, 133, 135, 137, 138, 139, 140-146, 171, 177
Russia 2, 106, 109, 116, 147, 153-156, 166, 172, 178

Saudi Arabia 13, 147, 166, 167, 172, 178
science denialism 10, 11, 22, 27, 93-96, 176
simulacrum 28, 44, 81
social constructivism 1, 9, 15, 35, 54
Sokal, Alan 43
Soros, George 71, 107, 152, 176
South Africa 61, 105, 147, 170
Soviet Union 13, 67, 73, 104, 156
standpoint theory 15, 39, 54

swiftboating   68
Syrian refugees   121, 128

tabloids   10, 12, 62, 84-86, 89, 129, 171, 174
television   11, 45, 50, 68, 71, 76, 77, 79, 81, 82,
    83, 84, 85, 95, 102, 103, 104, 111, 116, 119,
    125, 126, 131, 138, 140, 150, 161, 163, 167
tobacco industry   10, 29, 82, 83
Trump, Donald   2, 11, 13, 57, 68, 69, 71, 80, 85,
    89, 90, 91, 92-93, 101, 103, 104, 105, 106,
    107, 109, 110, 111, 112, 113, 114-126, 127, 128,
    129, 131, 132, 140, 142, 143, 144, 147, 149,
    152, 155, 156, 158, 162, 163, 164, 168, 176,
    178
trust   4, 8, 51, 52, 53, 65, 87, 88, 92, 94, 118, 137,
    150, 157, 159, 169, 174
truth decay   52, 175
truth:
– a priori and a posteriori   16
definition   3
linguistic origins   3
modernity and   20-21
objective truth   5, 6, 31, 43, 62, 65, 103
relativization of   9, 31-35, 38, 54

theories of   15-20
– uses   3-4
truthiness   5-6, 140
Turkey   12, 13, 130, 149, 166, 167, 172, 178,
Twitter   13, 86, 106, 109, 130, 154, 155, 156, 157,
    158, 160, 161, 164, 165, 166, 167, 168, 169,
    170

urban-rural division   12, 133, 144-145, 148, 172,
    177

vaccines   8, 10, 11, 13, 28, 53, 89, 90, 92, 94, 95-
    96, 105, 106, 107, 109, 124, 125, 126, 127, 156,
    157, 160, 163, 168, 171, 176
Venezuela   11, 112, 149, 163, 164
video news releases   82-83
violence   11, 22, 71, 76, 87, 109, 121, 136, 156,
    163, 168, 170

Welles, Orson   64

xenophobia   8, 13, 70, 132, 136, 149, 170

yellow journalism   10, 56, 62-64, 84, 89, 106

www.ingramcontent.com/pod-product-compliance
Lightning Source LLC
Chambersburg PA
CBHW070906270326
41927CB00011B/2479